AN INTIMATE UNDERSTANDING OF AMERICA'S TEENAGERS

AN INTIMATE UNDERSTANDING OF AMERICA'S TEENAGERS

Shaking Hands with Aliens

Bruce J. Gevirtzman

Westport, Connecticut
London

#2263308119

Library of Congress Cataloging-in-Publication Data

Gevirtzman, Bruce J.
An intimate understanding of America's teenagers : shaking hands with aliens / Bruce J. Gevirtzman.
p. cm.
Includes bibliographical references and index.
ISBN 978–0–313–34508–1 (alk. paper)
1. Adolescent psychology. I. Title.
BF724.G463 2008
155.50973—dc22 2008017595

British Library Cataloguing in Publication Data is available.

Library of Congress Catalog Card Number: 2008017595
ISBN: 978–0–313–34508–1

First published in 2008

Praeger Publishers, 88 Post Road West, Westport, CT 06881
An imprint of Greenwood Publishing Group, Inc.
www.praeger.com

Printed in the United States of America

The paper used in this book complies with the
Permanent Paper Standard issued by the National
Information Standards Organization (Z39.48–1984).

10 9 8 7 6 5 4 3 2 1

Contents

Preface   vii

Introduction   ix

1   I'm, Like, All…   1

2   The Rebel Paradox   15

3   Mirror, Mirror   28

4   Lily Munster…or Whatever's Cool   45

5   The Anti-Midas Touch   53

6   Dumb Stuff   65

7   Athletes, Arrogance, and Angst   79

8   The Slime Who Hurt Our Kids   91

9   When *Party* Became a Verb   104

10 Snitchin' Ain't Bitchin'   115

11 Hard-Bodied, Soft-Headed, and Stone Dead   129

12 Sex, Oral Sex, and "Hey, Everybody's Doing It!"   137

13 Devouring Junk   153

14 They Bombed Hiroshima, Didn't They?   170

15 Good and Plenty   186

16 You *Vil* Go to Ha'vid!   197

17 You Mean, When You Die, You're Dead?   216

18   It's a Matter of Philosophy: Remedies Times 10   228

19   Can't! Won't! Not!   242

20   When All Is Said and Done   249

Notes   257

Bibliography   261

Index   263

Preface

Humble people don't write books.

When a person thinks that he has a lot to say and boasts himself as *the* expert on a subject, not much room remains for humility.

That said: I can't even imagine any other adult in America who knows more about teenagers than I do. So with great pleasure—and, yes, some trepidation— I now pass along my intimate understanding of America's adolescents to parents, teachers, teenagers, and anyone else with either a vested interest or a macabre curiosity.

This is no time to be humble.

As I began to reflect seriously on this project—looking over my notes, collections, and memorabilia—one major theme stood out: *The problems teenagers faced 40 years ago are identical to the problems they face today.* A huge difference, however, is that *today the intensity of those problems is way off the charts*. Modern technology and more aggressive media pose challenges never conceived of in the past. The lives of teenagers have been severely complicated by negligent parenting, mix-n-match families, and an apathetic, inadequate education system. Instead of inadvertently burning down Daddy's woodshed after playing with fireworks, kids today are burning CDs about raping and mutilating women. Instead of parents *and* teachers *and* lawmakers *and* society looking out for kids, today's kids have been left to fend for themselves.

Those who wish to crawl into the minds, hearts, and souls of America's teenagers have opened the right text. The anecdotes will amuse you; the stories will move you; the conclusions will startle you—and the prescriptions I offer you come after countless hours of observations, reflections, and analyses. An extensive career as a veteran high school English teacher, baseball coach, play director, and debate advisor has afforded me an opportunity to do an insightful examination of teenagers from the last four decades, while concentrating on the most recent generation. I also divulge some secrets from my own experiences as a teenager, sometimes causing me to shrink with embarrassment, but always with a smile on my face.

Note: The students and other teens in this book are real. Their names have been changed, and/or they are composites of teenagers. Student writings and interview commentaries have been edited or paraphrased. Conversations have been recreated from my own memory, notes, and the recollections of others. All stories are true.

For a better understanding of the author's insights, those prescriptive sections that are aimed at parents should be examined by teenagers, too—and vice versa. All readers may benefit from the advice offered to teachers.

Introduction

"YOU MEAN, THEY'RE NOT BORN TEENAGERS?"

"They're *people*."

"Huh?"

"They're people. Even though they're not even four years old, they're still people."

I cowered; a mixture of guilt and fear surged through me. "But they still need to follow orders—to do what they're told by their father."

There! That would show her!

"They're little kids, Bruce. They're not robots or marionettes. Sure, they should listen to you, but you have to be careful about the *way* that you tell them."

As my wife admonished me for expecting our two small children to follow my directions, I found myself only half-listening to her advice. Of course our kids were people. And I thought I'd always treated them as people; after all, I wasn't standing behind them with a whip and chain, barking at them to build the pyramids of Egypt. Although sticking their hands into my bowl of cheese dip did not warrant a lethal injection, I figured raising my voice over this calamity *was* warranted. I had simply suggested the possible diseases that lurked on their unsanitary little mitts, and the chance they may actually *kill* somebody from not washing their hands and then poking them where they didn't belong.

I had waited until later in life to have children. Parents never really know what to expect before they bear their first child, no matter how frequently others have warned them, no matter how many baby books they've read or child-birth classes they've attended. When they initially notice that their tiny baby resembles a prune atop a corncob, they think it's the most beautiful child in the whole world.

And some parents believe this forever.

For me, however, there was only one major surprise at the moment of child-birth: *My new daughter had not arrived as a teenager!*

She wasn't 14. She was only 14 seconds! Rationally, of course, I knew my children would not be born teenagers; something inside me, however, told me they *ought* to have been born teenagers—because teenagers were all I knew. I'd taught high school for almost 30 years. I'd traveled with the debate team to other states and spent countless hours in cars and hotel rooms with teens. I'd spent six years coaching high school baseball, often being ejected from games by umpires because I had the audacity to defend my players from their incompetence. I'd read countless pieces of student writing that made me laugh and cry. I'd counseled teenagers about some of their most difficult problems. I'd directed teens in several plays I had written, mostly about adolescent social woes: drugs, sex, abuse, self-identity, and so on. I had been so close to these kids, I'd practically been one of them!

So as my own children entered the world, it was a huge shock that they had not come out already sporting baggy pants and bumpy pimples; instead, they were these miniature whatevers that only cried, spat, farted, barfed, and pooped. When I thought about how it was now my obligation to mold and nurture my crying, spitting, farting, barfing, and pooping baby into the kind of adult who would bring rave reviews of my fatherhood, I reeled in horror.

Mold my baby?

How would I do *that?*

For me, the baby years were the scary ones. Most people are afraid of what they don't know. I know teenagers; it's the little ones who have the inherent capacity to affect my episodes of acid reflux. This view may seem rather odd, because people dread teenagers more than they do babies. The number one phobia in America is probably public speaking, followed closely by the fear of death. I'll wager that right behind the fear of death is the horror of sitting at a Burger King with a couple of teenagers who are munching on cheeseburgers and punching keypads on their cell phones. Parents of younger kids worry about the future, when their children will have grown into adolescence. Parents of teenagers have empathy; they're already living it. And they constantly warn others:

"You think it's bad right now, Joe? You just wait. Pretty soon he'll be a... *teenager!*"

"Yeah, but not for 12 years."

"You gotta start preparing yourself now, Joe. Time goes a lot faster than you think."

"But how bad can it be?"

And the teenager's parent sends Joe a silent stare, as if to tell him, "You'll see, Joe; in good time, you'll see."

Many parents never catch on; they don't understand that anomaly of human development known as a teenager. Some parents are as much in the dark about teenagers as I am about babies—only worse, because babies have some rhyme or reason to them. Teenagers do not.

Teachers don't understand either. Most teachers only know these kids in the confines of their classrooms, content that all 15-year-old minds who sit before them are eager to digest their pompous utterances about Shakespeare, algebraic equations, or the Boston Tea Party. The truth, of course, is that teenagers have absolutely no desire to learn these irrelevancies, especially if they had just left the house as Dad was chasing Mom around the room with a tire iron—or they hadn't slept the night before, the result of dodging bullets in the latest gang-bang assault in their neighborhood. Real life-and-death issues tend to diminish the urgency of memorizing the periodic table of elements.

If I hadn't lived among teenagers for so many years, I wouldn't have a clue about the idiosyncrasies of teenage life; I would have been left fumbling in a maze of ambiguities, my own voice snarling: "What's with these kids!" And I would have echoed the words of my father—and his father, too: "Son, things were different, when I was your age...." As though profundities of this kind were going to change the lives of my students forever.

Now, I know better. In a sense, I have been researching this book for 35 years, accumulating stories, anecdotes, student writings, and memories—all of which have become indispensable. I actually look forward to parenting teenagers. Contrary to what a majority of parents think about themselves, I believe that I will do a far better job parenting teenage kids than I have done fathering my little ones (although I'm a pretty dandy daddy to my own kids, too)!

But I understand teenagers much better than I understand small children.

And I know what they need.

EARLY ENCOUNTERS

Long hair is back.

Pick a color: any shade of brown or black, with bleaches and dyes to match; frosted hair, streaked hair, highlighted hair; red hair of any shade; even green hair or blue hair or orange or pink hair—or any combinations of these colors.

Hairstyles abound: permed, curled, frayed; hair with droopy bangs, locks in the back, shaved on the sides, or a tall horn on top.

Cosmetic appeal has taken on some new—and freshly recycled—characteristics that have caught on with a vengeance: pierced ears, adorned with large looping earrings or shiny studs; ornaments that stick through any part of the face or body, including the navel and the tongue; the shaving of hair on every microscopic part of the body—even the head; manicures, pedicures, facials, tush reductions, face lifts, tummy tucks, pectoral implants, and moisturizing skin applications; full-hour appointments in the beauty salon for actual hairdos; and regular applications of facial makeup and eyeliner.

And these are the *boys!*

When Bob Dylan droned in the late 1960s, "The times, they are a-changin'," most of us shrugged our shoulders and smirked, "Yeah, right." We were somewhere in the throes of adolescence ourselves, and we figured we were smarter than anyone else and certainly could read the trends of pop culture better than the over-30 crowd that moralized to us with an insufferable redundancy. Besides, if the times actually were changing, this had to be a good thing, right? Wasn't change *always* good?

The hair and the clothes and the language: they're constantly changing. The trends are claimed by the generation that breeds them, and that same generation—eventually fearing conformity—renounces those trends later.

Teenagers haven't changed. When I first walked into a classroom as a high school teacher in 1971, I gazed at the kids in front of me and thought, "So this is how it is, and this is the way it's always going to be. From now on—from this day forth—teenagers are going to look like this. They're going to act like this, too. I already have them figured out. This is going to be easier than I thought." After all, I was barely out of the teen years myself. What could be so hard about relating to these kids?

And then I began my teaching career.

I learned immediately that I was no longer a teenager; I wasn't one of *them*. When I strode into my classroom on my very first day of teaching in my freshly laundered trousers, white shirt, plaid tie, and corduroy sports coat, I actually felt like an alien myself. For one thing, my head sported a crew cut. One of my male students thrust his fist into the air and shouted, "Sieg Heil!" And when I told him his comparison of me to Hitler was "utterly repugnant," he showed his remorse over the incident by asking me what utterly repugnant meant.

My students have provided me with a constant source of humor—admittedly, much of it unintentional. In valiant attempts to disguise their weirdness at this age, a lot that escapes their mouths is full of surprising truths that are, well, *funny*.

In the early eighties, I was helping one of my student speakers polish the delivery of an oration she had prepared for an upcoming competition. That sunny afternoon she practiced tenaciously, but nothing seemed to be working. She had cotton in her mouth, her body slouched forward in a manner that made her look like the Hunchback of Notre Dame, and she kept forgetting her speech. Just as she bolted toward me, I threw my pen up in annoyance, thinking she had decided to kill me, the result of her intense frustration. As I put my arms up to protect myself, she wailed, "Mr. G., you don't understand! I'm a really good speaker! I just can't speak in front of *people!*"

I'm still not entirely sure what she meant by that.

But it struck me at the moment—and still does—as very funny.

My introduction to teenagers, now from an adult perspective, confused me. Much of the residual weirdness from my teenage years had not worn off yet, and now working around adults—many of whom were especially *un*cool—made it difficult for me to take my job seriously. It was as though my students and I had journeyed here on a huge flying saucer from another planet. While on that flying saucer, we listened to music, danced, played softball, shared our deepest secrets, told jokes, and used lots of dirty words. Suddenly, we deserted the spaceship; I was asked to put on a coat and tie and become the boss. My foul language stopped abruptly. The others couldn't call me by my first name anymore, as my new status required them to address me as *Mister*. Since I was not that far removed from being an alien myself, I truly understood them; I knew exactly where they were coming from, but I was now surrounded by scores of other adults who didn't have a clue.

Complicated decisions had to be made. I wasn't going to stay 23 years old forever. Someday I would be really, really old—maybe 40 or something. If I expected to reach middle age working around teenagers, I needed to embark on a course that would satisfy my life's desire to make a difference in the world. But being a bona fide classroom teacher wasn't enriching enough: the fruits of my labors were rarely immediate and often nonexistent. So *involvement* was the key—spending large quantities of time with students was the formula for success. Involvement would allow me to monitor their music, read their books, watch their movies, attend their functions, and mend their social ills. The prospect of spending so much of my life among aliens now seemed real—*and absolutely insane!*

ON ANOTHER PLANET

In early 1991 after our military had entered Kuwait for the purpose of liberating enslaved and tortured Kuwaitis from the invaders from Iraq, one boy on my competitive debate team who always wore a denim jacket and some kind of creepy plastic necklace quipped, "Mr. Gevirtzman, I suppose you're happy now."

"Happy about what, Robert?"

"Bush [the elder] is killing people."

"No, Robert; it's the Iraqis and their leaders who are *murdering* people."

"Yeah, right."

"Yes, Robert," I persisted. "It's absolutely true. We're not happy about killing anybody; we're actually saving some lives by our mission."

Robert didn't flinch. "You just like violence."

"No, I don't like violence. But I hate evil even more."

"You know, Mr. G., one of these days we're gonna send thousands of troops to fight in Iraq, and lots of our guys are gonna die; it'll be like another Vietnam. And you old people who support war and killing…"

He stopped just short of accusing me of starting the war myself.

I flashed a knowing, pompous smile and winked at the other student debaters. "Don't worry, Robert. We're not going to fight in Iraq for long. Mark my words: Americans aren't going to be in Iraq after this year [1991]. Trust me."

Whoops.

Almost 15 years later: Robert, now a commissioned officer, has come home from another war in Iraq, after his second tour of duty.

So much for being able to trust the teacher's enlightened sense of world politics.

On Robert's opposite political pole were boys like Jack: Jack came to class wearing military fatigues every day; he drew fighter planes on his desk and pasted stickers representing different branches of the military on his notebooks. If anybody even hinted of disillusionment with America, Jack clenched his two fists and fought to control his anger. Jack contended that anything America did was good, and anything any other country did was bad.

That was in 1986, about the time President Reagan got ticked off at Muammar Gadhafi of Libya and blew up some of his family. Most of the teenagers didn't really care about Libya; they were too busy listening to Cyndi Lauper and planning their spring break in Grandma's swimming pool. They would then lie to everybody about how they got their great tans while romping on the beaches in Ft. Lauderdale.

Twenty-some years later, Jack's story has been written: Jack never joined the military; right after graduation he impregnated his girlfriend and left the state, denying any responsibility for his new daughter. He took odd jobs around various communities, and around 1989, he simply vanished from the planet. To my knowledge Jack didn't return for his class reunions, and he never helped to raise his kid.

Due to the complex nature of teenagers, teachers can't predict with much accuracy the destinies of their adolescent students. Only on the surface are certain traits obvious, and sometimes these so-called obvious traits are misleading; American adolescents are just too peculiar. The kids on the debate squads, in the theater productions, on the baseball teams, in various clubs I sponsored came from all walks of teenage life; I've had the experience of meeting thousands of teens, most of whom my mind had already reduced to an adolescent stereotype.

By the middle of the 1970s, I was still young enough to be cool; unfortunately, my personality, the product of a too-protective Jewish mother, and my character, the result of a truth-driven Polish-German father, brought not the slightest ring of *cool* to my persona: I still liked fifties doo-wop music, enjoyed dialogue in film, defended baseball as America's pastime, found politics exciting, adored cats, loved books, and coveted being alone; I didn't care for living out of suitcases, drove a 10-year-old car, preferred live musicals over rock concerts, and frequented Denny's Restaurants. I looked forward to the Academy Awards more than I did the Super Bowl, and—check this out—I viewed President Carter as a man with an exciting vision for America!

I was not *cool*.

Things that aren't cool bother teenagers.

Giving speeches isn't cool at all. Twice students have fainted in my classroom, both times over the stress of oral presentations. Once, a boy swaggered to the front of the room, his flowing blond hair radiating coolness; he walked like a man on a mission—to wow us with his every utterance. The girls smiled, eyeing him with admiration, in awe of his confidence. He had mustered the courage to give his speech—away from his trusted skateboard.

As the blond bomber reached his destination a few feet in front of a green chalkboard, he turned to face the class. He paused, made fleeting eye contact with a cute redhead in the front row, and then opened his mouth to speak...

It's never pretty when someone faints.

The boy's eyes suddenly became glassy; he rocked backward from his toes to the heels of his feet. What had been a slight smirk of confidence was now a barren visage. His body fell backward, his head slid down the chalkboard, and he crumpled to the tiled floor.

He now faced the most humiliating moment of his life so far: utter mortification, horrific embarrassment in front of his peers!

And in the blink of an eye, he had lost all of his coolness.

After the security guard finished cracking jokes and carted the unlucky bugger away, the other students began making sarcastic quips (which continued for the next six months):

John finally found a way to drop out of school!

Mr. Cool!

Encore!

It's the hair!

Beautiful! The three judges—9, 9, and 9.5!

Do it again! Do it again! We like it! We like it!

For weeks, just as someone went up to speak, another student would invariably chide, "Careful! Don't pull a *John!*"

Making any kind of oral presentation is definitely not cool, so the kids usually hate it. The general teenage population—especially the popular kids—gazes at the competitive debaters as though they had just been snatched by one of the pods in *Invasion of the Body Snatchers*. They see the speech kids as totally weird—geeks, nerds—hopelessly retarded in their social development.

On the other hand, the debaters don't quite understand why the popular teens don't enjoy traveling to speech tournaments on weekends and then competing against hundreds of other talented teenagers. Both groups of kids eye each other with curiosity, disdain, and—a little bit of envy.

But whichever group they happen to be in, the other one is weirder.

When I first entered education, most of the adults I knew, including the parents of teenage kids, shrugged their shoulders and sloughed off this strange, unpredictable age as "one of life's phases they would grow out of soon." But I was stuck on the thought that approximately five or six years for a *phase* is a very long time, especially when we consider all of the changes teenagers undergo: the development of their sexuality, minds, bodies, sexuality, social awareness, sexuality, spirit, and sexuality. (Did I mention their *sexuality?*) If a kid becomes an alien at age 13 and then starts to shed her alien status at age 18, imagine all the eardrum-thumping music that has permeated her auditory receptors, not to mention all the bad pizza she has consumed during those years.

I had to do *something* to affect the trends, to mold the masses, to sway the future.

To make a difference.

Our mission to better understand America's teenagers will not always go smoothly; occasionally, we will shudder, as a scary chill runs through us. This often happens when we brace ourselves for the unknown. But as I have so richly discovered, the rewards for our courage can be immeasurable.

So: Onward! Into alien territory we march!

1

I'm, Like, All...

CLUELESS: A SCARY TRUTH

If and when creatures from outer space land on Earth, they will have a language all their own. As a kid I watched those early science fiction movies from the 1950s, and I wondered how those guys from Mars were capable of speaking perfect English, even better English than most of my classmates. Did that creature in the tight silver pants with the slick white hair really take courses in other languages before he began bugging people around our galaxy? Hey, maybe *everybody* in God's universe spoke perfect English (except for teenagers raised in Brooklyn)!

My first real introduction to an alien language—not including when my parents hid their discussions from me by speaking Yiddish—came in 1971; in fact, my first adult *personal* encounter with *Teenagese* (my term) occurred the very first moment I opened my mouth before a classroom full of students: "Okay, uh, let's see, I, uh..."

Not exactly the most articulate utterance during those opening seconds of my career, and then a lovable chap from the middle of the class asked, "This guy— a poser or a hodad?"

Let's see...I was still young and hip (I'm a lot hipper now, but this is measured in body mass, not in coolness), so what was I missing here? What was this twerp asking about me: *a poser or a hodad?*

Was he asking *me* a question?

Was he even speaking English?

This guy: a poser or a hodad?

I already knew from my own high school days something about the word *hodad*. A hodad was a guy who dressed like a surfer, walked like a surfer, talked like a surfer, but had never surfed a day in his life; in fact, he probably didn't know *how* to surf. Later, in 1973, *hodad* still connoted a phony but was not as bad as *poser*, someone who actually *thought* he was the real thing; in other words, these kids kicked off my career by refusing me the benefit of the doubt. I had auditioned for them that day as either a liar or a phony.

Take your pick.

And from there—for the rest of that first year—it was downhill.

Teenagers have a language of their own. Teenagese is parodied and idolized at once by media stalwarts who make mucho bucks from doing so—and mimicked by old farts who have forgotten that hundreds of years ago they were teenagers who had their own language, too. Those who chastise kids for their unique language advertise some jealousy, their haughtiness a weak camouflage for an utter disdain of getting older. Old people have no language of their own, unless it has to do with arthritis, flatulence, or their frequent bouts with constipation.

Critics hailed the 1995 film *Clueless* as an original—a jewel of creative thought and biting satire. I also loved this movie, but not exactly for those reasons. All students of film—and literature—know there's a fine line between the satiric and the real, and effective satire manages to posture itself barely on the acerbic side of that line. Sometimes it's difficult to figure out whether the literature is true life or a commentary on true life through the art of parody. *Clueless* had me stumped: On the one hand, the movie was funny and imaginative, as it depicted teenagers' customs, values, and codes of conduct in a caustic, humorous manner; on the other hand, my first viewing of the movie left me shrugging my shoulders (and laughing) over what I had seen. I thought it entertaining, but a social satire on modern high school kids?—I had my doubts.

This film came dangerously close to the truth. The teens were depicted as sex-crazed, party-hardy, air-headed, compulsive, impulsive, obsessive, possessive, narcissistic, materialistic, trendy adolescents, whose every other word fit a stylized, personalized vocabulary for teenagers in 1995.

What's satirical about *that?*

Experts tell us that it's easier to learn a new language when we're young. Unaware of the fundamentals of language acquisition, over decades American teenagers have unknowingly acquired newer (and better) ways of saying things. English is still English (sort of), but as these words have passed through generations, they have inherited entirely different definitions and usages. Like the white-haired guys—the ones from Mars—wearing the silver pants, generations of American adults have eventually learned the necessity for language understanding and idiom adaptation when it comes to teenagers.

FROM *FANTABULOUS* TO *TIGHT*

Two ramifications of developing language may pique some interest: first, decades of change in teenage slang, and second—a more serious topic—significant generational communication barriers (or, "Ohmigod! If I only knew what you *meant!*").

Never in my life has anyone mistaken me for a cowboy (Jews and horses don't mix). Despite this, I thought I had a pretty good idea how to describe a dude, even though cows weren't my thing either, and I found them appealing only when they sat docile on my plate at a Black Angus Steak House. But around 1980 my male high school students began calling me *dude*. As I noticed this growing habit, I cautioned them that I was not now, nor had I ever been, a rancher. However, failing to comprehend my little play on words (which, admittedly, was not that funny, especially since I had said it 5,000 times), they persisted in their greeting: "Hey, dude, what's up?" After which, I would look up and say, "The ceiling. That's what's up." Which was very uncool—so uncool that they occasionally laughed about my nonexistent coolness.

I did, however, learn the rules: (1) A *dude* is a guy. The person who said *dude* was the cool guy, not necessarily the person to whom it was directed. (2) Only males may use the word *dude*. A female using *dude* sounded like she shouldn't be a female (thus, an immediate deterrent for any girl desiring to use that word). (3) Jokes about this trendy slang word were off-limits. Adults who acted smug or ignorant about its application in conversation did not look brighter, smarter, or hipper. They simply looked like geeks. Around teenagers, many adults look like geeks no matter how hard they try not to look like geeks. Perception is everything in the teenage world; and since adults are perceived as geeks from the get-go, associated adult behaviors will serve to augment this perception.

Today *dude* is part of our culture; I probably use it more than his first name when I refer to my son. In the 1950s if teenagers thought something or someone was especially cool or hip or noteworthy or fantastic, two predominant words described that thing or person: one of those words was *fantabulous*. Notice the clever combining of the words *fantastic* and *fabulous*—although no generation of teenagers would have been caught dead elevating the use of the word *fabulous* to any level of coolness.

An example of its common usage: *Albert threw a fantabulous pass to his favorite receiver.*

Or, *How do you feel, Jack?*

Fantabulous!

Obviously, *fantabulous* wound up higher on the usage priority charts than *fantastic* or *fabulous*, both of which were forbidden words anyway.

Another word kids used for *fantabulous* was *bitchin'*.

An example of its common usage: *Albert threw a bitchin' pass to his favorite receiver.*

Or, *How do you feel today, Jack?*

Bitchin'!

Although the word *bitch* had other connotations, not the least of which were unpleasant or downright derogatory references to women, they were mild when contrasted with the meaning of the word *bitch* today. Teenagers, mostly through the predominant use of this word in modern pop culture—mainly rap music—have incorporated it as part of their daily vocabulary.

Recently, my students were quietly reading their books in class, when outside the room a young male voice summoned loudly and clearly, "Hey, bitch, get over here!"

The timing provided some irony: I had just finished a rather poignant lesson about the power of words and the ugliness of some of today's commonly used slang. Even I had to grin, since the good timing of the kid's gross comment amplified a valuable lesson about irony. But despite the gallows humor, I was saddened; a boy, presumably a decent teenager who attended our better-than-average high school, had casually called a girl—someone he probably knew—by this name.

And he thought nothing of it.

Worse, the girl ran to him with a big smile on her face. It was acceptable, if not customary, for a boy to call her a *bitch*.

I may go to my grave believing—despite opinions to the contrary—that the single worst influence on adolescent speech habits and, therefore, the principal impediment to linguistic decency among young people today is the influence of rap music. This music is packed with appalling grammar, incessant swearing, and blatant misogyny. When the Rolling Stones sang in 1965 that they couldn't get no satisfaction, I cringed. During college I was already enough of a grammarian to abhor the use of double negatives. A decade earlier, every time I heard Little Caesar and the Romans croon, "Those oldies but goodies *reminds* me of you," I shrank in despair. My verb-subject-agreement-loving, eccentric self recoiled with the anguish of someone whose life had just been threatened. Don't get me wrong: these were good songs—classics—but they had poor structure, awful syntax, and unacceptable grammar.

Then it got worse.

Much worse.

Pimp has turned out to mean something good. Where I come from, if someone is a pimp, he buys and sells women who are called *prostitutes*. This is a *bad* thing; therefore, a pimp is a bad man. Today it's good to be a pimp, as in, "Hey, Johnny, whatcha up to, pimp!" This means, Johnny has had sex with a lot of girls—or at least, he gets a lot of girls to come after him—right? Another: "Yo, bro! Wanna pimp my party!" This means the party I'm throwing is not very much fun—kind of boring actually—and a guy like you, with your elevated social stature, could make it a heck of a lot more interesting.

Whatever.

The word *pimp* stands for something superb—all anyone really has to know to see that the language has changed. The original culture of all this, by the way, is rap music. Pimps rule rap. Pimps strut their stuff on the rap videos, sometimes with scantily clad young women hanging on both arms. Pimps dress in expensive clothes, wear ostentatious jewelry, and drive fancied-up luxury cars. Twelve-year-old boys throughout America share grandiose dreams of someday becoming a pimp: to rule over women, to have sex with sluts, to slap around bitches and hoes.

Yes, *pimp* has become the modern version of *player* or—I'm going way back now—*playboy*. Only, being a pimp is better: it's rougher, tougher, leaner, and meaner.

On another level, more benign changes in word use among teens have displayed an uncanny evolution: Take the word *bitchin'*, for example. We've already discussed how this word eventually took on new, unpleasant meanings among teenagers and the rest of our culture. What could possibly fill the vacuum left by *bitchin'*? Some held *fantabulous* as a possibility, but young people frowned upon this option; in fact, think about how nerdy the word *fantabulous* sounds today. Since its roots go back to the early sixties, something eventually had to replace a word that meant "really cool, utterly wonderful, way off the charts super"; in fact, *super* itself sufficed for a little while:

Hey, Jane, how ya doin'?

Super!

These days, when someone answers the question, "How ya doin'?" with "Super," we figure he's at least a hundred years old. This term reeks even more than *swell*, which makes all teenagers sound a lot like Wally Cleaver, a fictitious teenager who has been aberrant to every aspect of American culture except the sitcoms of the late fifties.

So, what came after *bitchin'* that stayed in the teen culture for a very, very long time?

Nope. Nice try, but *Far out!* didn't come until much later—maybe five years or so—and it stuck around for quite a while, since so many of us thought the expression was, well, so *far out!*

The actual replacement for *bitchin'* was . . . *boss!*

No, this had nothing to do with an employer; it was all about being cool!

Hey, Ben, you got a boss-lookin' girlfriend!

Thank you, Ben would answer.

Oh, Janine! You should see Jack's new car! It's so boss!

And if you *did* happen to have a high-caliber employer, you might hear the following: *Johnny works at Yummy Burger, and his boss is really boss!*

Well, maybe not. But right here in southern California the most popular radio station among teenagers during the sixties and early seventies was (amazingly) an AM channel. It was not uncommon for teens to listen to a loud, obnoxious D.J. who screamed, "This is 93-KHJ, Boss Radio!"

And what replaced *boss*, after its very good run as the king of teenage slang? *Groovy.*

Boss and *groovy* ran almost simultaneously. *Groovy* did not command the limelight as long as *boss* did, having its high-water mark in 1966, when the Mindbenders released a number one song entitled, "A Groovy Kind of Love." But the Mindbenders were one-hit wonders, and *groovy* fizzled out with hippies, after hippies adopted *groovy* into *their* vocabulary. This, of course, was bad, since teenagers wanted to share nothing in common with hippies. Hippies, since most of them were in college or of college age, were *too old!* And then ...

Enter *radical.*

This word *radical,* evolving from *fantabulous, bitchin', swell, boss, far out,* and *groovy,* became popular about the time I started teaching at a public high school. It sounded familiar; after all, I had been a part of the hippie movement and a keen observer of the political spectrum. So why were my teenage students using a word that seemed to have little or no application to social politics? *Radical* had nothing to do with extreme left-wing ideas. It was not about "Hell no! We won't go!" It *was* about, "Ohmigod! You should see Dee's radical new clothes!" And this didn't mean she now had clothes that made her look as though she hung out on Telegraph Avenue in Berkeley; it did mean, however, that her clothes were, well, *bitchin'.*

Radical very quickly was shortened by the culture to *rad.* Everything was either *rad* ... or it wasn't:

What a rad idea!

Lucy has a new boyfriend; he's so rad!

Rad lasted for a long time; right through the eighties, *rad* enlightened us about what we should appreciate and savor, as opposed to what we should overlook and shun. It became the mantra for acceptance. If you weren't *rad,* you probably hadn't been accompanied to the prom, asked to a party, or involved socially at lunch. *Rad* meant *cool* at a time when *cool* had become the registration card for even a minimally tolerable teenage existence; *cool* dominated the thinking of every teenager on the planet, a leading gauge for social acceptability.

Finally, something happened to *rad.*

When I finally acquiesced and reluctantly began to use it, it died; evidently *rad* had died long before I even realized it. Kind of embarrassing, I know. And when I said something to my students like, "Hey, guys, I got a rad idea," they looked at me piteously; I once again had been way out of touch with the hippest language norms.

Moving into gear, I began to emulate my students' descriptions of the cool and the utterly fantabulous to new levels of teacher stardom. I started to say the word *dope*, as in, "You did a really dope thing last night"—nothing to do with narcotics either. It was all about coolness. I felt *so* cool:

Louie, you got a dope friend!

Which is quite different from having a friend who is *a* dope—or worse— who *uses* dope. *Where* a teenager places a word in a sentence can mean everything. A *dope* friend is good. A friend who *is* a *dope* is bad. And having a *doper* friend is even worse (which places a lot of responsibility on that *-er* suffix, doesn't it?).

This awkward use of words that have dichotomy-like meanings goes on and on. More recent trends in Teenagese have given us:

da'bomb—"Mike's body is da'bomb!" Silly me, but I figured if something "bombed," it was a bad thing. Oh, yeah. The reference here is to *da'bomb*. (Flash! My students have just told me *da* is no longer a viable prefix to *bomb*. Now they say, "His body is bomb." In some nations they lament, "He blew up his body with a bomb." Who knows what they'll be saying by the time you read this!)

sick—"We want Kevin on the debate team; he always comes up with sick arguments." Again, something normally very bad turns out to be exceptionally good, although a few people still may think using *sick* as an adjective presents a negative image. Silly them.

bad—"You should have seen that movie! It was bad!" How something bad can wind up good is the mystery here. Alas, simply remembering we are examining the language used by aliens solves this mystery!

My most recent research on this subject identified still another change in the cool-word label. The next word to take on *cool* in adolescent dictionaries is *tight*:

Jennifer, I aced the geometry test today!

Tight!

I'm not too happy with what I found out about this word's derivation, so I now bolt from the subject by challenging you to figure out how this word may have originated, as your imaginations run straight into the gutter.

WHAT THEY SAY—WHAT THEY MEAN

Teenagers gossip—gossip freely—and gossip without a conscience; they have cornered the market on gossip. Teenage girls love to gossip; some girls have made this the cornerstone of their lives. Teenagers are very difficult creatures to communicate with, and even among those who favor verbosity, there is a tendency for an indiscreet warbling of ideas—an interminable, indiscriminate chatter. As a result, only an in-depth study of teenage communication can enlighten us about what kids *really* mean when they say something. This may come in handy when trying to figure out what teenagers actually think about adults; it also could be helpful when unearthing a kid who is slowly destroying his life with drugs.

Usually, though, communication goofs are not this serious. And we don't have time to conduct that in-depth study anyway; so let's become enlightened by the most popular teenage expressions—those offered by girls during a typical gossip session—and what their words *really* mean to the astute, discriminating ear:

Gloria, age 15: "Karen, I really love your new hair! It's so different now, but, like, in a good way!"

What Gloria means: "Karen, it's about time you did something with that crappy hair! None of us girls can understand why you had your hair like that in the first place. Not that it's so great now, but anything would be better than before!"

Kristin, age 16: "I told her what I thought, and she was, like, all...and then I go, 'So what's your problem?' and she's like, 'Nothing,' and then I'm all, like, 'Okaay!'"

What Kristin means: "I informed her of my own opinion, fully expecting to offend her. She reacted the way anyone in her position would react to such an insult, but I feigned surprise at her sensitivity, so I would appear to be bold and daring in her presence. She shrank in her defense, backing down to my admonition."

Brianna, age 16: "He's, like, so hot! I can't believe you don't wanna hook up with him! I mean, I'd, like, be with him in a minute, but...like, I see where you're comin' from. You have morals....I understand."

What Brianna means: "He's much better looking than a lot of boys, and I'm really attracted to him. I'm a little mystified that you don't want to date him and possibly be his girlfriend. If you won't—which you probably won't—I'll have sex with him....Of course, you always were a girl of character, of integrity, of high moral fiber....You loser!"

Amber, age 15: "Come on, Jenna! There's no reason why we shouldn't go to that party. It's gonna be so fun, and everybody's gonna be there! Sometimes you just gotta do what you wanna do and forget about what other people tell you is right for you. You need to do what's right for you, Jenna!"

What Amber means: "Jenna, I want to go to this party, and I'm not going alone. What I need to do is sucker you into going with me. Yeah, there are going to be some vices there—booze, drugs, sex, and probably some fights the cops will have to break up—but doesn't that sound like fun! Besides, Jimmy Reed is going to be there, and I've been waiting for this opportunity! Sometimes, Jenna, you should stop listening to your head and what you think is right, and just go with the flow."

Teenage girls: you needn't comment on the four previous interchanges. Your red faces (I can see them!) provide tacit support for the authenticity of the girls' remarks and the validity of my interpretations.

CURSED BY WHAT THEY HOLD IN

It's not that boys don't feel or think; they just don't like to *talk* about their feelings and thoughts nearly as much as girls do. They gossip less and tell fewer stories about people and things; teenage boys converse about *ideas* and *tangibles* (the risks of surfing, police misconduct, unfair teachers, etc.), but they are not into the psychological realm. Trying to bring a teenage boy into this orb is like asking him to pull his wisdom teeth when he's 50 years old. When teenage boys have a disagreement, they duke it out and then go outside and play basketball together; when teenage girls have a disagreement, they revisit their old grudges at their 50-year class reunion.

Girls emote.

Boys suppress.

Scott wallowed in his secrets. He was like an overinflated tire: crammed with air, bulging on the sides, ripe to burst; so after he began angrily stomping his right foot during baseball practice, digging his cleats into the hard soil around home plate and making a crater that would someday rival the Grand Canyon, I called him into my office.

"What were you thinking out there, Scott?" I chided my stocky second baseman. "Do you realize how ridiculous you looked at practice today?"

His jaw clenched and his face turned purple, but he merely nodded.

That was it: a nod. I wanted to provide him an outlet for his internal rage, but perhaps calling him *ridiculous* was not the best way to coax his anger out of him.

I found out later from his best friend (another player on the team) that the catalyst for Scott's outburst had been a series of arguments with his mother and her new boyfriend. Trying to push his way into Scott's life—despite Scott's revulsion at the idea of anyone replacing his father—the boyfriend had grown impatient with Scott's coldness toward him. He had moved into their home, and Scott's mother gave him the reins on discipline. Despite Scott's obvious aversion to their new living arrangements, his mother remained unsympathetic; in fact, she said nothing when her new stud—with a half-closed hand—struck her son about his face.

Miguel knew Scott better than anyone else; however, it was only *after* Scott had almost decapitated an opposing team's first baseman with a blindside elbow that Miguel came to me with information and sought some compassion for his friend.

"Scott's mother doesn't protect him," he revealed to me on the day of the elbow incident. Not only had Scott been thrown out of that particular game; our assistant principal, who happened to be the administrator in charge of the game that afternoon, subsequently handed Scott a three-day fighting suspension.

"Doesn't protect him?" I raised a brow.

"No," Miguel said quietly, "she lets her boyfriend beat him."

"Why didn't he tell me this?" I asked, clenching my teeth.

Miguel shrugged. "I guess he didn't think anybody cares." And then he paused, looking down. "Maybe Scott doesn't care anymore either."

The discussion with Miguel cascaded into my report to Scott's counselor about the possibility of child abuse. After gathering all the particulars, I filled out a complicated form that clarified very little: Scott lived in a home that neglected his needs—a situation where his mother's new stud sucked the marrow out of the love that had once filled Scott's life. Worse, Scott's mother clearly demonstrated that the needs of her boyfriend came before those of her son.

His loss, his pain—both physical and emotional—had muted him.

Some teenage boys are garrulous (won't stay quiet), but the vast majority of boys must be prodded with cattle irons before they squeak out their feelings or divulge their idiosyncrasies. Despite knowing that boys shut up and shut out, rather than share their inner secrets, society still contends—for inexplicable reasons—that it is *girls* who barricade their needs and problems from busy parents and distracted teachers. Sad, but through all the laughs we adults have enjoyed about the quirky language of teenagers, we still haven't found a more successful scheme for effectively communicating with our most wary, introverted adolescents.

MR. G.'S HOME-GROWN ADVICE

Several times during my teaching career I have said to myself, "I give up. I can't understand these kids; I will *never* understand them. They speak funny, intentionally look weird, and do the most baffling things! They either talk too much or they clam up and don't talk at all. They often say the very opposite of what they really mean. They have a language all their own, and just when I've begun to understand some of it, it changes."

I quit!

I haven't quit, of course. I'm a very tenacious man, and quitting my lifelong dream, working with teenagers and teaching them the skills they will need to live successful, ethical lives, doesn't figure in my plans; so I keep going, fighting my frustrations and agonizing through the whole process of living with—and understanding—teenagers.

Parents

First and foremost: While they're *young*, encourage your children to open up to you. Remind them often that there's nothing they can't tell you. Every time you scoff at them, belittle them, or ridicule their ideas or language, you are constructing barriers between you and your kids. And by the time your children have grown and become teenagers, they will have erected communication barriers of their own. It will be your duty to get through these barriers—fast—providing some damage control. Your teenagers will need to trust you, rely on you, and *talk* to you. Your own exhaustion and everyday frustrations are not excuses for becoming inert in this critical aspect of parenting. Yes, it's exhausting work, but you volunteered for the job.

Teachers

Let your students go! (No, I'm not Moses groveling at the feet of Pharaoh.) You don't have to tolerate profanities (and *should not* tolerate them), but carefully reexamine your intense focus on grammar, punctuation, and slang language. Sure, teach the proper styles for writing and speaking; and, sure, guide your students in the processes for finding their own voices. But never refuse to listen, even if they choose a form of communication you don't agree with or perform with a level of adequacy below your expectations.

Never humiliate teenagers for not saying it the "right way."

All good teachers know there is a fine line between suggesting and rejecting, and often that line is blurred. Good teachers—the ones who actually *care* about the futures of their students—work diligently to find out where that line is and how to straddle it without damaging their students' psyches.

Encourage your students to speak up, even when you know they're going to be wrong. Reward them for oral participation, especially when an exchange of heavy ideas is the order of the day. *Involvement is the key:* with their hearts and their minds and their souls. More than occasionally I have said things in class that I *knew* would infuriate my students, forcing them to respond—sometimes from sheer anger or frustration. As a teacher, you have the power to make or break your students in this most vital of life's arenas: their willingness to express themselves.

Teenagers

If you face any of these communication obstacles, whether they result from your own noncommunicative language or from ill-spirited, narrow-minded adults, here are some pointed suggestions:

1. Love the language that *you* use. Like your teenage predecessors, your language is all your own. Enjoy! If others criticize you—and they will— or make fun of you (as *I* often do), *tough*. You won't be a teenager forever, and one of the pleasures you're going to miss later is your silly, slang-riddled language. When you're all grown up and a daddy of two kids, you will crack your children up, as you describe the way you used to talk. Remember, however, that every so often you also will have to employ a formal voice; for example, writing on a college application, "Yo, dis place's got some sick buildings! It's da'bomb," probably isn't going to get you into Princeton.

2. Speak up. Just when you're thinking you have absolutely nothing to say, nothing to offer anyone else—that everybody else will just laugh at you—these are precisely the times you need to speak up. Say something. If it's wrong, it's wrong. If it's silly, it's silly. If it's irrelevant, it's irrelevant. Part of breaking through communication barriers is being able to absorb criticism and rebound from abject embarrassment. Remember Nietzsche: "That which does not kill us makes us stronger." Good philosophy.

3. Read. Read a *lot*. Read anything! Reading will make you speak and write better; you will have more to say and many additional ways of saying it. Good word use rubs off on us. And reading itself becomes habit-forming—even a better habit than biting your fingernails or smoking weed. So…*read!*

4. Take a speech class. Some of you would rather be at ground zero of the next terrorist attack than take a speech class; the theory behind my suggestion, however, is quite simple: Instruction in public speaking consolidates language use, tears down communication barriers, and alleviates a lot of fears. My competitive speech kids could sling the slang and *get down* with the best of them, but they also knew how to stiffen their speech habits and act formal, stilted, and boring when the situation required them to do so. Taking a speech class is not a sucky idea;

after you have completed the course—not during—you will bless me for prompting you to have done it.

5. Find an adult confidant. Your communication problems do not stem from the language you use; they come from your inability—or unwillingness—to find an appropriate ear. You can use all the Teenagese you want, and most people, even adults, aren't going to care. They *will* understand you when you say, "I had a bad time at the dance Friday night." They'll know you actually had a *good* time at the dance Friday night. The key is to find someone—preferably a parent of the same sex, a teacher, a counselor, a minister, or an older, *hot* cashier at the supermarket—you can spill your guts to. Even a good friend your own age cannot replace the wisdom of the older, hot cashier at the supermarket.

6. Go right to the source: A friend is talking about you behind your back? He's not your friend. *Tell him that.* Without an apparent reason, the teacher picks on you? *Ask her for her justification.* You want to ask that cute, suntanned blond to the movies? *Call her today.* You need a job and are terrified of the interview? *Immediately schedule the interview for tomorrow and march in there as though you held the world in the palms of your hands.* You're embarrassed because your mom is not behaving as a dignified mom should behave? *Explain your concerns and tell her that she embarrasses you.* Get the point? Go to the source—stutter and stammer if you have to—and get the job done with the words that *you* want to use.

7. See a professional. No one enjoys constipation. Emotional and verbal constipation prevent us from getting rid of bad stuff that needs to come out. Good therapists, psychologists, and psychiatrists have been known to perform miracles, extricating the emotional demons from people of all ages. Trained professionals coax their clients to relax, performing their nonjudgmental therapy. Many of you would benefit tremendously from this kind of help. Getting therapy doesn't mean you're nuts; it means you're a normal American teenager.

8. Become good at something. What do you do well? Get even better at it. Teenagers who involve themselves in permissible passions lead better lives than teenagers who don't. Find groups that share your interests and skills and make new friends. Sports is an obvious outlet; having hobbies (fishing, train collecting, theater, etc.) is another. You may be surprised how well you communicate with people who speak the common language of your passions. Eventually, you will have to fan out to other areas of interest, but slashing down some of those communication barriers today could unlock some doors for you tomorrow.

Like, Final Thoughts

A few years ago, a local teacher carefully studied the reasons why young people generously mixed the word *like* into their everyday conversations. He concluded that they lacked personal confidence and commitment; for example, if someone asked you the directions to the local pizza joint, you would answer: "You exit the parking lot, make a right, go to the end of the street, and then turn left."

A modern teenager may say: "You, like, go out the parking lot, make, like, a right, go, like, to the end of the street, and then, like, turn left."

The teacher's explanation made sense. Teenagers sprinkle their sentences with the word *like* because they don't wish to commit themselves to anything. When, *Make a right*, becomes, *Make*, like, *a right*, we show our indecisiveness. Increasingly in society, people are unwilling or unable to commit to *anything*. (No wonder some kids view married people as self-deluded buffoons.) Our teens see a lack of commitment all around them, and this image rubs off in their language use.

Supposedly, English is one of the most difficult languages to learn. Replete with zillions of rules—with as many exceptions to those rules—studying the English language can make even the toughest grown man cry. Throw in the ever-changing language of teenage America, and even intelligent life-forms from outer space would surrender in their endeavor to understand America's adolescents. Adult Earthlings face these challenges all the time. Their successes or failures in bringing up children, teaching students, or handling society's wayward young people are determined by how well adults and teens communicate with each other.

Kudos to those who succeed in meeting these challenges.

And woe to those who fail.

2

The Rebel Paradox

DAN THE VAN

In his masterpiece *Annie Hall*, Woody Allen alludes to the legendary comedian Groucho Marx, who quipped something about not wishing to belong to a club that was lousy enough to accept him as a member.

A strange paradox facing modern teenagers embodies this philosophy. Kids fiercely wish to belong; yet, they desperately desire to stand apart. They don't want to be different; yet, they despise being the same.

Dan the Van exemplified this paradox. Learning about Dan the Van and what motivated him can enlighten us; for a little—perhaps, a lot—of Dan the Van lurks in all teenagers.

Dan the Van did not come into this world as Dan the Van. Dan the Van had a very normal name: he was born Jarrod White. Evidently, his first-grade teacher mistakenly kept calling him Van, mixing his name up with another student's. Dan *liked* to be called Van, but the *real* Van didn't like this at all, so they compromised: one went by Van the Dan; the other by Dan the Van.

Nobody knows what happened to Van the Dan.

By the time he joined the debate team in his sophomore year, Dan the Van already stood more than six feet tall and weighed around 160 pounds. Despite his height, Dan the Van did not project muscularity or athletic skills; he did not exude confidence in his speaking ability. His physical appearance was sloppy, his gait slovenly.

Dan the Van definitely lived on a planet of his own. Extremely knowledgeable about material nobody in his right mind would seriously care about, Dan the Van could toss around the most worthless information with the best of them. Back then, games like *Trivial Pursuit* were thriving. But nobody on the debate team wanted to play trivia games with Dan the Van. He'd slaughter them by actually *knowing* the answers to questions such as, "What was the name of the Dallas nightclub Jack Ruby owned on the day President Kennedy was assassinated?" I mean—really—who cared about *that?* (Kennedy assassination geeks know the answer: The Carousel Club.) What's worse, Dan the Van would later caustically recap his opponents' botched answers and provide background information on the same topics—the ones nobody cared about in the first place.

Dan the Van was cursed with terrible coordination. Once he fell down a few steps leading to the parking lot outside my classroom. His timing was impeccable; he had just finished telling me that he needed to participate more in his gym class, or the PE teacher wasn't going to let him miss Fridays in order to attend speech tournaments. Immediately following his enthusiastic confirmation of a new commitment to his physical development, Dan the Van proceeded to topple down three stairs, his face meshing with the gravel in the parking lot.

I can sum up the *exterior* Dan the Van this way: He possessed little or no talent for competitive speech. He never spoke to girls. He complained bitterly about liberals and Democrats, although he demonstrated a political IQ of about −50. A worse athlete I had never observed. A greater propensity for an abrupt display of anger (to my knowledge, always expressed verbally) I had never known in a teenager. Dan the Van dressed like a geek and walked without purpose; yet, he plumed his feathers like a peacock.

Dan the Van was one very strange dude.

Although the following exchange occurred more than 25 years ago, it seems as though it was only yesterday when Dan the Van shuffled goofily into my classroom on the Wednesday afternoon before Thanksgiving.

"Mr. Gevirtzman," Dan the Van addressed me with a formality reminiscent of our very first meeting. "We need to talk."

This kid really bugged me. A rare opportunity to catch a movie on the way home had presented itself, and I needed to hurry. Here was El Weirdo holding me up—and for what inane reason?

"I'm on my way out, Dan," I told him, trying to mask my impatience.

"I need to talk," he said, setting his jaw firmly.

Not fully aware if a support existed under me or not, I sagged; fortunately, my desk chair caught my collapsing body. "Okay, Dan. You've got my ear for five minutes."

"Not enough time," he persisted.

"That leaves about *four* minutes, now."

"Not fair."

"Three. You have *three* minutes left."

"Mr. G., I'm going to kill myself."

"A tad of an exaggeration," I shrugged, masking the chill that ran through me. "When *my* teachers didn't have time to speak with me, say, for example, on the *Wednesday afternoon before Thanksgiving*, I didn't take it to heart. I just figured they were jerks."

But he didn't bat an eyelash. "I'm going to hang myself with bed sheets, just like they did in *Cool Hand Luke*."

I'd seen *Cool Hand Luke* three times; there was no hanging with bed sheets; the closest Paul Newman came to offing himself in that film happened when he stuffed himself like a pig in the hardboiled egg–eating sequence. Of course, this wasn't exactly the time to contest Dan the Van's movie aptitude; he'd just threatened to kill himself. Already, I was legally bound to report his comments to school administrators.

Before I could gather my thoughts and respond, Dan the Van went on, "I'm doing it right after turkey tomorrow night. Right after turkey, I'm going to blow my brains out in my dad's bedroom. I know where he hides his gun, and...."

Hadn't Dan the Van just informed me that he'd decided to use bed sheets (just as they *hadn't* done in *Cool Hand Luke*)? And now he's going to shoot himself in the head?

What gives?

I looked at him with an intensity that managed to conceal the exhaustion I always felt this time of year. "What are you saying?" I asked him. Actually, I knew what he was saying; I just didn't understand what he meant to do about it.

"I'm saying," he responded, suddenly raising his voice, "that I'm going to kill myself tomorrow night."

I decided that a long, thoughtful pause should precede opening my mouth and making the irreversible error of putting my foot in it. After a few seconds, I knew it was my turn.

"What could be so bad that you would want to do something like that?"

"I hate my life." He remained stoic; his earlier anger had quelled.

"Right now, things aren't going too well? Is that it?"

He didn't respond.

I continued, "But what about later? What about all the things you have to look forward to in the future?"

"Like what?" he whispered with a heartbreaking softness.

Should I make something up or tell him the truth?

I compromised. "You're smart; you're tall. Lots of guys would like to be tall. I wish I were half your height...." I suddenly perked up. "Let's make a deal; I'll swap with you. I'll give you an inch of bicep (I was a bodybuilder), if you give me three inches of height. Fair enough? Muscle for height. Sound good to you?"

My not-so-clever method of distracting him had failed big time; it may have reminded Dan the Van how awkwardly tall and underdeveloped he was.

"It's either myself—or you, Mr. G.—or my mother. I hate my mother; I don't hate you. I just hate *her*."

Through the prattle of his last statement, some clarity surfaced: *Dan the Van had just threatened my life*. Uneasiness enveloped me. What if he pulled a little gun out of his pocket right now and shot me? He'd be arrested and on the news; I'd be dead. We'd both get lots of publicity, but he would be able to soak it all in—in person—while I sat in an urn on my mother's fireplace.

Something told me this was not the time to sound timid or halting. "You just threatened to kill me, Dan the Van."

He nodded, sending a spooky gaze in my direction. "I'm not sure that I did that."

"And kill yourself."

And then he reiterated, "I'm not going to do it until tomorrow night. Right after turkey."

I looked cautiously at Dan the Van. I'd always been aware that on some level Dan the Van had been hurting inside, although I didn't know how much or why until later. Dan the Van on the outside was quite different from the Dan the Van on the *inside*: scared, confused, inadequate, hesitant, and besieged by loneliness. Unfortunately, the Dan the Van who said he was going to kill himself was the Dan the Van on the *outside*—and the outside pulls the trigger on the gun.

Subsequently, Dan the Van received treatment for his depression; and for his threat on my life, he was expelled from our school district. In this crazy system, when a kid is suspended from one public school district, another district takes him in by trading one of their worst offenders even up; it's sort of an equal opportunity juvenile delinquent swap.

I never heard from Dan the Van again. I expected to find out that he'd been killed doing something irrational, or that he wound up in prison with guys meaner than he was. I did, however, learn enough about Dan the Van to understand his head-trip: Dan the Van lived alone with his mother in a single-bedroom apartment; evidently, they both occupied the same bedroom, but Dan the Van slept on a couch in the living room. Dan the Van's mother depended on him for everything, including grocery shopping and cooking meals. Through this unorthodox arrangement, he struggled with a self-loathing that had evolved from his failed obsessive attempts to find purpose through his *mother's* happiness. *Dan the Van tried to fit in and stand apart at the same time*. Most teenagers crave simultaneously these disparate, mutually exclusive conditions. Confusion and chaos usually follow, and that explains why some teens look perpetually stoned.

"HELL NO! WE WON'T GO!...OR WHATEVER"

James Dean's movie, *Rebel Without a Cause*, had been a huge Hollywood blockbuster before I became a teenager. The reason it skyrocketed to the top of the cult classic genre is that it spoke to teenagers of all generations. Kids are enthralled with the idea of being rebels; and if they can be a "rebel without a cause," well, that's even cooler. Some boys long to be rebels because they know that girls like rebels. When a guy is a rebel, he receives lots of attention: from girls, from friends, from teachers, from parents, and from the police. This attention may not be good attention; it could be criticism or ridicule, *but it's attention* nonetheless. For many boys, any kind of acknowledgment is better than no acknowledgment at all. When the teacher yells at them in class, they cringe inside. But, hey, at least *somebody* noticed them!

Boys come running to rebellious girls like dogs go after leftover meat on a discarded bone; they expect rebels to throw their sexual inhibitions to the wind. Tougher, meaner-looking girls tend to be easier—at least, their reputation says they're more sexually available. Rebellious girls often get tattoos in titillating places on their bodies. And tattoos broadcast that a girl is more willing to put out than a girl without tattoos. Tattoos are a sign of rebellion; and in general rebellion wears a very positive reputation among teenagers.

Rebellious teenagers behave in ways that hurt themselves—such as drinking, drugs, promiscuity, crime, body mutilation, excessive weight fluctuations, isolation, licking glossy pictures of Zac Efron, and suicide; in addition, rebellious teens command so much unwarranted attention, they capture the wrath of their teachers and parents. The credo of the rebellious teenager: Figure out what authority figures demand as appropriate behavior...*and do the opposite*.

I obtained some comments from several teens about rebellion, conformity, and those gray areas between the extremes. After each comment I provide some brief analysis:

> Joy (10th grade): I usually get frustrated when too many people are telling me what to do, so I wind up getting mad and give up. Sometimes I just do what I want to do—and forget about what everybody else expects from me.

Joy desires to gratify too many people. Since she can't please everybody, she decides to please nobody. It's also a good excuse for indulging herself, no matter what unsavory form this may take.

> Jackson (10th grade): When I feel lazy, I get rebellious; I just try to piss people off!

Jackson rebels out of anger, but the rage is directed mostly at himself. Jackson, however, is perceptive enough to see his problem: he's lazy. To disguise this condition as well as he can, he lashes out at others, as though their nagging were the real culprit.

> Jenny (12th grade): I usually do what my parents want, except when it comes to my boyfriend. They don't like him; I figure, it's my life, and they don't have the right to tell me who I should feel happy being around.

This is classic rebellion, but aimed at a particular audience (parents) over a particular issue (boyfriend). In addition to being typical teenage rebellion, it also embodies the standard adolescent cry: "I know better than anyone else what's good for me!"

> Alyssa (12th grade): We learn from our mistakes. That's how we get better. When parents and teachers control us too much, it's natural for us to go in the other direction. They say, "Do this; do that; do this; do that"—and you're all, well, "I'll do whatever. Just get off my back!"

It's typical for kids to react defensively when they know they've done—or are about to do—something wrong. The old standby is, "We gotta learn from our mistakes." The teenager who is only minimally rebellious hopes to make only minor mistakes and learn valuable lessons. That's why so many teenagers actually *like* it when people in authority set clear boundaries and enforce those boundaries. Ask a high school student which type of teacher she likes better: a teacher who is loose in his classroom management, or a teacher who sets down strict rules and procedures and makes sure they're followed consistently and fairly. The structured disciplinarian wins—hands down.

> Mark (11th grade): Being different is usually good. But sometimes it's bad. It depends on what it is.

In a larger sense, Hitler was a rebel. He stood up for what he believed in; he took grave chances, offered huge sacrifices, and made bold moves. Do we admire Hitler for being rebellious or different? The answer, of course, is that sometimes standing up for what we believe in can be evil, *if what we believe in is evil.*

Many teenagers esteem "different" just because it is, well, different. With disregard for morality, ethics, dignity, and integrity, awe comes when standard norms are rejected. Teenage girls smile and giggle when the teacher chews out the bad boy. Who cares if the bad boy she is laughing with—and somewhat attracted to—is more likely to later send her to an abuse shelter than is the passive, obedient, horn-rimmed glasses–wearing geek who sits behind her in algebra class. The rebel is *hot!* He stands out! He gets attention! He's not like everybody else! He does his thing! He's a rebel *without* a cause! And, frankly, a rebel *with* a cause is not very attractive to girls—since having a cause renders him less of a rebel; perhaps, a rebel *with* a cause isn't really a rebel at all.

AND THE WINNERS ARE...

Dan the Van epitomized the rebel paradox. He yearned for attention; yet, he also sought normality. In our youth culture, normal does not get noticed; no one takes heed of normal, and normal reeks with boredom, especially when surrounded by other normal.

Visit any public high school in America, and you will find a rich pool of attention-seekers. Physical appearance deceives; there's no doubt about that. The deception, though, is not always as overt as people claim. No matter what some kids do—or what they look like—they disappear the minute they walk into a room. They may go unnoticed until the next Ice Age; they've been doomed by nature or genes or whatever to merely blend into the furniture.

Dan the Van wins hands down for the *strangest* teenager I've ever come across—much of that strangeness ensconced in rebellion; however, aside from a rebel's unusual hair, the obvious attempts to shock with profanity, the grungy attire, the outrageous music, and so on, here are my choices for the top five rebels of my teaching career (in reverse order of their audacity).

Rebel #5

Jarrod walks into my classroom for the first time on the third day of school. He wears a black hat with the insignia from an infamous professional football team on its front. His move is more of a swagger than a walk, and he radiates that he hates being here. He plops into a desk in the back of a row. I finish taking attendance and quietly go to where he's sitting. We have school and classroom rules, and Jarrod obviously has missed the lecture in which I spelled out those rules the initial day of class. I'm about to inform him of his first infraction: Rule 74 B-6, Little A, Section 4: "If you wear a hat in a classroom, you will be executed."

"Jarrod," I whisper discreetly, because I don't wish to embarrass him, "you need to remove your hat."

Not even hinting that he is willing to remove his hat, he offers a dull stare.

"Huh? Why?" he manages to semi-grunt.

"Because it's a school rule."

"School rules suck."

Hmm. This one may turn out tougher than I thought it would—certainly tougher than it needs to. "It's my rule, too: no hats."

"Your rule sucks, too."

By this time, most of the class is eavesdropping. Especially during the first week of school, teachers must establish themselves; this means absolutely no flexibility for bending the rules. It also requires a tough teacher strut.

"Jarrod," I respond, half-trying to contain my increasing impatience, hoping this has become obvious to my other students, "you have three seconds to take the hat off. Just do it; it's not worth it."

What did I know in 1985?

Being a rebel *was* worth it.

Jarrod makes not even a feeble attempt to take the hat off, so I'm compelled to write one of my infrequent discipline referrals (this one for defiance). He is removed from my class by the assistant principal.

Jarrod drops into permanent obscurity.

Rebel #4

Monica's story is strikingly similar to Jarrod's, but with a few notable differences that put her higher than Jarrod on my list of infamous rebels. Monica, too, stands out. But in this instance, it's the first day of school, a time for me to present rules, regulations, and procedures to all students.

Monica, a petite brunette in the back of the class, finds intolerable my limitation on the number of days I would accept makeup work after absences. She interrupts me from her seat. "What if we need more time?"

"Easy," I shrug. "Just let me know why. I'll probably give you more time."

"What if we don't want to tell you why we need more time?" she asks.

"Why would you not want to tell me?"

"Because it might not be any of your business."

This girl irritates me; I unsuccessfully try not to show it. "Well," I counter, gritting my teeth, "if you miss the deadline, I guess you won't be able to turn in your makeup work."

"That's stupid."

I narrow my eyes. "I think you need to see me immediately after class."

"Fuck you!" she sneers.

I'm not sure that I actually *hear* what I think I hear; however, if I'm correct, this is a scene out of a bad movie about teenagers—the kind in which the kids go to the teachers' houses and torture their families with screwdrivers, profanities, and bad grammar.

I come back at Monica with a real zinger: "Uh, excuse me?"

She stands, grabs her backpack, and retreats toward the door. She flashes me an exaggerated middle finger salute, one she has clearly mastered over several years of practice. The fact that she is no more than 15 years old makes this even more impressive, and I somehow refrain from hurling back, "Fuck you!"

Needless to say, I write Monica up on referral; she is tossed from the school and sent to another high school in the district.

Our assistant principal takes *fuck you* seriously.

Rebel #3

Ronnie would never shrink from the prospect of nonsensical, unmotivated rebellion against any authority: Ronnie knows that he owns status as one of the handsomest kids in the school. Closely cropped blond hair, accented by his even July tan from the scorching California sun, does nothing to deter Ronnie from his quest to win over the summer's cuties. His *up yours!* smirk and bad-boy persona are enough to attract girls like sugar cookies attract children during the Christmas holidays.

Unfortunately, like most teenage rebels, Ronnie manages to ignore one fact: He is his own worst enemy.

I first meet Ronnie during the summer of 1997. He defiantly marches into my classroom, besieged by the daunting task of still having to pass 9th-grade English. About to embark upon his 11th-grade year, Ronnie's frontline defense against humiliation is machismo pride. He becomes agitated when he senses someone does not like him; yet, almost every move he makes is seemingly designed to thwart his likeability. He cusses in the classroom, even after repeated warnings. He deliberately disregards my mandates to hand in assignments on time (or at all), as he stands out in this summer session as the student least likely to complete a homework assignment.

I have to fight my conflicted self; a teacher, after all, is supposed to be fair. The problem here is that Ronnie is extraordinarily likable most of the time. But he has a penchant for blindsiding me with a sudden pompous attitude and unenviable talent for spewing profanities.

I scowl; Ronnie gloats without saying a word.

The girls swoon.

And then I receive this journal entry:

My father tried to kill me last night. He found marijuana under my bed. The thing is, I didn't put it there. I know who put it there. My dad's girlfriend. She can't stop drinking and smoking pot, but he seems to overlook that fact. So she stuck me for the dope, and my dad beat the shit out of me.

By the way, did I mention that my dad is a cop? He used to steal the stash from the station and then come home and hide out in the bathroom all night smoking pot. Then his girlfriend, Pat, started, and she won't stop. He takes it out on me by cussing me out and slamming me around the room. I love my dad. I hate him! HATE him!

So much potential there! Ronnie's assertiveness could have been channeled into positive athletic endeavors or a prized leadership position. But Ronnie is destined to fail the class and, perhaps, wind up in serious trouble—maybe with a third-party boyfriend or even a husband who wants to rip him apart. A self-centered, unreasonable father has screwed him up, and now Ronnie pays the price for it.

The following September Ronnie requests to be put in my English class. When I first see him, I'm glad that he's doing better. I know he's inwardly appreciative that I had reported his journal entry to a guidance counselor; she conveyed its content to the proper authorities, who managed to help bring some safety and peace into Ronnie's household.

Later Ronnie provokes a fight with one of the athletes, and I'm reminded that he is a terrible influence in the classroom. The football player leaps furiously over three desks to get to Ronnie, who has become trapped by a wall. I interrupt the bloody pounding and badly strain the pinky finger on my left hand. Both boys are expelled from our school, but because of Ronnie's dismal discipline record, he is ostracized from all other schools in our district.

He is released into oblivion.

Rebel #2

Sarah sports cheers and smiles wherever she goes. Beautiful, in a sophisticated, mature sort of way, Sarah possesses an electrifying smile, one that jolts energy into any room previously worn down by the tedium of a mandated high school curriculum. Sarah's charm is contagious, so hardly anyone dislikes her.

But Sarah balks at conformity.

"Hey, Mr. G., you wanna go to the prom with me?" she asks me half-jokingly.

The fact that a girl who looks like Sarah would grovel for a prom date is in itself a bit peculiar. But grovel she does. She likes one boy in particular: his name is Fernando. He's tall and has tattoos; he doesn't come even close to Sarah in intelligence and appears to be headed for a lifetime of pumping gasoline.

So, why does Sarah yearn for Fernando?

She explains it this way: "There's just something about him. Something mysterious. He's not like other guys, always trying to impress girls, planning to make tons of money and live in a big house surrounded by a white picket fence."

Translated: "He's a bizarre dude who has very few goals in life, has little patience for courting females, is dirt poor, and means to stay that way."

On this earth there are lots of Sarahs; they're extremely pretty, highly intelligent, and very amiable. Girls like Sarah, however, thrive on nonconformity. Being unlike the hordes of other attractive, brilliant 15-year-olds is a top priority; so Sarah sends signals to good boys that she *doesn't* want them and to bad boys that she's *interested* in them. The bad boys, however, never approach Sarah, because they're afraid of her; she broadcasts unavailability. And let's face it: no teenage boy feels comfortable around a girl who is 20 times smarter than he is.

Sarah doesn't go to parties; she doesn't dance, and she doesn't hang out at the mall. She dresses conservatively, remains a virgin, and declines to use profanity. In essence, Sarah gauges the coolness level of any idea, fad, pattern, or movement among her peers...

And does just the opposite.

For Sarah, rebellion is an avocation.

An aside: Sarah tells me years later that she never dated *once* during her high school years. Two months out of high school while attending college in Berkeley, she meets a rich oil executive who is considerably older than she is, dates him for five months, and gets married.

They now live in San Francisco with their two teenage children.

Rebel #1

The best way to describe Gus: conspicuous.

You can't overlook Gus—for anything.

Gus is now 49 years old, has failed to hold down a job for more than a couple of months, lives with his aged mother (on and off), and currently weighs more than 400 pounds. Gus would describe himself as a political liberal; he's an avid baseball fan and can recite batting averages in his sleep. He's loudly outspoken (often obnoxiously) and admits that he is very lonely. Gus tells me directly that if his father hadn't deserted his mother and him when he was six years old, his life today could be quite different. His mother, a tremendously strong, courageous, and honorable woman, tried valiantly to raise Gus by herself, but she can't be a father, too: she's not a man. Gus says that he doesn't relish blaming his fatherless home for his abject failure in life, but he seems to wallow continuously in his victimhood.

Despite this, I like Gus.

He is charming and funny and adept at contributing to intelligent conversations. Despite his hard exterior and his enormous size, Gus projects an inner sensitivity that endears him to people who get to know him well.

Still a rebel, Gus is slowly but surely killing himself.

I first meet Gus during his sophomore year, when he and his bulk (yes, he is way overweight at the age of 15, too) strides into my classroom for 10th-grade English. He stands out: Beyond the obvious, his weight, Gus wears an Angels baseball cap wherever he goes; since the Angels are also my team, I immediately discover something in common with this unusual youngster.

I learn of Gus's sadness over his father's abandonment, and I also meet his mother, who picks him up from school every day. She's a dedicated, committed mother; yet, she isn't a man, and no matter how hard she tries, she can't be a father to Gus, too.

The three of us quickly become friends.

The main consequence of Gus's withdrawal and rebellion is his weight. He can't fit on a regular scale; he uses a freight scale. The other kids ridicule him constantly, calling him nicknames such as "The Cargo," whenever he gets into a car. We all enjoy Gus's sarcastic quips, melancholy perspectives on social issues, and extreme political views, which lead to inspired conversations on the way to debate tournaments. But around Gus there is always an aura of sadness.

Gus's propensity for rebelling is enormous. Everything he does, he does to excess: his passions, his loyalty, his politics—and, of course, his eating.

Recently, I have a conversation with Gus about where he has landed in life. He tells me, "If I had a dad, things would've been different. I wouldn't have become so angry. I wouldn't have needed to get attention the way that I did. All my life I've traded my dignity to get attention."

Reluctant to look me in the eye, Gus simply lowers his head.

MR. G.'S HOME-GROWN ADVICE

Gus knew that his rationalizations for failure didn't impress me. As with all rebels, it's particularly difficult to figure out motives and make reasonable sense of their behaviors. For most rebels, there seems to be little excuse for their conduct; *the act itself has intrinsic merit.* Their rebellion is judged by the methodology of their acts and the size of their deeds—not the *reasons* they rebel. To have an actual *cause* is not to be a true rebel; it is an interloper, a protester, a hippie—volunteering to be scrutinized on the dreaded geek scale: a hideous, unintended consequence of rebellion *with* a cause.

Since rebels cry out for attention—any kind of attention—it's crucial that parents fill up their kids with love. This is done mostly by the amount of *time* they spend with their children—not just at an early age—but while they are adolescents. When her teenagers arrive home from school, Mama should be standing at the white picket fence with Spot the dog and warm chocolate chip cookies.

Someone needs to be there; preferably, this someone is a loving parent.

Listening to teenagers—*actually acknowledging what they have to say*—could deter some of them from acting out in negative ways in order to garner adult attention. Blatantly defying authority figures is one way of turning the spotlight on the self; however, a few compliments about anything at all (how they're doing in school, the way they've parted their hair, the smiles on their faces, their energy level, their enthusiasm for special activities, their civilized manners, their kindnesses to others, their industry, their loyalty to friends, their depictions of right and wrong, their wisdom for making sound decisions) earn only positive reactions.

Teachers need to reinforce the benefits of *civilized* social behaviors. Some teachers only yell at kids for the things they've done wrong. Children learn that the surest way to remind other people that they're alive is to act out in a manner (usually an ugly one) that brings them attention. Remember: the goal of the rebel is to be *noticed*, validated, recognized as someone who matters—regardless of what he has to do to reach that goal.

We all need people to confirm that we exist. We *crave* to be noticed; it's an aphrodisiac. Some people nonchalantly substantiate that we're important; others *fill us up* with their attention. Human beings depend on other human beings to bring us security, warmth, and love. And protecting our children and soaking them with security, warmth, and love constitute our primary duties as parents. Without these, kids have a void that—one way or another, for better or worse—*will* be filled. Look at the lengths to which Dan the Van, Gus, Monica, and the others would go *just to have someone notice them.*

I hope someone finally gave Dan the Van the time and attention he craved, and he somehow made positive strides in his life. I'd like to think Dan the Van survived in a world that has not been too kind to its rebels.

3

Mirror, Mirror

MIRROR, MIRROR—AW, SHUT UP!

I'm never pretty enough. If I'm with my boyfriend at a movie and there's this really hot actress on the screen, I sit there, going crazy in my mind. I know he's lusting for her. I know he's thinking that she's hotter. I put my hands down and touch my thighs and feel how fat I am. It disgusts me.

Ever since Laura wrote these words more than 20 years ago, I have shared her journal entry with thousands of my students.

Laura is not an aberration.

In March 2007, while preparing the manuscript for a play about teenagers and self-image, I asked hundreds of junior and senior high school students to look into a figurative mirror and anonymously write down what they saw in their reflections:

When I look in the mirror, I see a young woman—confused—and afraid I will never be loved.

When I look in the mirror, I see a guy who tries too hard—and is still never good enough.

What happened? I used to be a zero and now I'm a four. Gross.

I eat and eat, but I can't gain a pound.

I see a skeleton.

I see a tub of lard.

I'm a Christian boy, but my sinning is off the charts, man.

You give up too easy, dude. . . . You're a failure, failure—failure!

Chubby cheeks. Not cute either. No one would want to pinch 'em.

That's a really white person I'm looking at. Too white...way too white.

Dimples.

Pimples.

Has that bump on my nose always been there? Has it always been that big?

My friends get all the chicks. Why can't I get even one?

All my friends have boyfriends. I'm still the girl without the boyfriend.

I gotta succeed—as much as my older brother.

Get into a good college...or else.

I'm the guy without a dad whose mother is married to the biggest jerk. How embarrassing for me that she stays with a man like that!

I see my mother in the mirror, and it disgusts me.

Look, dude...just remember one thing: you're never going to be like your father. You can do much better than that.

My friends think I have the weirdest family. I need to hide my family from my friends.

What I can do to attract boys? I'll do anything.

I ask, "What do girls want?" And I try to be that.

Not pretty enough. Not good enough. Not smart enough. Not enough. Never enough.

I'm weird.

I want to be different.

I hate being different.

I alter myself all the time to fit in—and then I never fit in.

Disgusting. You disgust me.

Would I want to be my friend? No!

Would I want to be my boyfriend?

Studying seven days a week, seven hours a day....Look at those rings under my eyes. I'll just hide them with some makeup.

Black and proud.

More American than Mexican.

My muscles will never be cut like my brother's.

I'll never be as pretty as my sister.

Blunt.

Scared.

Lonely.

Tired. I'm so tired!

Why don't I get off my butt and do what I'm supposed to? I'm so lazy!

When I wink at myself, why don't I wink back?

Am I pretty enough for him?

Straight teeth. Brushed hair. Pretty cool. I look good, but do I look good enough for her?

Why can't I appreciate my family more? I'm such an ingrate!

I get distracted; I'm messing up my life.

I want to take care of her.

I'm such a little girl; I'm waiting for someone to take care of me.

Nothing. A nothing under all this makeup.

The product of divorced parents.

Why are you alone? Because you're not a size two.

You're ugly, dude.

You're all face—mostly cheek and chin.

You're lazy—and lazy because you're fat.

Lazy made you fat. Exercise! Get off your butt!

Heeeew! A zit!

Flab…Flab—flab—flab—flab—.

Yuck! Yellow teeth!

Let it out! Suck it in. Let it out—suck it in!

No breasts.

No muscle.

No boobs.

Small neck.

Big feet.

God, I pick the jerks!

I'll take any girl. Any girl is better than no girl at all.

Will I ever find a good guy? What's wrong with me?

I'm attracted to the wrong people.

I only eat when I absolutely have to.

I can't stop eating.

I can easily go two or three days without eating.

I can't stop thinking about food.

Food is my enemy.

Scars. Surgery is in my future.

Burns.

Acne pits.

Crater face.

Does being adopted make me different?

Will any girl ever like a nice guy like me?

Why is my voice still so high?

How come my left eye is smaller than my right eye?

I've stood next to teenagers, as they've moaned, groaned—and swooned—over their own reflections; I can relate to what they're going through, although my own teenage years are mostly a blur. In May 1966, I was looking forward to my senior prom; unfortunately, 10 minutes before I donned my flashy turquoise tuxedo for this highly anticipated occasion, I glanced in a real mirror.

Huge mistake.

That gargantuan red blob of—whatever—that sat in the middle of my forehead stood out like a Christmas bulb; and when I covered my eyes with my hands, I mistook myself for a cyclops. After trembling like a chilled newborn, I identified my latest head ornament: an enormous, newly formed *pimple!* I looked like one of those guys in *Ben Hur* who hid in dark caves because he had leprosy. I just stood there and watched my zit shine like it had a Double-A battery inside. I swear—the dang thing began to pulsate!

I even entertained thoughts of asking my girlfriend if we could call the whole thing off: "Hi, Pamela, this is Bruce. Would it be okay if we didn't go to the prom? I have a zit the size of a shot-put on my forehead."

The small, faded color picture they took at the dance tells it all: Pamela, with her dark hair piled about 40 feet in the air, dressed in a stunning, blue, low-cut gown, a dazzling smile lighting up her face; I, in a dorky turquoise tux, a size too large for my bony frame; a forced smile; and an engorged pimple lighting up my shiny forehead. Even 40 years of oxidization couldn't conceal one of the ugliest—and most untimely—disfigurements that had ever burdened me while I was a teenager.

For years my students have heard this story; I want them to understand a crucial concept: *They'll get over it!* The zit will go away. The other kids at the prom that night had problems of their own, many of which were far worse than springing a puree boulder on their foreheads. Even in those days, dads were beating up moms, sisters were announcing they got pregnant by the grease monkey who lived across the street, and 50-year-old fathers were coming home from work, grabbing a beer and a cigarette, settling in to watch a ball game—and then dropping dead from a heart attack.

Abusive dads, pregnant sisters, and sudden death: they would have to take a back seat to the *crisis* of the moment. Those were mere abstractions. My 20,000-centimeter pimple: now *that* was reality!

MY DAUGHTER, MY BARBIE, AND MY PIG

The reality for millions of America's teenagers is that they don't *ever* like what they see in the mirror. They can't be tall enough, skinny enough, tan enough, muscular enough, or pretty enough. They want blond hair, but they have black hair—black hair, but they have blond hair. They augment their breasts because they're too small and shrink their noses because they're too large. Their entire lives are wrapped up in the vanity of their appearance, as they tangle with a nebulous, fleeting concept known as *self-esteem.* Every day breeds another battle to keep up with the Heathers or the Jennifers, while the self-worth of a teen is contorted by the media and the goddess-like bodies of Jessica Simpson, Jessica Alba, and Jessica Biel (so many Jessicas to compete with)!

And this is not merely theoretical: Rachael finally had worked up her nerve to make her move for Pedro; after all, the junior-senior prom was only three weeks away. Mortified by the stark realization that she may have to attend this vitally important high school social function with a group of her girlfriends or—horrors!—*alone,* Rachael decided to announce her intentions by the not-too-subtle method of passing a note to Pedro during her fifth-period chemistry class. Mr. Simore's boring lectures usually slid the entire class into a comatose state, so dispatching a folded piece of notebook paper would certainly go unobserved by the teacher. Unfortunately, as the note came to a shaggy-haired dude who sat two desks in front of Pedro, it fell unnoticed to the floor; neither Pedro nor the goofball in front of him had the slightest idea the note existed, even as it lay on the scuffed and worn tiles of the chemistry lab.

Rachael panicked. What if Mr. Simore, who had read other intercepted notes aloud to the entire class, discovered *this* note? With seemingly no time to spare, Rachael raced through an aisle of student desks toward a fallen piece of lined paper—one that promised an entire lifetime's worth of adolescent angst. But just as she came upon the folded object of her concern, her foot grazed the backpack of a classmate, causing Rachael to lurch forward, her ample weight unable to thwart the laws of gravity or inertia.

Yes, Rachael managed to get her hands on her note to Pedro; unfortunately, she also lay flat on her face with that note clutched tightly between her fingers. She never delivered the note to him. She never attended the prom during her senior year. She never wrote another note in high school to a boy again.

Much later, Rachael told me, "It's not what the note said; feeling like I had to use a *note* to ask him to the prom humiliated me. Looking back, I see how desperate I was—how my self-esteem was so wrapped up in going to a stupid *dance!* I didn't even *want* to go to the prom that year. I thought I'd better, though, if I didn't want to hear all the teasing from my friends—even my *mother.* Nobody thought a boy would *ever* ask me to the prom. I was always the jovial chubby kid—good for a laugh with the girls—who didn't know how to handle the scene with the boys. I would always freeze up and not say much....I knew if he had another option, he would choose *her.* He would always choose *her.*"

Rachael's desperation stemmed from a disquieting source: Her father—although he had remained with the woman he married, worked hard, and did everything he could to support a two-parent, intact family—barbed Rachael relentlessly about her physical appearance. Rachael said later, "He wanted a Barbie doll, not a daughter. I never fit the bill. Once, at a Fourth of July picnic, I was eating a hot dog. My father stood there with his mouth open and stared at me; there was such disgust on his face. At that moment he hated me. It's like he was telling me, 'You're a pig. You eat too much, and you're a pig.' All right. I was overweight; I admit it. But it was the Fourth of July and a big picnic and everybody was stuffing down hot dogs and cheeseburgers like there was no tomorrow. I guess he wasn't looking at his Barbie doll at that moment; he was looking at his pig."

Rachael stood around five feet four inches and weighed around 130 to 140 pounds. This is not obese. But as long as Rachael defined her net worth by such a small amount of portliness, she had doomed herself to despair. Compared to the Jessicas, Rachael was Porky Pig. And no teenage girl wants to be Porky Pig. Thinking of yourself as Porky Pig makes getting dates for the senior prom a dreaded, dishonorable, dastardly experience.

Ironically, it's not the "fat girls" who shoulder the burden of self-repression and self-designated victimhood. Death rates from anorexia, for example, can be as high as 25 percent.[1] Young women actually *die*—as in, like, *dead!* They didn't keep enough vital nutrients in their bodies to sustain themselves; sometimes their organs simply shut down.

The actual total of young people afflicted with anorexia nervosa is difficult to know. Like so many cases of physical abuse, rape, or molestation, many situations are never reported because of fear or embarrassment. Teenage girls don't brag about sticking two fingers down their throats after dinner, so they can dump their half-digested cheeseburgers in the toilet. What we do know, however, is that an enormous number of girls between 12 and 18 think that they will never get thin *enough*. A Los Angeles physician, Dr. Robert Moxie (the father of one of my religious school students), said, "When it comes to eating disorders, all semblance of logic goes right out the window. The frustration is when we try to fight this problem with logic. Telling a girl who weighs less than a hundred pounds that she's not fat is like telling a policeman that he's not a sanitation engineer; it's abundantly obvious, but she doesn't care."[2]

Diane's graceful stature earned her a reputation that not a lot of other girls acquire. Standing almost six feet tall, she contributed to the remarkable success of our school's girls' varsity volleyball team. Diane appeared lanky, not skinny or razor thin, as so many of her friends and teachers labeled her. Looking back at the early part of 1987, the still photo in my mind of Diane brings to life the smiling face of an energetic, bubbling personality; yet, with it, an aura of sadness. A line from a short story, "Winter Dreams," by F. Scott Fitzgerald comes to mind. In relating a conversation between the very beautiful Judy Jones and Dexter Milwood, her desperate suitor of several years, Fitzgerald wrote, "Judy laughed sadly, without sadness."[3] In other words, she falsified her empathy. I have discovered that for too many teenagers the reverse is true: They *try* to fake their *joy*, while their underlying despondency belies them.

To her shame, Diane's legendary battle with her eating disorders became the talk of the volleyball team and eventually the gossip of the whole school. She later quit the team in order to fight her demons. Thank God she had lots of support from her parents, because it turned out to be quite an uphill battle; she was dying inside a little more each day, but no one could know that by looking at her. Fortunately, the generous love of her parents and friends filled Diane's life to the brim, ultimately helping her to dodge a bullet.

Diane emerged as one of the lucky ones.

THE CORNELIA SYNDROME

Cornelia is now an actress who has been seen on television and in the movies. By any standard Cornelia was gorgeous (and can still be described in those terms). Huge, almond-shaped brown eyes radiated such a constant passion and exuberance for life that when her eyes were *not* bulging with fervor, everyone else figured something had gone terribly wrong for Cornelia. Long, dark brown hair complemented her African-Latina persona, making her the fantasy of almost every boy in the school. She dabbled in cheerleading for a while; she also participated successfully in speech and debate. But her true passion was for theater.

Ordinarily, when Cornelia spent time in my classroom after school, it was to help with recording grades (she was a student teaching assistant), or to practice a dramatic monologue that she would later take into competition. This afternoon, however, there were no grades to record and no pending speech tournaments.

As she entered the classroom, I looked up from behind my desk. Cornelia never presented herself as an annoyance; her cheerfulness and catchy smile were always welcome.

Upon this visit, however, there were no catchy smiles—and cheerful, she was not.

"Something tells me you have a problem," I said before she could address me. She forced a smile. "How did you know?"

"I know you."

"Yeah," she uttered, sliding into one of the student desks that had some green goop of unknown origin fixed on top.

"Boy trouble?" I guessed.

Cornelia shook her head. "Not this time. Cornelia trouble."

"What?"

"The problem is with me and only me," she explained. "Mr. G., did I ever tell you that I had an uncle who kept telling me how ugly I was?"

If this were true, he should have been named *Uncle Moron*.

"Yeah," she went on. "Every time he'd come over to our house—when I was little—he kept telling me it was clear that I hadn't taken my ugly pills for a while. It really got to me, you know?"

"Cornelia," I smiled, "I mean, it's obvious your uncle was telling you how cute he thought you were. Verbal irony."

"But I was only six or seven, Mr. G. How did I know what verbal irony was? All I knew is that he told me over and over again that I was ugly."

I shrugged. "So, now you know that he was kidding around, like uncles often do with their little nieces. Are you telling me that this made a permanent scar on your life?"

Cornelia's eyes suddenly filled with tears; I'd seen this from her before, but only when she stood on stage or presented one of her gut-wrenching dramatic monologues for competitions. This time, however, the tears were sincere—not part of her act. I had long ago realized that my job as a teacher and coach had ramifications that went far beyond the borders of the academic or competitive arena. My relative youth, bachelor freedom, and overwhelming charm (okay, a lie) afforded me the time and opportunity—and access—to help these kids in ways that truly mattered.

Teaser! We'll get back to my visit with Cornelia a little later.

Every year, 5,000 teenagers kill themselves.[4] Many more than that *try* to kill themselves, but any numbers here are suspect, because defining *attempted suicide* becomes problematic; often kids dramatically grab attention by staging what appears to be a suicide attempt. Real or threatened, too many American teenagers lose their battles with their despondencies. What brings so many of them to the point that they want to take their own lives—and sometimes do—is not always apparent. Anecdotal discussions with kids who have threatened to die at their own hands or with parents who have suffered this horrible loss have not conclusively proven anything. Sometimes these acts defy logic. Strangely, despite their tendencies for hormonally based, emotionally driven decisions, girls are less likely to commit suicide than boys are; boys are also more prone to self-mutilations (more about this later) and acts of violence against others.

Generally, high levels of self-respect produce happy, successful teenagers. While self-loathing usually doesn't result in suicide, it does materialize in other forms of self-destruction—inducing alcoholism, drug addiction, smoking, depression, complacency, or self-mutilation. The excuses teenagers give for the deterioration of their lives are not reached by calm, logical analysis; and ultimately, their actions have been driven by emotional, illogical rationalizations. I wish I had a taco for every time I told a downtrodden teen, "You can do better than this. This is such a waste!" And *meant* it. But the kid somehow dropped though a maze of paradoxes, contradictions, and absurdities to arrive at the bottom of the heap. Sometimes that "bottom of the heap" turned out to be as low as he could go.

Back to Cornelia:

I studied her before I spoke. How could a girl like Cornelia have *any* problems? "You're okay?"

She shook her head and added with irritation in her voice, "I already told you: 'No.'"

"Okay," I sighed, "I'm listening."

"Am I ugly?" she asked me without acknowledging the astonishment in my face.

"If you're ugly, I'm Godzilla." My feeble attempt at an analogy produced its usual lack of success.

"I feel ugly," was all that she said.

"Well, of course, you do know that anyone hearing that assessment of yourself would be inclined to wonder about your mental condition," I teased, slowly losing her trust with my pathetic attempts at humor.

She wiped a tear. "Then what is the matter with me, Mr. G.?"

Time to get serious: "There's nothing about you that's ugly, Cornelia. You gotta already know that. You're beautiful from your skin to your heart to the depths of your soul. So, what's going on?"

She looked confused. "I am, huh?"

"*Ugly* would be the furthest word from a person's mind while thinking about you."

She paused for a few seconds, contemplating the veracity of my comments.

And then she looked up at me with her eyes full of tears, ready to bare her soul.

Unfortunately, we'll have to get back to Cornelia's bare soul a little later. Patience *can* be such a virtue!

A billion or so years ago, when I was a boy growing up in Southern California, I worried a lot about what other people thought of me. I was one of the tallest kids in my eighth-grade class, and then I stopped growing at all, finally formatting into the midget that I am today. This bothered me—a lot. Everybody in high school seemed taller (and, of course, they actually *were* taller), and I probably spent way too much time dwelling on it. But boys in those days (and, remember, I'm speaking of centuries ago) did not focus as much on their physical appearance as they do today; in fact, males caring about how they *look* is a concept that I stumbled upon rather recently. I had been telling my students for years, "Girls agonize over how they look—how pretty they are. They become body conscious at an early age, because they know boys are looking first and foremost at this part of them, not because boys are shallow or mean, but because of biology. And while boys may be a *little* bit worried about discovering a new zit or two, they typically find ways of attracting girls, other than their bodies, hair, or jewelry."

I have told my students this forever.

And now I'm beginning to have my doubts about its accuracy.

Richard wrote this in a recent free write: "I think girls are becoming a lot more like boys. They care too much about the physical stuff. So what is a boy supposed to do nowadays? It could be getting a manicure, having his hair done professionally, or buying colored eye contacts. Girls say that the guys on the reality shows like *Real World* are hot. I'm pressured to compete in ways that boys didn't have to before."

Huh?

Boys get a manicure? When I was a teenager, I bit my fingernails a lot, mostly because I was a nervous little runt. Wasn't that a good way to keep them trimmed?

Boys get their hair done? When I was a teenager, I went to a *barbershop*. It took about eight minutes for the whole thing and cost about three bucks.

Boys get colored eye contacts? When I was a teenager, some boys may have bought those, but they were also the boys everyone else beat up.

Today teenage boys care a great deal about how other people visually perceive them. The result: fat boys, short boys, pimply boys, big-nosed boys—boys with floppy ears, droopy chins, pudgy cheeks, pale skin, stubby hands—boys who consider their physical appearance mediocre have doomed themselves into tangling with even graver self-image issues throughout their adolescence.

In a sad way, boys are catching up with girls.

However, boys have not *yet* caught up with girls in the realm of narcissism (in the most literal sense of the word) and self-flagellation. When it comes to teenage girls, take all the characteristics of "it's my body" worship and then multiply their intensity about six zillion times: The Jessicas will have begun to look like witches flying in on their broomsticks, for the Jessicas have dug in their knives and twisted deep and hard inside the self-image wounds of teenage girls across America.

Cornelia's watering eyes had lost their effect on me. I figured the drama queen was getting ready for another one of her solo acts; it became increasingly difficult to take her seriously.

"Chad's going to the prom with someone else," she whimpered.

My mouth fell open. *This* is what she agonized over: going to a dance with Chad—the skinny dude with *bangs* down to his eyebrows?

"His loss," I shrugged, apparently (at least to Cornelia) callously.

She recoiled. "My loss, Mr. G.! He's, like, the perfect guy!"

Perfect? Yeah. As a stand-in for Ringo Starr.

She continued in a broken, emotional tone, now taking a more analytical approach. "But he only goes out with the sluts. You know the ones. They dress like sluts; they act like sluts.... But they're all pretty. Really pretty. Somebody told them—probably their moms—'If you got it, flaunt it.' And they do."

I hoped Cornelia was wrong about their moms. "I doubt they're any better-looking than you are, Cornelia. Sounds rather impossible, if you ask me. They just push it all out there because they're so insecure about themselves; they think it's the only way they can hook a boy."

"Worked for *her*."

"Temporarily," I told her. Of course, this was only a hopeful guess.

"Mr. G.," Cornelia said, settling back, seemingly resigned to her denouement, "I have to tell you something—something I've never told anyone else before. Not even my parents know this. No one does..."

Sorry. Cornelia's secret (sigh!) will have to wait.

According to students at my high school, several key issues about self-image stand out. Here is my list of the 10 most significant self-identity concerns, in their ascending order of frequency and qualitative importance.

10. maturity level (Boys deny that they're more immature than girls.)

9. dress and style (Both boys and girls like to dress trendy and cool.)

8. sexual identity (Especially boys are nervous about being gay.)

7. religion (Boys and girls equally share religious identity issues.)

6. academic success (Used to be boys; now mostly girls care about this.)

5. attitude and toughness (Testosterone makes this a top concern for boys.)

4. race or national origin (Both boys and girls care—although girls a bit more.)

3. family (Surprisingly, boys are more sensitive about family identity.)

2. body image (Clearly, girls care more about how their bodies look to others.)

1. overall physical appearance (The boys are racing to catch up.)

The first-, second-, and third-place self-image concerns would probably have led the list 40 years ago, too. Although the issues haven't changed much during the time I have taught high school, self-image tragedies have multiplied and intensified due to mass technological communication, greater media exposure, and wider parental detachment.

Finally, back to Cornelia:

"I throw up," she said, barely uttering the words. "I eat; then I go into the bathroom or wherever, and I stick my fingers down my throat and throw it all up."

She waited for a response. I'd heard about this sort of thing before; I'd never dealt with it, though. "So, you don't gain any weight." I declared the obvious.

She nodded.

"Do your parents know?"

Silence again, but this time she shook her head.

"Well," I sighed, "You already know the possible consequences of what you're doing. I'm not going to bore you with that. Or…is that why you came to me? Do you want me to—?"

"No," she interrupted. "I already know about all that. What I want from you, Mr. G.—what I want from you—is to get me to stop."

Counselors and psychiatrists get compensation for this type of work; I was paid mainly to teach English to high school kids. I knew next to nothing about eating disorders. I had been bumbling and fumbling in my attempts to help Cornelia. What could I do? After reassuring her how gorgeous she was—which was the absolute truth—and then reminding her of the harms of bulimia, my arsenal was depleted. Having confidence that they would get her the professional help she clearly required, I recommended to Cornelia that she immediately tell her parents everything that she had just revealed to me.

Some teenage girls cannot be pretty enough; unfortunately, if they compete in society primarily with their physical beauty, sooner or later, they *will* lose to someone else: The actress on the screen will be incredibly gorgeous; the model on the magazine cover will appear absolutely flawless. Eventually, as the teenager eases naturally into adulthood, someone younger and more beautiful than she is will gather more attention than she does.

Guaranteed: Someone younger and more beautiful will come along. *Guaranteed.*

MR. G.'S HOME-GROWN ADVICE

In 1968 teenagers longed to be different; yet, they yearned to fit in with the rest of the crowd.

In 2008 teenagers longed to be different; yet, they yearned to fit in with the rest of the crowd.

But here's the major difference between those times and these times: Today's longing for camaraderie through conformity infests a teenager with a potentially malignant form of narcissism brought on by peer pressure and media contamination. Her obsession with superficial qualities—breast size and weight measurement—brings her to irrational levels of concern: about her body, about her face, about her sex appeal. Many kids today are wasting their lives by focusing on the trite and meaningless, rather than by enriching their lives through indulging in the unique and the profound.

Parents

Your role modeling frames the values that you teach your children. When *you* make the trite and meaningless important, so will your children attach artificial significance to those values. Each time you suggest to them the critical importance of someone's physical features—even their own—you plant the seeds for their hypervaluing those same qualities about *themselves* when they become teenagers. This doesn't mean that you never throw a casual comment to your little girl about her cuteness; it does mean, however, that you are more circumspect about those 60,000 times you've already told her that she should be featured on the cover of every fashion magazine in the galaxy.

Consider my wife's scolding about my cooing over our seven-year-old daughter (who, by the way—from the onset—has been the cutest, loveliest, most adorable little girl in the entire history of children who have ever been born in the whole Western Hemisphere!).

"Stop that, Bruce," she told me in the voice that always halts me from doing whatever stupid thing I happen to be doing at that moment. "You're going to give her an attitude."

Not exactly sure what my wife meant, I offered my usual scholarly probe. "Huh?"

She narrowed her eyes. "Do you want her to worry so much about the way she looks that she doesn't care about how she treats people? Do you want her to be all hung up on her beauty?"

I thought to myself, "Hmmm..."

But I answered, "Of course not."

"Then," Mrs. G. scolded me in her professorial style, "you need to stop constantly telling her how cute and pretty she is. Say more about her character and less about her cuteness."

Of course, I could do that; it wouldn't be nearly as much fun, but once again, my wife's wisdom on child rearing trumped my emotionally driven methods of dealing with my precious (now for *character* reasons, of course) little daughter.

Lots of times health concerns and appearance issues coalesce, so it becomes difficult to address one without coming to grips with the other; for example, when you tell your 10-year-old that she is putting on weight, you are voicing worries about her health *and* the way she looks. Both concerns carry value, but which one will help your child more? True, dedicating one's entire life to festering over her being sick or not being sick (the *health* issues about being fat) is not a good thing; however, obsessing about her body size (the way-she-*looks* issues about being fat) could mature her into an anorexia or bulimia candidate. Let's face the truth here: Adolescents don't want to hear about how they will live 90 years longer if they just lay off the Oreos for the rest of their lives; likewise, they don't want to hear about the anatomical theory of organ shutdown because of the diversion of vital nutrients from certain parts of their body.

They don't *care* about that; they care only about how they *look*.

As a result parents should educate their young children about the dire consequences of eating too much, eating too little, and eating wrong—and how this will determine whether they will be sick or healthy until the day they die. If parents focus on saying, "Jill, if you eat another ice cream cone, the next boy who glances in your direction will also be throwing a harpoon," they will have demonized eating. Emphasizing the *fat* and *ugly* aspects of improper eating generates more scary possibilities: that *food* equals *fat, ugly*—not that food equals *good health*.

So, parents, the Twinkie is in your court. *Food is good.* Food doesn't have to mean useless layers of lingering lard; in fact, food makes us stronger, taller, and more radiant. It helps us to glow with a healthy vigor.

Teachers

Volumes can be written on the teacher's ubiquitous dilemma: "How do I, as a teacher, bolster the confidence of my students, while communicating to them that there is definitely room for improvement in their schoolwork and in their character?"

The problem for us teachers, however, goes beyond benevolently telling Johnny that two and two do not equal five. Teenagers are so different (yet, the same—that paradox again), even trained veteran teachers err while diagnosing serious maladies and self-esteem problems in their students. Yes, I can point to girls in my classes who wrap up their entire self-worth in how sexy they look to those oily-haired juvenile delinquents on street corners or skater dudes they have just met at the suburban malls. I preach and nag and sermonize almost daily to my students about the importance of having passions, interests, and successes that they have control over. I tell them how much more refreshing and liberating it is to concentrate on the life's lessons they acquire from the books they're reading, instead of the life's anxieties they get from the boys they're fantasizing about.

Critical for teachers: Inform your students that high school lasts for only a *little* while—they will have lives beyond high school. Only *four* out of a possible hundred years of their existence are spent in the agony of high school. While what happens at school may now *seem* to them of critical proportions, the relative importance of these events is minor: their friends, families, interests, politics, and worldviews—all of these will change. Wrapping themselves up in issues and values that are short-term, self-absorbed, and me-focused is common—but pointless. Teachers, you must tell your teenage students the truth: The problems of their youth are a miniscule part of the overall scheme of their lives; after they graduate they will hardly see their high school friends anymore; their teenage romances won't endure; and their "D" in geometry will *not* disqualify them from someday running for president.

Your students need to discover what truly matters in life and latch on to *that*; the inconsequential and the irrelevant have to go. *You* are the teacher; *you* guide them in discerning the momentous from the frivolous—infinitely more life-altering than knowing the difference between a gerund and an infinitive or the names of the Axis powers during World War II.

Teenagers

About 20-some years ago, one of my most successful speech students decided to write her oratory about something that "freaked her out." Of all the things she could have spoken about in her competitive rounds, the matter that bothered her—truly *bothered* her—was what she called "America's obsession with the Super Bowl."

Isabel did not have a reputation for hiding her feelings: "I can't stand this country!" she blurted out one afternoon, while we brainstormed ideas for her oration.

"Those are harsh words," I suggested. "Maybe you ought to consider a speech on *that* topic."

She paused, realizing that her brazen attitude did not reflect her true view of America. Then she fretted, "People here are weird. I mean, making such a big deal about a football game! I mean, like, who cares! A bunch of overstuffed goons running up and down a grass field with a piece of pigskin! Is that crazy or what?"

"Isabel, why do you care?" I asked calmly.

"Mr. G.," she continued, now standing in wild gesticulation, a patented characteristic of her flamboyant speaking style, "Our Marines were massacred a few months ago in Lebanon [this was about three months after that event in 1983], people are dying all over the world because they don't have enough to eat, crime is soaring...and Americans are in suspended animation over a *football game!* This is worse than when everybody couldn't wait to find out who shot J. R. Ewing [the previous year on a popular television series called *Dallas*]!"

Isabel was on to something interesting, I thought. The speech she eventually developed and presented in competition—of national championship caliber—was about society's tendency to care too much about events that don't matter—at least, not in the overall scheme of things.

Take that to heart. High school comes and goes, but you're here every day. In 20 years will you care more about popping that pimple on your nose or about putting food on your family's dinner table? When you go to your 20-year class reunion, who is going to remember that you weighed about 30 pounds more in high school than the weight charts or fashion magazines dictated that you should weigh?

And will you even remember the Jessicas?

Have a life. In order to do this, you have to lay the groundwork now: Work hard, study hard, and play hard. Help other people; let other people help you. You can make a difference, but parading through the mall with your breasts protruding through a bikini top will not carve out your special place in the world—at least, not one you'll want to brag about to your own children two decades from now.

Care about your family and friends, and *don't sweat the small stuff.*

About 30 years ago, one of my students wrote an essay describing the petty annoyances brought into her life by her younger brother. But later in that same paper, Annette dropped a bomb on me: The previous summer her little brother had been killed while riding his bicycle. Now the former irritations of her brother had taken on new meaning. And these words from her essay have stayed with me for three decades: "What I wouldn't give to hear my little brother tattle to my parents about when I pinched his arm. What I wouldn't give to yell at him for leaving his smelly socks in my bedroom. What I wouldn't give to see—just one more time—his funny, little face with the crooked baby teeth that are ready to fall out."

When you're doing the undoable, challenging the impossible, seeking the unattainable, you *are* striving to make a difference. And the self-*respect* you receive from the face staring back at you in the mirror goes far beyond what you ever could have gained from the likes of Britney Spears, Paris Hilton, or Lindsay Lohan.

Millions of people, without any knowledge of that private conversation between Cornelia and me about her eating disorder, have seen her glowing, confident face on the silver screen. Somehow Cornelia made it through her crisis; somehow she figured out that Chad didn't deserve *her*, correctly concluding that she could do much better. It scared her, too; for if her whole life depended on being pretty enough for this particular boy to ask her to this particular dance, well, maybe he *did* deserve Cornelia. And maybe she deserved *him*, too.

For teenagers, life is all about mirrors.

4

Lily Munster...or Whatever's Cool

PLEASE! NOT THAT GUY!

Whenever my seven-year-old daughter wears her earrings, she exudes cuteness. I am so overwhelmed by her adorableness, every part of my body immobilizes. What I had formerly thought to be endearing now pales by comparison.

My daughter wears only those fake earrings that we buy for a buck or two in the cheap store at the mall. My wife and I have made a united, adamant decision that our daughter will not have her ears pierced until she is 42 years old. (Okay, that may be 12 years old, but it will be at the sole discretion of her *wanting* to have a sharp, *maybe* sterile needle passed through her ears, for the sake of dangling a piece of overpriced metal from her earlobes.)

The decision to poke holes—or not to poke holes—should be reserved for adults. At least, that's the way I see it.

Today all girls wear earrings—and (sigh) so do some boys. When I asked teenagers to tell me where they got the idea that boys should wear earrings, I found it very tough to get any answers; weird, because for almost every other question that I posed I received willing and reasonable responses. However, try these on for size:

Why not? (Don't you just love it when you ask someone a question about what motivated a particular behavior, and they answer with the non sequitur, "Why not?")

None of your business! (An unusual response, considering the teens hardly ever responded in those words to anything else I asked them.)

Girls wear 'em. Why can't we? (Girls do a lot of things. Why can't *we*?)

You should be able to wear what you want. (Okay! I want to wear a Speedo bathing suit. How disturbing is *that* thought!)

I look better in those (earrings). (Better than what?)

It's part of my culture. (American culture?)

My dad hates it, so I do it. (Scary.)

My dad wears 'em. (Even more scary.)

The chicks like it. (Sorry, I don't buy it.)

It's the style. (And *I* can't wait for Speedos to be in style!)

All the guys in my family wear earrings. (And the point is…? Some of my ancestors wore moustaches—and I'm referring to Italian *women*.)

My overreaction to young people wearing jewelry is rooted in my many encounters with teenagers who have overdone the piercings bit. Old buzzard that I am, I recently ranted and raved about unusual youth attire to the producer of Phantom Projects, an incredibly enlightened youth theater group. Steve Cisneros is around 30, so his young ears were not very sympathetic to my self-induced antagonism. Before I launched into dogma, I checked him carefully to confirm he wasn't wearing any of those weird little trinkets on his own face or body.

In a tone that let me know he didn't want to irritate me, he said carefully, "It's what the kids are doing now: those piercings. More have them than don't."

Which was particularly instructive, since the new play that I had just written for Steve's company poked fun of kids who pierced their whatevers; I had attempted to trace nose rings, tongue studs, lip diamonds, and belly button stones to a carefully crafted, subversive, Soviet Communist plot. But Steve's help with the editing of my scripts has made the plays better. Eyes that used to be in tune with youth pop culture trends were starting to blur with age, and I had to face the fact that my withdrawal from what was truly hip and happenin' began to affect the way I viewed the world—such as my unconcealed intolerance for boys who wore loop earrings that were so enormous they could be used by gymnasts for their rings exercises.

What it boils down to is this: I'm out of it—*out of the loop.* I grew up in the sixties, so I'm used to weird stuff, especially unorthodox clothing and peculiar body ornaments. I have taught high school for a long time—maybe too long—so nothing should faze me anymore, especially the youth shock factor. But what continues to gnaw at me is not the insanity of kids who puncture gross holes all over their faces and bodies; what bothers me are their *reasons* for self-mutilation. Maybe I have become another one of those old guys we see in rocking chairs on front porches: the guys who terrorize the five-year-olds who stand on their lawns and glare at the teenagers who walk on their sidewalks. Have I become *that* guy?

"Kids these days! I tell ya, Mable, back in my day…."

Please—oh, *please*—tell me I haven't become *that* guy!

WEIRD THEN—WEIRDER NOW

High school, circa 2008: several cliques, groups, and factions have become prevalent. Reminded of years gone by, I can't help but glimpse a couple of the more prominent sects *then*, as well as today's rather—shall we say—*interesting* young people who populate teenage America.

Surfers

Since the fifties, all generations of teenagers have claimed surfers as their own. Back then, the surfers wore medium-length blond hair, parted to one side (bleached or natural); they sported longer hair in the sixties—still blond. But the late eighties gave us the crewcut surfer. Today's surfers come in all hair colors, lengths, and styles (some even have bangs down the front—bleached and natural—but now dyed). The surfers got the chicks; they introduced new slang (*woody, dude, hang ten*), and they bore their bruises and broken bones as badges of honor. Best of all: the surfers gave us surf music. I can't imagine growing up unacquainted with the Beach Boys, Jan and Dean, or Dick Dale and the Deltones. A few modern movies have spotlighted female surfers; however, despite claims to the contrary, surfing is still an activity dominated by boys and young men.

Hodads

They looked like surfers; they talked like surfers; they listened to Dick Dale music like surfers. The only real difference between the hodads and the surfers was that, well, the hodads didn't surf. Ever. Most of them stayed far away from the beach. And don't ask me why we called them *hodads*; today that label would have a completely different connotation—and reaction.

Goths

In the early sixties, Fred Gwynn popularized the Frankenstein's Monster look on the television series *The Munsters*. Good ideas in television usually led to similar programming, so *The Adams Family* came next. Hardly anyone realized that this motif of pallid skin and black clothing would soon become vogue for generations of teenagers. The white, crusty makeup, dark blue eyeliner, black overcoats, capes, and dresses suggested death—certainly an appearance of "grave" despair. These kids didn't need to find costumes for Halloween; they were already fitted.

Own Drummers

Doing her *own* thing, an Own Drummer acts a certain way or does a particular action simply because it's different. She may be correct, and the action righteous, but *nonconformity*—not righteousness—is the mantra of an Own Drummer. She may be characterized as being strange, weird, bizarre, abnormal, or extraordinary; an Own Drummer doesn't usually care about *correct* or *righteous*. He may wear his hair like a shark—the Mohawk thing. He may color his hair blue or purple or pink—or all three at the same time. He may wear a ring in his nostril, a stud on his lip, or a pin in his eyebrow. He may collect guns, play hooky, or eat tofu. He may tattoo his entire neck, shave his full body, or paint his whole face. Over the years Own Drummers have changed their look, but they have not changed their philosophy: "I do what I do. I know what I like. I know how I am. This is how I express myself." Every generation of Own Drummers has its critics or Doubting Thomases. "Sure," say the Doubting Thomases, "you think you're expressing who you are through a weird look and lifestyle, but we know better. Your weirdness is because you don't know who you are." Are Own Drummers expressing who they are, or are they still searching for who they are?

Or maybe they're just incredibly strange.

Sea of Black

Forty years ago few kids wore black. Black, considered a dingy color, represented poverty—and so did white. White meant that you were poor, too—even poorer than black meant. A good example of the trashy white look was epitomized in the sleeveless white undershirt worn by men. But white showed off their tans. Guys could pull on a tight white T-shirt and wear a trim, fit look; this white contrasted nicely with the brown or red skin they had manufactured at the beach. So while both black and white attire projected drabby and lifeless, white began to make a little headway into the *cool* category, especially during the beginning of the surfer era; that is, until...?

It's one thing to look around me at school or the mall and notice that almost every teenager is dressed in black clothes; it's another thing to pinpoint the exact—or near exact—time this came to fruition. Just as the Goths appeared out of nowhere (*The Adams Family* doesn't get official credit—or blame—for the Goths), the Sea of Black suddenly just happened. American classrooms now look like funeral parlors. The industry that sells black T-shirts spools in delight: Black is cheap to make, easy to keep clean, and set to match with anything. I've heard stories about parents who have prohibited their teenagers from wearing black to school, and the kids changed clothes—into all black, of course—immediately upon arrival at school. Kids have told me it really began with the Oakland Raiders football team of the eighties. But why would a teenager in Bismarck, North Dakota, give a rip about the Raiders? No, it's much simpler that that: Black is a cool color now; it casts nothing bright or optimistic or cheerful. And for lots of teenagers, keeping out the bright and optimistic and cheerful gives them a semblance of control over the kinds of moods they wish to perpetuate. They wear green to school only on St. Patrick's Day, so they don't get pinched; then they switch into their black shirts just before they go to the mall.

Sluts Ahoy

The *tramps* or *trollops*—labels assigned when I was a teenager—are no longer rare. My trusted T.A., Richard, told me, "Well, Mr. G., it depends on how you look at it. Since most girls are having sex these days [an assertion I've been stubbornly reluctant to accept], it boils down to the girls who have sex *in* their relationships and the girls who have sex *as* their relationships—which means with whoever and whenever—sorta like what boys do." Evidently it's a lot easier—and more acceptable—to be active these days, since oral sex has become so common. After all, if you can have sex with a boy and not risk pregnancy, you are being, uh, *responsible!* Oh, I'm sorry: I forgot that oral sex is not really sex. Just ask former President ("I did not have sex with that woman!") Clinton. Blossoming numbers of teenagers have bought into this perception, and now young girls (I've been informed) are servicing boys in record numbers. From what the kids have told me, it doesn't work both ways either. Boys who love *receiving* usually consider repugnant the act of *giving,* and, therefore, find ways of *receiving*—exclusively. The boys know how to find the sluts—or they simply blackmail their girlfriends, intimidating them with threats of "other girls will," at the slightest hint of their reluctance. Although a minority of girls in high schools and middle schools across America may have the same base nature as boys when it comes to sex, the majority of girls relinquish their power when they adopt the *eager* or *willing* persona. In the name of gender equality, did feminism help to create as many female sluts as there are male players? How ironic, if it did!

Emos

No, Emos is not the better half of Andy. Emos define themselves by the kind of music they listen to. This has something to do with an alternative form of rock music (Isn't it *all* an alternative form of rock music?) that purports serious passion and overwhelming emotion. Since all music claims to do this—to my knowledge those are basic characteristics of music—I asked a couple of my self-proclaimed Emo students to bring in a CD to illustrate: "The best kind of emo!" they billed it. "You might like this, Mr. G.!" I listened, retched, and told them that I could barely understand a word of the music; that the beat was too fast—I figured it would be sloooww and emotional, perhaps, romantic. I expressed my disappointment.

In fairness to the Emos, the style of their music never should have surprised me. Anything particularly tame would have come off as an incongruity. One of the Emo boys apologized and offered that we hear something else—presumably, uh, slow and romantic—but I politely declined. It's easy to confuse an Emo teenager with other rebel types; however, the physical characteristics of Emos pop right out at you: dyed, long black hair that hangs over their foreheads and sometimes over their eyes (you wonder how the kid can possibly see anything); an ultrathin physique; eye shadow and/or eyeliner on boys (no kidding); an abundance of piercings, especially in the lips, eyebrows, and tongue; black T-shirts—usually sporting the weird name of a band that no one else has heard of before and hardly anyone else cares about—displaying an embarrassing (for anyone who looks) picture. These kids are soft-spoken in class, but gregarious among their own. I once sat in the Jacuzzi at the gym with an Emo kid from another high school; I suspected he was an Emo, because the steam moisture caused his mascara to run, and he had that identifiably forlorn look about him. Quiet but friendly, he displayed amazing self-control by not allowing himself to laugh at my casual jokes about his appearance. He sat there, listening to my humorous quips—and never so much as punched me in the nose!

Recently, I asked one of my classes about stereotypes. The students were instructed to stay away from specific putdowns and lambastes at groups of odd kids. The teens who spoke up seemed to argue that whichever group *they* identified with possessed superior attributes to those who belonged in the *other* groups. Since the strangest teens were polarized according to the genre of music they preferred, their biggest putdowns of others were about music. Styles of dress also attracted criticisms, although the differences in appearance were sometimes so subtle that their rambling condemnations of others' clothing surpassed my understanding. As with most subjective views—especially among America's adolescents—persuasion through logic played absolutely no part. Here, therefore, was the view of one high school student describing another. Keep in mind that girls tend to be more vicious, especially when alluding to other girls. The girl who gave this description did not fit into any of niches relevant to this chapter. She was one of those kids who tries to do well in school, has a general idea of her future plans, does not face extraordinary difficulties at home, and is concerned—above and beyond anything else—with her social status and overall popularity.

Meg commented about Goths: "They're too weird. They're always quiet and don't assert themselves too much. . . . They have pale skin all the time, like they're dead. I know that's their whole point, but sometimes their white makeup gets on my nerves, because you don't need white makeup for anything; it just makes you look even weirder."

One of the "white" fads when I was a teenager had to do with lipstick. Hoping to look more tanned and earthy, some girls smeared a hideous white stuff all over their lips. *The Mod Squad* was a hit TV show, so we guys not so cleverly referred to these girls as *The Ghoul Squad;* the lipstick had made them look like corpses. Fortunately, the white lipstick craze lasted about another five seconds and then faded on its own. Looking back, I realize the girls did not look so bad; actually, they looked pretty good, except for the ones who smeared the lipstick all over their faces. Many teenagers stray to the weirder and stranger, simply because they know that no matter what they say or do or wear, other kids are going to mock them, and adults are going to admonish them. So why not go for the gusto! Why not *really* give others something to talk about! Right now in my first-period class, a boy sits in front of me, proud of his long, *pink* fingernails, multicolored hair, tight-tight shiny black pants, and a T-shirt peppered with skeletons. If he had somehow planned on jolting my senses—it worked!

MR. G.'S HOME-GROWN ADVICE

Being weird, peculiar, eccentric, anomalous, odd, unusual, or bizarre is *normal*—at least, in the world of teenagers. During my lifetime many odd ramblings have emerged from my mouth, so what I am about to say next does not sound strange to me: "I can't make suggestions for fixing something that is perfectly normal." Discussing screwball teenagers is simple; actually *curing* them may be akin to an antidote for—I don't know—swallowing lye. Like most anything else, we should be suspicious of any foreshadowing behaviors that portend serious consequences. Otherwise, seeming abnormalities are a part of the growth and development of a kid—a rite of passage. Teenagers who do not have at least a few weird qualities are suspect—perhaps, a bit strange—themselves.

Beware: Has this teen's behavior and/or appearance changed drastically or abruptly? If so, something more heinous than typical teenage rebellion or peer copycatting may be involved. Nobody changes radically on a whim: Something or someone motivates her. A normally conservative 15-year-old boy who suddenly walks in the door wearing a black trenchcoat, right after having his eyebrows throttled with 42 piercings, clearly has been influenced by others. Most kids do not spew vulgarities and profanities out of the blue; they don't wake up one morning looking like Lily Munster, unless they have previously projected gradual hints of their soon-to-be wacky appearance.

Is this teen a rebel? Since most teenagers are rebels in one form or another, we should ascertain whether *this* teen's rebellion would end with benign—or malignant—consequences. Lawlessness, drinking, drugs, sex, and extreme lethargy: they should be off-limits. Examine those behaviors closely; they hurt the teen himself, and they adversely affect other people. Having abortions, vandalizing property, and guzzling booze are not appropriate, healthy forms of rebellion.

Does the teen believe that if something is different or weird it is *automatically* good? Teach him the speciousness of that argument. Kids need to know that being bizarre is not good *unto itself*. A boy walked by my classroom every day, and all that my students and I saw through the window was the top of his hair. Since he wore a Mohawk, it always looked as though a shark were swimming by the room. Most of my students thought this was so *cool*. And why? Because *it looked radically different*. To a teenager, *different* rules! What if somebody walked by the room, and all we saw was a Ku Klux Klan hood covering his head? "The guy with the racist hood! Ha! Ha!" Certainly a different look for our school, but would that have been unbelievably cool, too?

Drawing the line—as a parent, a teacher, or a friend—can be difficult. How do we know the difference between the normal (conventionally weird) and the dangerous (abnormally weird)? The demarcation should revolve around those behaviors *that do harm*. Every parent and friend is a protector: First and foremost, they must decide which hill (of abnormalities) they're going to die on, fighting for the physical, mental, and emotional health of the children they love.

Too provocative clothing and shocking body ornaments are not allowed in my family. Basically, my wife and I tell our children what they can wear and what they can't; they have a range of choices about their hair and apparel, but that's it. Ultimately, we are responsible for protecting them from dangers—emotional or physical, perceived or real—and as parents, we're required to act on our value systems and sometimes our instincts. Yes, I worry that other kids, teachers, and the general public will stereotype my children, based on their physical appearance. How they are perceived and judged by others may eventually determine their lot in life. But when it comes to the images they project to others, teens really don't always know what's best for them.

Some people have told me that my kids are going to do what they want, dress how they fancy, and pierce where they will, no matter how my wife and I have brought them up. I admit, even the slightest possibility of this gnaws at me to no end. If we had thought this were true—that we treaded at this level of impotence—my wife and I never would have mustered the incredible amount of courage that it took to become parents.

And without our children—and yours—the world would be deprived of its splendor.

5

The Anti-Midas Touch

BENIGN HUMILIATION?

Just before school began in September 1980, word spread quickly that Sura, one of my former students, had shot herself in the head. Sura was *not* one of those kids about whom teachers and other students said, "I can't understand it! She had everything going for her!" A bit of a wallflower and an obscure blend in her classes, Sura seemed to have no more challenges than other kids; yet, for Sura, *bad* had reared its ugly head in the worst possible way: suicide.

So what happened?

Everyone knows an adult who can't do anything right, who loses at virtually everything she attempts, even meaningless board games. Unlike King Midas (as the story goes) who could not touch anything without it turning to gold, some people have the opposite effect—the *anti-Midas* touch: everything they touch turns *brown*.

So it goes with teenagers. Their teachers label them losers, other kids call them losers, they even dub *themselves* losers, deeply plummeting into a quicksand of Loserdom. Once branded with the anti-Midas touch, everyone—without exception—knows who they are. Other teens relentlessly gossip about them behind their backs, as they spawn more jokes about nerds and geeks than anybody else in the entire school.

Jake competed on our speech team for four years—from the beginning of 9th grade until the very end of his 12th-grade year—without ever winning *anything*. While there had been many other students on my speech teams who managed to go winless throughout their inauspicious careers as speech and debate devotees, nobody brought more conspicuous attention than Jake did to the fact that he lost *all the time*. On one memorable occasion in which only 15 students were competing in Jake's "best" event, original oratory, the tiny size of the tournament guaranteed that 14 of the 15 competitors would advance to the semifinal round.

Only *one* orator missed out.

Guess who that was.

At another tournament, this one a major event in the forensics community, the adult awards presenter blurted out Jake's name for *first place* in original oratory! The rest of the auditorium honored Jake with a smattering of polite applause (as they usually did for speakers from other schools who won trophies), but our own team sat quietly, looking at each other with raised eyebrows and open mouths, baffled by Jake's placing at the top of the heap. Jake actually had been eliminated from the tournament the day before, managing, as usual, not to make the oratory cut to the semifinal round, let alone the final round, a prerequisite to placing in the tournament.

So Jake stood up, bent at his knees, completely bewildered. Had he actually competed in the esteemed final round of oratory at this prestigious tournament *and not remembered anything about it?* Could he have been so stressed by his competition—not to mention *shocked* by his success—that he had numbed himself into denying the reality of his unforeseen victory? In other words, had Jake been languishing in La-La Land?

Uh…no.

The unfortunate truth of what happened to Jake evolved from a careless error that his speech coach had made during the registration process. Pressed into doing a multitude of duties in the tally room (where the results of the competition are scored), I had inadvertently assigned Jake's name to the wrong speaking code number. One of my other students had won first place—not an unusual or shocking occurrence for *her*—but Jake, much to his embarrassment, had been given the credit. The girl who had actually won, but whose name did not get mentioned, took the whole thing in stride, opting to have a good sense of humor about it.

Jake, however, sighed, shook his head, and sank into the soft, padded chairs of the auditorium, trying to find another rock to crawl under—not an unusual or shocking occurrence for him either.

Then I then made another clumsy mistake. Feeling just awful about the mortifying ramifications of my blunder, I later purchased a nice trophy for Jake and presented it to him in front of the speech class on Monday morning. Jake bristled when I called his name; the kids in the class, reminded of what had happened at the tournament, cackled.

And Jake stormed out the room.

Sometimes we just can't fix those things that need to be fixed—even when we're the ones who broke them in the first place.

THUMP! OUCH!

My father couldn't make any money; he failed at a dozen different business ventures. My mother, sweet and encouraging of her children, offered no such treatment to her husband. Once, when my father arrived home from a trip to the bank to secure another loan for the sole purpose of paying delinquent bills (possibly the fourth or fifth loan he had taken), my mother roared, "Some men, they—I don't know—they manage to keep their families above water. But you— you manage to let us sink deeper and deeper!"

"I do my best," my father pleaded.

But my mother would not relent. "Take Daniel [our next-door neighbor and father of three children]; he invests in a dinner club [a topless bar], and he becomes a millionaire. You invest in a small coffee shop, and we all become paupers!"

"Daniel was lucky."

"Lucky?" My mother charged. "Lucky? Everything that man touches turns to gold. He's like King Midas."

"I try," my father mumbled feebly.

But my mother dug even deeper: "And *my* husband? Everything you touch turns to shit. You're the opposite of King Midas. You are the *anti*-Midas!"

Hmm, I thought to myself, even though I was only five years old: the name for a chapter in a book I will write in about 50 years—about those teenagers who can't do anything right. Unlike King Midas, everything they touch turns to, well, *not* gold: They fail almost all their classes; they misspell the very first word in spelling bees; they can't get dates for big dances; they're excluded from most social cliques; they freeze in their most important job interviews; they trip while riding escalators at malls (usually right in front of the people they most want to impress); they ostracize their own families from their lives by mortifying them; and they can't point to even one interest or passion that excites them enough to pull them out of their beds. Even the athletic kids: they strike out with two outs and the bases loaded in the bottom of the ninth inning, or bounce a potential game-saving shot off the rim right at the buzzer. They're the kids who are caught sneaking into R-rated movies, or trying to buy cigarettes at convenience stores.

It *starts* funny, but soon the humor dissipates. Anti-Midas teens are often depressed teens, and adolescent depression rarely winds up in a funny punch line: Besides the suicides, several hundred thousand teenagers will indulge in binge drinking during parties or at unsupervised homes after school hours. Countless others will engage in severe drug dependencies that will ruin their lives and their families. Teenagers don't deal well with depression, and not because they're unlucky at winning Monopoly during family game nights. Simply put: Many kids have become discouraged, disgruntled, or disengaged due to their own perceptions of themselves as total losers.

And some teens fall off the deep end.

Every time a young male with a gun marches into a school and blows the students to smithereens, investigations later reveal troubling information about the youngster's life—a horrifying profile that stretches far beyond the usual bout with acne or a wayward parent off the wagon. These young people have an unbearably lowly perception of themselves; they see no future, can't remember their past, and look askance at their present. For them life has become so excruciating, they lack the energy to drive forward and compete with the forces that have encumbered their ability to succeed. The different personality types and genetic dispositions may explain—at least, to some degree—why their surrender to their own antisocial idiosyncrasies sometimes manifests itself in acts of horrific violence. Some kids wind up shooting up Columbine High School; others never physically harm even a fly, though they may dress like they are auditioning for a haunted house exhibit.

In my own career, I have come into personal contact with fewer anti-Midas types than a lot of other teachers who have taught high school for more than three decades. After all, baseball coaches, debate advisors, play directors, and honors English teachers meet only a very few of these self-identified, so-called loser types during their careers.

Right?

Meet Harold. (I know. His name sounds so cliché. I wish I could tell you his real name; it was even more cliché than *Harold*.) Harold loved horses; he hated any other animals. Harold was that way; he either *loved* something, or he *loathed* it. Rarely did a middle ground exist for Harold when it came to any topic or person.

I knew Harold from his stint as the boyfriend of one of the star debaters on my speech team. One of the most perplexing high school romance matches in history had taken place that year: Jeanie stood about five-feet-two, her long, sandy-blond hair always immaculate as she swayed when she walked down the hall. *Adorable* described Jeanie. Her blue eyes radiated energy and mischief, accenting her fire and passion for life. Deceptively brilliant, because Jeanie didn't wish to turn off the boys by acting *too* smart, she played her role well. She was smart enough when she had to be, and dumb enough when she wanted to be.

Jeanie asked me—pleaded with me—for my permission to bring Harold with us to the Novice Championships. After all, she contended, he was just like one of us anyway; and he could even judge, since he wasn't a novice competitor himself.

I pointed out to Jeanie that Harold hadn't ever *competed* in speech tournaments, so he couldn't judge. But, yes, he was welcome to come along and sit in the rounds Jeanie was judging. Although Harold had the word *quirky* written all over him, he was smart, extremely verbal, and somewhat charismatic; perhaps he would enter a tournament next year as a senior.

Big mistake.

That afternoon on a street in front of the host school, a car clipped Harold while he was in a crosswalk.

Harold's injuries were mostly of the emotional variety. The driver anticipated that Harold would step in front of him, so he tapped his brake. Harold did walk in front of the car, and the driver swerved around him, barely nicking his arm with the driver's side mirror.

Harold sprawled; the car stopped.

And the director of the speech tournament said to me, "You are responsible. *You.*"

I was still too shaken from the mishap to put up any kind of defense for myself. He continued, wagging his finger. "You're supposed to be supervising your students at all times. That's the rule. You know the rule, Bruce; you've been coaching for years. What's *with* you?"

What's with me? When I traveled to speech tournaments with my students, I always made certain each kid had a parent authorization slip on file. In the event of medical emergency, doctors would not (could not) touch a child—even to deliver life-saving medical treatment—unless his parent had signed a consent form. But now I had no defense. Somehow I had managed to convince my speech students that they shouldn't walk in front of a two-ton moving vehicle; obviously, Harold had never been taught that strategy. I immediately hurled my wrath on Jeanie, which wasn't fair. Jeanie didn't share any responsibility for Harold's stupidity. His parents should have signed a permission slip, stating something to this effect: "Having been Harold's parents for the past 16 years, having a pretty good idea how stupid he is, and having knowledge that he lacks any common sense whatsoever, I absolve the school, the speech tournament, and especially Mr. G., if Harold is run over and killed."

Jeanie and Harold broke up about a week later. Jeanie went on to bigger and better things in speech; she also starred in a couple of stage productions. She sang beautifully. She became a mother—probably too early in her life—and has remained beautiful for a long time. We stayed in touch.

Harold, on the other hand, dissolved into thin air.

And then 10 years later, while in a pizza joint with another one of my speech teams, I ran into Harold. He scampered up to me breathlessly, as though I were an old, lost friend. Wide-eyed, he grabbed my hand and shook it. "Mr. G.," he cried, "do you remember me?"

Remember him!

"Sorry," I lied, as I shook my head and feigned embarrassment. "So many students...over so many..."

"Of course," he smiled politely. Harold was all grown-up now; he had filled out rather amply. He went on, "My name's Harold Kreiger. I got hit by a car at a speech tournament while you were supposed to be watching me."

I just nodded and ordered my pizza. Not be appear impolite or ungrateful, I had no desire to rehash old times with a former student who brought back such unpleasant memories. When I see my past students, they usually bring a warm glow to my heart; a few, however, send a cold chill up my spine.

Harold definitely fit into the latter category.

MR. G.'S HOME-GROWN ADVICE

There are two breeds of anti-Midas teenagers in the world: the *merely annoying* and the *unfortunately lethal*.

Deciphering the meanings of these labels requires all of us to make some rather gross—perhaps, unfair—generalizations; however, it comes down to this: Anti-Midas teenagers, those kids who seem to fail at anything they attempt and whose self-image deflates with every tick of the clock, usually do not wind up in the trash heap of civilization. Many of them go on to do wonderful things with their lives. Some of their anti-Midas tendencies are benign, manifesting themselves in mere annoyances. But the bigger problem comes with the *malignant* anti-Midas kids, those who cause tremendous harms to themselves and others. These teens have fallen into an abyss of losing. Sometimes they resign themselves to their lots in life; other times they panic, ultimately leading to more expedient forms of self-destruction. Trying to rescue themselves, they often wind up trapped in a morass of confusion and despair. Whether this is simply bad luck (as some experts have testified) or a self-guided path to obliteration, the result is these two groups of anti-Midas teenagers: the annoying kids, those who are laughed at, tormented, or ridiculed; and the doomed kids, those who transmogrify into addicts, convicts, or corpses.

Parents

Pay attention to your children. Fridays are board game nights at our house. My seven-year-old daughter loves Monopoly, because she craves the thrill of owning property and buying things. My five-year-old son digs chess, because he likes having the control over the movements of the pieces. My son loathes Monopoly because of *Go to jail; go directly to jail.* That jail part horrifies him. My wife is so busy with her responsibilities as banker and game rules guru, she hardly pays any attention to her own strategies (which are practically nonexistent). Once, after I hooted and howled over her proclivity for landing her game piece on my Boardwalk hotels, she pulled me aside and scolded, "Don't you realize that every time you laugh at my misfortunes in these games, you encourage our son to be terrified?"

"Terrified?" I asked. "Of what?"

"Of going to jail. Of losing."

Then, as my usual poor judgment in these situations would have it, I flashed one of my patented, obnoxious smirks. "You're just mad because you keep losing."

Stupid me.

Narrowing her eyes, my wife's usual grace and dignity, next to my usual aloofness and cockiness, reigned superior. "Bruce, we need to teach our kids how to be good losers and good winners, because they're going to do both in their lives. You're unintentionally giving them license to become obnoxious winners and dread even the thought of losing. Is that what you want to do?"

What was I supposed to say *now?*

Here's the bottom line: Parents should instill in their children a competitive fire that entertains losing *and* winning with dignity and grace. Instrumental in those lessons is providing children with the knowledge that—yes—they may *lose* at something today, but tomorrow they may *win* at something else; additionally, parents should offer some tools for their kids to bounce back from their losses: pride, tenacity, outside support, a shifting of priorities, a wiser perspective (not every game, not every endeavor, is a matter of life and death). Going to jail in Monopoly is not that bad, when compared to what happens to Daddy in real life after running a red light and crashing into another car. Parents can help to prioritize their children's time, so they will not embrace the destructive tendencies and temptations that seem to follow the anti-Midas teenagers around: addictive substances, slothfulness, bad peer outside influences, and a disinterest in learning.

Here's the scoop on a boy named Sam:

How would you have defended yourself, if you were Sam's parents?

About 15 years ago at a social gathering, I met a woman named Myra. Myra proved to be amiable enough, although I eventually discovered her more devilish, sardonic side. She was the boss at a local ice cream parlor (one of those large chains). In the process of hiring new workers for the parlor, Myra was rummaging through several job applications. Suddenly laughing, she handed me an applicant's submission form; the information seemed ordinary: name, birthday, previous employment, etc. One of the questions, however, asked the prospective employee this: "Why do you want to work here?"

An easy question, especially if you're expecting it. If you're not expecting it, you may be forced on the spur of the moment to speculate just how saccharine you have to be in order to impress the boss; after all, this is *her* store—*her* baby! So, having wound up for what, I'm sure, was the most profound job application answer of his life, the teenage boy had written this response:

"Cuz I like iceceem."

That's all.

Not "I wish to work here because I like ice cream" (which would have been insipid enough)—but "cuz I like iceceem," in all its sentence-fragment, improperly punctuated, misspelled, inarticulate, unsatisfying splendor.

So, of course, I laughed; Myra laughed, too. Together the iceceem—excuse me— the *ice cream* boss and I heartily chuckled, both of us shaking our heads, the kind of laugh you have when you find something especially funny. Maybe we were into something here; perhaps, this was the start of something big between us!

And then I noticed the name of the student on the application: Sam Gergamister. Sam Gergamister, varsity football player on a terrible football team that had come away victorious only once during the entire season. Sam Gergamister, who previously had been dumped by Jeanie, my star debater. Sam Gergamister, *a student in my fourth-period sophomore English class!*

So as soon as I saw Sam's name on the application, I felt my chuckle grinding to a halt. I'm afraid my once-hearty hoot had dwindled to an embarrassed cackle. It was mortifying for me to admit that *I* had been teaching Sam how to read and write English—and *this* was the fruit of my labors.

Could Sam have been *your* son? Would you have allowed him to hold down a job scooping ice cream at night, rather than practicing his writing and spelling at home? Boys from homes like Sam's exhaust the teaching community; no parent should have let Sam work at a job until he's able to write "I like ice cream" (not an articulate answer by any means) on his own. It's the minimum a parent should demand from a 16-year-old, or her kid will wind up scooping *iceceem* for the rest of his life.

Teachers

Very simple: if you pass Sam to the next level of your course, you should lose your teaching credential. For the sake of the kid, *someone* needs to display some guts for a change. "But," you contend, "if I don't pass Sam, he will turn out to be even a bigger loser." This is all a matter of perspective. Sam may ultimately become a winner in life, because someone finally had taken the initiative to teach him the skills he needed for survival.

Or not.

Teachers, therefore, have the following seven responsibilities to students with the anti-Midas touch:

1. Teach your subject *well*, so young adults will acquire the skills they need to prosper. If they don't get it the first time, give them another opportunity. They can take the course again. It won't hurt them; in the end, you actually will be doing them a favor.

2. Provide a *venting vehicle* to kids who think they're in trouble. It doesn't have to be the teacher, but you should be ready, able, and willing to refer the teen to where he feels safe about getting help.

3. Role model good citizenship, effective study skills, and healthy habits.

4. Guard against putdowns, teasing, and bullying. *Open your eyes.*

5. Raise *expectation* levels for your students and provide any needed assistance, so that your students can meet those expectations. Making certain that the expectations are high shows your students you have confidence in them. But expectations that are out of sync with reality construct unreasonable barriers to success.

6. Offer places for students to succeed, *other than* the confines of the academic curriculum. One example of this is class *team* competitions such as spelling bees, trivia contests, and subject-related bingo. Somebody always loses; however, somebody always wins, too. I don't believe everybody should win a trophy for just showing up, but if they play enough, if they hang in there, *something* good is more likely to happen to more kids.

7. Praise a lot. But have a sense of *humor.* When the kid who always seems to trip on the invisible line in the sidewalk stumbles *again,* joke about it. Eventually this sort of awkwardness comes with a badge of honor. (If the kid happens to break his neck, please ignore this suggestion.)

Teachers provide crucial leadership in helping anti-Midas teens develop some *self-respect,* while allowing these kids to maintain more than a semblance of their *dignity.*

Teenagers

When you stand out like a sore thumb, you feel like a loser; when you don't stand out like a sore thumb—blending into the background—you feel like a loser. Here's an old-fart expression you may have heard: "Damned if you do; damned if you don't." The point is this: All kids are certain to feel like losers during various stages of their teenage years (also at different times during their adult lives)—but what you actually *do* with your comprehension of this concept may be the predicator of your future happiness.

Your life will be what you've made it. Adolescence is a very hard time. You're not an adult, though most of your bodies certainly look like adult bodies; you're not a child anymore, though a lot of the time others treat you like you're still a child. That's why I call you *aliens.* I'm really not quite sure what you are, but you don't fit into a typical classification system. Aliens are strange, different creatures, normally associated with outer space. The word *alien* itself means foreigner; so to that extent, teenagers *are* foreign—not of this world—but of *the human race.* This is not a bad thing; in fact, every one of us has had to travel though adolescence. I remember my alien years and how horrible they seemed at times. I was sure there were moments I couldn't do anything right: If I needed to get up at 6:00, I woke up at 7:00; if I guessed on a test answer—even when there were only two choices—I always picked the wrong one; if I liked Becky and wanted to take her to a movie, Becky didn't like me; *Donna* liked me, but—of course—I didn't like Donna.

Being a teenager means up is down and down is up. It means being scolded for things you didn't do, and feared by people you've never met. It means yearning for love from parents who have given up on you, and being devastated by parents who are splitting from each other. Being a teenager requires you to obey your elders, listen to your teachers, and care for your siblings. It engenders impulsivity, passivity, and rigidity. You must make decisions you are not sure of, and plan for a future you are not aware of. Being a teenager throws you a curveball just when you're looking for a fastball, and then labels you as a failure for not guessing the pitch correctly.

Being a teenager is *tough*. And it's natural—*expected*—that you will lose more than you will win; that you will fail more than you will succeed.

So here's what you have to do: Each time that you lose—that you fail—you have to shrug it off and remember that *it's just a part of growing up*. Every soured attempt is a stepping-stone to success in the future, because it gives you perspective. You will never realize the joy of winning or succeeding if you have no failures to frame that perception for you. If you choose to gear your mind in another direction—wallowing with every loss, fretting over every failed attempt—you will wind up joining countless other teenagers who have fallen into an abyss of despair. Those kids truly possess the anti-Midas touch, because, in a sad sense, they have fulfilled a self-proclaimed prophecy: *They have determined themselves to lose, to fail at everything that they do.*

And lose they did.

More than 30 years later, I still don't know why Sura killed herself. I vaguely remember Sura as a quiet, withdrawn kid who had very little to say in class and rarely voiced her opinion in writing. She left no suicide note. She had no breakups with boyfriends or her closest friends. She didn't do drugs or drink, and she had never been in trouble with the law. She was a pretty girl who probably dealt with some of the usual challenges teenagers face every year of their lives. From the information I garnered, the police were stumped, and so were her parents.

Whatever Sura's motivation was for ending her own life, devastating her parents and friends, and depriving society of her potential contributions, one thing was abundantly clear: Sura saw herself as a loser. I never thought of her that way, and other students didn't either, but *she* held that impression of herself.

You can't afford to fall into that bottomless gulf. People don't automatically know what is going on inside you, what you need, or what you want. Adults with the best of intentions are often frustrated by you, because they want to help you—and can't. They wish to convey to you that you are important; that your life is special, and your soul is precious. And becoming the popular or successful kid people look up to at school does not automatically make you a winner; that kid has problems, too. What sometimes separates the people who are happy in their adult lives from the people who are miserable in their adult lives was their ability to hang in there—learning and maturing—when they were teenagers. It's called *tenacity*: bouncing back from a setback, getting off the floor and dusting yourself off, working hard to finally travel forward instead of backward—these qualities turn around young lives and help teenagers like you to live up to your potentials.

Carl auditioned for my new play about masculinity. A cinch to get the part, he created perfectly a caricature of brainless—yet idolized—manliness: tall, brawny, aloof, and crass. I knew Carl only from a sophomore English class, but he had obvious talent for reading aloud; he also matched the rugged physical requirements for the role.

"Yeah, man," Carl beamed, "I'd like to get up there on stage and strut around with my shirt off to 'The Macho Rap'! Cool!"

"Then you've got the part, Carl," I promised enthusiastically. Discovering this kid for the play was like raising a treasure from the secret depths of the ocean. "Can you make all the rehearsals?"

He hesitated. "Uh, well, except for the weekends."

"Oh," I muttered, somewhat disappointed.

"And except for after five o'clock on the weekdays."

"What!" I exclaimed. "Then you can't make any of the rehearsals!"

"Well, I can, Mr. G.... if you will talk to my probation officer and get me out of jail. But just for during the rehearsals."

What?

Carl told me that he'd been convicted of residential burglaries but was trying to turn his life around. Whatever motivated him to rob from people, he wanted to change. Both of us saw promise for altering Carl's life through the vehicle of theater. His academic counselor and I managed to get permission for Carl to participate in the rehearsals and all nine performance nights. Ultimately, Carl became a tremendously successful member of the speech team, qualifying to compete on the national level. After graduating from high school, he landed a leading role on a new CBS sitcom (that didn't last very long); since then, Carl has been featured on several television shows (such as *Who's the Boss?* and *Married with Children*), and a few motion pictures.

Carl discovered what so many other teenagers have failed to discover: life's perks and rewards can be obtained through hard work, tenacity, a strong will, and—yes—some good fortune. Even at a kid's lowest point, there remains the potential for "turning it around" and finding purpose.

Yes, brown really can be turned into gold.

6

Dumb Stuff

ADULTS KNOW BETTER...RIGHT?

Albert Einstein warned, "If the Third World war is fought with nuclear weapons, the Fourth World war will be fought with sticks and stones."

As a kid, hearing these words scared me. The potential horrors of nuclear annihilation alarmed most people, but impressionable teenagers lacked the mental maturity and wisdom for understanding the intricacies of such a dastardly scenario. Adults have the capability to venture beyond the emotional bondage of such a nightmarish vision, better able to see the whole picture. Scare tactics—the kinds that were used in the fifties and early sixties—discouraged a lot of teens from rationally coming to grips with the melodrama of doomsday prognosticators; consequently, we questioned the sanity of our parents when the overwhelming majority of them refused to build underground bomb shelters or pack up the family and drive off to Switzerland.

The truth here, elucidated by my observations and various experts' analyses, is that America's teens have an odious record for using bad judgment. Their bad choices are fueled by their lack of maturity, underdeveloped wisdom (mostly because they haven't lived long enough), and their proclivity for impulsive decision making.

Had I been living solo (without my parents) when I was 16, I would have not only built that idiotic bomb shelter, I would have lived in it; I also would have spent all my money on Beatles records and driven my car 110 miles per hour in residential neighborhoods. If I had not been guided by others who knew more than I did about, well, *everything,* my amount of dumb stuff could never have been recorded on—or in—anything available at that time (no personal computers existed); there would not have been enough space for me to confess my stupidity.

Teenagers do even more dumb stuff today, because fewer adults than ever are watching them. I wish I had a one-pound box of dark chocolates for every time I was forced to say to a student or player or actor or debater, "Do your *parents* know what you're doing?"

With the usual response: a grunt.

WRINKLED TOILET PAPER, SMASHED FLOWERS, AND TWISTED METAL

Monique looked at Paulina with an air of confidence, mixed with a shade of mischievousness. "He'll never find out," she conjectured with a self-assurance that Paulina didn't share. "And even if he does, big deal."

"I don't think we should," Paulina cautioned. "What if his parents, like, sue us for damages or something?"

"*What* damages?" Monique pressed, excited about their pending scheme. "Toilet paper can't hurt anything!"

Paulina knew that draping acres of toilet paper around the landscape of a former boyfriend's home would not constitute a capital offense; yet, she had an inkling that this sort of stunt often produced repercussions, if nothing more than tit-for-tat retribution from the targeted person.

Paulina and Monique solicited the help of two male friends and then thoroughly papered their prey's home. Toilet paper now hung from everywhere around the dwelling: from the two tall trees near the front windows; from an enormous elephant plant in the pathway to the front door; and from an array of bushes around the parameter of the front clover grass. When the foursome returned to Paulina's house for a celebration of their mischievous deed, Monique breathlessly rejoiced, "I've done like, oh, 25 toilet paperings, and this one was the best one yet! Great job!"

Paulina scrunched her nose and hesitated. She, too, had given their efforts high marks, but her misgivings lay in being caught and any retribution from the victim's family. "Do you think anybody saw us?" she wondered aloud.

"Paulina," Monique smiled, "what's he gonna do about it? Like he already dumped you. He can't dump you after dumping you! What? Are you still hoping to get back with him?"

"Nooo," Paulina replied deliberately.

"Then don't worry about it. Wouldn't you love to see the look on his face after he walks out the front door in the morning? And his parents are gonna, like, make him clean the whole thing up. They're gonna be so pissed!"

In reality, Paulina's ex-boyfriend's parents did not fuss about the attack. After they awoke in the morning for church services and stepped outside to get in their car, they totally ignored all the toilet paper; they weren't bothered by it at all.

Paulina's ex-boyfriend's parents may have had a different response, however, if the girls had papered *their* home!

Directly across the street from Paulina's ex-boyfriend's house lived a policeman, his wife, and his two future police academy teenage sons. Understandably, *they* did not take kindly to the incident. But they, too, may have been indifferent to the prank if the house across the street from *them* had been papered—and not *theirs*. They filed a police report for vandalism, after finding one of the boys' wallets (with condemning identification) in their garden. They unleashed verbally on Paulina, Monique, their two friends—and all of the connected parents. The cop and his family claimed the kids damaged their peach tree and demanded its replacement. They also pointed to smashed flowers in their front garden and tiny particles of toilet paper that could not be removed from the crevices of their plants without doing harm to the plants themselves.

After the dust (and the Charmin) had settled, the bill for this fun-filled, raucous night of entertainment amounted to around $2,000.

Monique said later, "I didn't think anybody would take this sort of thing seriously."

And Paulina reminded her, "We did the wrong house!"

To which Monique observed, "That was kinda stupid, Paulina! After being with a guy for three months, you shoulda known which house was *his!*"

"He *showed* me the wrong house! We used to park in front of it—well, the policeman's house anyway—at the curb."

"Then he lied to you," Monique accused, long after having lost her sprightly, confident grin.

Paulina ended the exchange. "Yes, he did. And if you didn't have such a dumb idea, none of this woulda happened in the first place!"

Teenage girls dramatize everything. They add an energy and immediacy to events most normal people see as commonplace and bearable—events whose seriousness most normal people have no difficulty at minimizing.

I am quite surprised that teens still go about their prank-filled evenings throwing around toilet paper; I'm also rather pleased. On the list of dumb things to do, hurling toilet paper rolls on someone's front lawn pales next to, for example, racing cars on city streets. Drag racing sped into the limelight right around the time Jim Stark (James Dean) forced that mean dude off the cliff in *Rebel Without a Cause*. About 20 years after *Rebel*, the glamour of drag racing motored its way into American moviegoers' sensitivities when John Milner (Paul Le Mat)'s souped-up Chevy flipped violently into a ditch in *American Graffiti*. Only in *American Graffiti*, the good guy lost the race and almost got himself and a couple of his friends killed; still, racing looked like a pretty cool thing to do, and when something appears to be particularly *cool*, teenagers swarm around it like bees near a honeycomb.

The effects of drag racing are *not* cool. I've had no personal contact with students who have been killed while drag racing. But looking at the numbers of casualties for this ridiculously careless and stupid pursuit forces a sobering thought: Illegal road racing fatalities went up 87 percent in just one year (2000–2001).[1] Frankly, anyone who claims that *this* is really keen qualifies for a serious mental examination.

A contributing writer to the "Letters to the Editor" section of the *Los Angeles Times* punctuated these thoughts with an exclamation point. After a long night of partying, two teenagers had died while drag racing on a city street in the wee hours of a Sunday morning. No one disputed the idiocy that lent itself to these senseless losses; however, the man who took the initiative to write to the newspaper decided to take it one step further: He wanted something of tangible value to come from the death of these teenagers; after all, he argued, nothing would bring them back—so, perhaps, their demise could prevent others from duplicating their recklessness. He suggested that videos of the carnage from high-speed wrecks should be shown at the funerals of young people who had died in drag racing crashes. Hundreds of teenagers at these funerals would see—up close and personal—what *really* happens when two tons of steel, careening along the highway at speeds in excess of 90 miles per hour, collides with other objects: mangled, bloodied bodies, and the requisite twisted metal and shattered glass.

The writer's ideas—obvious hyperbole—should be taken with a grain of salt. But his heart was in the right place. Teenagers, especially boys, do not understand the grim realities of life-and-death decisions they make on a daily basis. Their perennial desire to hurl their macho selves around the highway landscape sometimes begets serious consequences.

When I read that letter suggesting horrific videos at funerals to my classes, most students recoiled in amazement; some notions of blasphemy surfaced. The idea of parading the deaths of teenagers at—of all places—the *funerals* of other teenagers fizzled like a match in a windstorm. The very first comment made in class that day—and I remember it well—came from a boy who scrunched up his nose and asked belligerently, "Did you make that letter up?"

I walked over to his desk and handed him the freshly cut-out copy of the letter. He grimaced and then asked rhetorically, "Isn't it weird that a newspaper would print something so stupid?"

I didn't want my class to miss the lesson. "What about the stupidity of the boys who raced their cars on a city street?" I pressed.

He looked at me in silence.

But he had also raised a valid point: How *do* we cope with the senseless losses of young lives that come from impulsive, shortsighted, idiotic decisions? Do we honor the dead by vacating our notions of good sense and common decency in a desperate attempt to make some meaningful sense of the horror? "Take a look: Here's what happens, kids, when you succumb to peer pressure or refuse to reconsider some of your own very, very dumb ideas."

Not all dumb stuff is lethal—or even that harmful. Much of it is just extremely embarrassing. Some dumb stuff provides the material from which memories are made—that people laugh about decades later at class reunions. Sometimes we say much later, "No harm, no foul." Other times we sigh, "Whew! Now, that was a *close* one!" And no particularly awful consequence had resulted.

Lethal or benign, and in no particular order of dumbness, here are some of my clearest memories of dumb stuff from bygone years:

The boy quacked like a duck; I thought it *was* a duck. While waiting to practice his speech on a Saturday afternoon, the boy had climbed to the roof of my classroom. He risked life and limb to distract the speakers and me with his rather authentic duck sounds. I had to laugh at this one. As much as I verbally chastised him, he was still talented enough to pull a fast one; it was cute. Dangerous and *dumb*, but cute.

The girl hit the deck; the tardy bell had just rung, and in a last-ditch effort to get to my class on time, her grand entrance manifested itself in the form of a darn good belly flop. Head first, she skidded along the carpet. Thirty teenagers burst into laughter. I howled. She slowly rose from the floor, also laughing (sort of a choke/laugh sort of thing), but through a preponderance of tears. When I observed that the entire underside of her right arm had been stripped bare of its skin, I abruptly stopped cackling. The students, however, continued to whoop it up; for them, the sight of blood and mangled flesh had somehow made it even funnier.

Melissa, wildly gesticulating, wrapped herself in conversation with her friend Grace. Juicy gossip was her forte. With her head tilted slightly to the side so that she could see into Grace's eyes, she ranted, she raved, and she roared. And then she crashed head first into a steel pole. She did this without breaking stride and without deference to the pole. Since she was not looking in front of her at the time and did not notice what lay ahead, the first indication of anything remiss (like colliding her head into solid steel, for example) came with a loud thump: her bony head smashing into an unyielding pole. The excruciating pain that followed was the second hint she had done something unwise. The third sign of her foolishness reverberated in the laughter of a dozen kids who were standing right there and observed the mishap. Melissa laughed about it later, only semiglad that her inattention hadn't killed her. To a teenager humiliation often seems worse than death.

Terence stood more than six feet tall and had the gangly build of a basketball player; Denver was four inches shorter than Terence but outweighed him by over a hundred pounds. They loved to horseplay by wrestling on the floor. One day—Terence tells this story, so I take it only semiseriously—the two were up to their old antics, when Denver sat on Terence's face. Since Terence's face did not welcome pending suffocation by more than 300 pounds of buttocks, he became petrified. Terence says that he actually lapsed into unconsciousness and then woke up a couple of minutes later with the dry heaves. Whether his heaving was due to the dramatic curtailment of his oxygen or the odor emanating from Denver's buttocks, suffice to say, Terence will not be playing World Wrestling Association with Denver any time in the near future.

Roger liked to play games, and he welcomed all sorts of challenges. But here's one for the record: a game in which the participants bang their heads as hard as they can against a concrete table! And how does one *win* such a game? Roger said, "Well, the guy who slams his head into the table the hardest wins." And how does one know who bangs his head the hardest? Roger shrugged, "Well, you just listen for the thump. Usually the loudest thump means the biggest bang." Which leads to this hypothesis: The guy who wins by ultimately making the loudest thump on a concrete table probably has the least to lose when it comes to the value of his head.

Speaking of games, Mario has a game he likes to play with his friends: it's called "The Choking Game." This dandy contest exploits a teenager's impulsivity; it also begs the question: If an adolescent is dense enough to tie a rope around his neck and allow someone else to squeeze the knot until he is on the verge of drifting into unconsciousness or death, should he be allowed to breed (more like him) later? When some of the kids described this "game" to me, it was as though they were nonchalantly giving instructions on how to tie a shoe. I was more than delighted to hear that Mario later quit playing "The Choking Game" and took up the concrete table head-bashing game instead.

Rick possessed the best sense of humor of any student I taught during the 1990s. However, his pleasing, affable personality, combined with an acute ability to tick people off—especially authority figures—made Rick a complex kid to deal with. He also craved danger. All of these ingredients came together to form, perhaps, one of the saddest (but preventable) incidents that occurred during my teaching career.

RICK

Remember the quacking duck on the roof of my classroom? That was Rick. He had a fondness for getting my goat, while cracking me up at the same time: an interesting dichotomy, for my laughter often paralyzed my ability—or willingness—to reprimand him for his antics, and I felt reluctant to punish him.

Rick's parents divorced when he was five years old; he lived with his mother. She constantly smoked in my presence, even while attending speech squad activities; later I learned she also was quite a boozer. Rick's father rarely saw Rick or spoke with him—but he adored his father nevertheless, always speaking of him in the most glowing terms. Rick did practically anything to get attention from *anyone*. He loved to make people laugh, and he was quite good at it; he possessed a subtle, sarcastic sense of humor, somewhat highbrow, that mostly the smarter kids understood. Although Rick felt more comfortable around the talented, cerebral speech students, he rarely missed a chance to tell a joke or act silly enough to drive his less academic-minded friends into hysterics, too.

Then came that night: It happened just before midnight on March 31, 1994.

Rick had been smoking pot with two of his closest friends. (During my investigation of that night's events, nobody admitted to using anything more than marijuana.) The small group smoked grass near a railroad overpass, not too far from one of the boy's houses. On other nights they had enjoyed the absolute rush, the high, the joy they received after they lined up about five feet from the tracks and let a huge freight train whoosh by them. They stood like statues, their hair waving from the warm air of the train rushing to its destination. Sometimes holding hands, their building, intense fear caused them to laugh nervously—all part of the fun. Immediately following the passing of the train, they fell to the ground like small children who were having an amazing play date—and with so much energy stored up inside, they hardly knew what to do next with their bodies.

On this night events unfolded in a predictable fashion.

Until disaster struck.

Rick's friends adored him. Lori, a pert, curvaceous teenager, was the only girl there. She had a brilliant mind, a strong head on her shoulders—hard to believe, when one evaluates her conduct that night. Rick's best friend at the time was Milt. Milt stood almost six feet tall and had a set of piercing blue eyes and dimpled cheeks. Once Milt's body filled out—he was two years younger than Rick, who was now nine months out of high school—Milt would surely monopolize the chick market.

The cooling night air did not diminish the teenagers' enjoyment of marijuana. Toking away, they giggled and joked near the viaduct that would soon accommodate the large freight train that rumbled its way through the area at precisely the same time—midnight. The kids knew that; having greeted the train so often, this had become a ritual for them. The high they received from the train—especially when already high from pot—could not be duplicated.

And it certainly gave them something to look forward to!

"You shoulda called up Rodney," Lori barked. Her comment, tinged with a slight amount of antagonism, was directed toward Rick.

"I told you," Rick snapped back. "I called him this afternoon, and he told me he couldn't come. He's gonna be with his girlfriend tonight."

"Whatever," Lori shrugged.

Milt assumed Lori had a crush on another guy, Rodney, even though Rodney already had a girlfriend. The problem was both Milt and Rick had a thing for Lori, even though they both claimed her as their platonic friend.

Rick looked at Milt. "Turn the music up, dude."

Milt upped the boom box volume, raising the level of the anachronistic sounds of Slayer. None of these kids were into the hip tunes of the day, when rap music had settled into its huge impact on the youth market. Rap was not for them; they liked the heavy metal sounds of the seventies and eighties. That music drove harder and picked them up, well, higher.

Milt said, "The choo-choo should be here in a couple of minutes. Might even be late now." He took a cursory look down the track that wound into the darkness. "I can't see any engine lights."

Those last few words uttered by Milt would come back to haunt him later—maybe for the rest of his life.

"I gotta stop doin' this, man!" Rick said in jest, an enormous smile lighting up his freckled face. "I mean, how often can a guy get wasted and then let a big motherfuckin' train shoot right by him? Something's gotta give, man!"

"You know you like how it feels," Lori teased him. "You know you like it!"

Rick turned from Lori's sexual innuendo and moved abruptly down the small hill to the brush that covered the terrain below them. He called back, "Yeah, I like it! *I like it!* But right now, I gotta take a leak!"

And he disappeared into the weeds, just a few feet below the trellis and the small area of gravel where the others stood waiting for the train.

Just as Rick had begun to relieve himself, wobbling on his two feet, trying to stand straight and avoid spraying himself with his own urine, he heard Milt's voice call from above. "Hey, Rick! Get up here, man! Train's comin'! Hurry!"

Milt evidently hadn't noticed the train's headlights when he had peered down the track before—not until he heard the engine in the distance and then saw the light growing larger in the darkness.

Lori squealed with delight and anticipation.

Their plan was simple: join hands just a few feet from the track and let the whizzing train do the rest as it went by them. The rush was indescribable!

Milt yelled, "Hurry up, Rick!"

Milt and Lori had already taken their places along the tracks. Rick darted frantically up with hill with his pants still halfway down his legs, simultaneously trying to run to his place along the tracks and pull up his trousers.

But then he stumbled in front of the charging train.

Neither Milt nor Lori remembers any sounds coming from Rick during those final seconds. Lori thought Rick was smiling, but the night had been very dark; the only lights were the distant glare of the street lamps from the highway and the flickering headlight bulb on the approaching train engine. As the train roared toward them with blazing speed, Lori and Milt turned to face it, assuming Rick would be there to grab Lori's hand and join in their quest for the biggest high ever.

Lori's first sense of panic came when she realized Rick had not grabbed her hand with the train only a fraction of a second from the bridge. In that short instant, Lori was saddened by the thought that Rick would miss the zooming madness of the powerful locomotive. But this millisecond of reflection was replaced by the sight of her friend flying into the air and landing violently on the gravel near the base of the track, the multiton freight train having slammed into his comparatively tiny body. According to Lori, the whole world hung in suspended animation.

Rick lay motionless on the asphalt.

The investigators found later that the engine had barely made contact with Rick's body, but the damage from even a slight nudge of a mighty train would have been instantly lethal.

Lori and Milt remained frozen in horror, thinking that the cumulative effects of marijuana and the euphoria from the rush of the train had temporarily tricked their brains. Then the reality: Milt immediately ran to his best friend and lifted Rick's head off the ground, cradling him in his arms. "Just a bruise on your forehead," he thought. "You can't be dead. You can't die from being hit by a train that only left a little bruise on your forehead!"

But the force of the train had killed Rick—instantly. What to Milt looked like a comfortable state of slumber was, in reality, a catastrophe—another wasted young life. What appeared to be another teenager who had passed out from drinking too much was, in reality, a teenager who was dead. Rick and his friends had made the single, most costly decision of their young lives, and in less than a second, those lives were damaged forever.

All of this occurred during Easter break, while I was visiting Las Vegas. I returned home on Thursday, April 5, and clicked on my answering machine. The third voice I heard was Rodney's, Rick's friend, the boy who had been with his girlfriend that fateful night. "Mr. G.... This is Rodney.... I'm, uh... I have something to tell you.... Uh, Rick's dead. Rick died last night. He... [a long pause] was killed in.... There was an accident, and Rick was killed. Please call me at..."

At the very moment I returned Rodney's call, he was attending Rick's funeral. I tried in vain to reach the church, but the services were already over by the time I arrived. A couple of days later, I picked Rodney up from his dormitory at a local college, and he took me to the site of the incident. Small droplets of dried blood, now brown and crusted, still clung to some of the gravel stones. I pictured how it must have happened—how easily our lives can end in a single instant, in a brief moment of utter carelessness; I imagined Rick charging up the hill: how he must have tripped at the last second—maybe on the rocks or possibly because his pants were not pulled up properly—and when he fell forward just a *little* bit, the train grazing his head hard enough to kill him.

"You know, Mr. G.," Rodney said tearfully, "Rick was my best friend. All that stuff we did together on the speech team, all the fun we used to have... the shows we did together.... But you know what? *I wasn't there for him that night.* . . . And Milt... he held Rick when he died.... And he can't forgive himself."

"Can't forgive himself? For what, Rodney?"

"For not seeing the train. When he first looked, he didn't notice the lights of the train. If he would've seen the train, he would have told Rick, and Rick never would have gone down to pee; he would have just stayed there. And the way Milt figures it, it never would've happened."

I simply nodded in agreement; there was no point in contesting Milt's perspective.

All of the events and decisions that led up to that horrible moment—*those* were not the mistakes. The *real* mistake wasn't picking the wrong moment to urinate in the darkness; the *real* mistake was getting high, and then playing Red Rover with a freight train.

MR. G.'S HOME-GROWN ADVICE

For a boy, catching a dare is one of the most important challenges to his budding manhood. A double dare is even more intimidating. This generalization comes from personal memories of my own youth, but it's also formed from decades of observing teenagers who have dealt with dares and double dares. As kids get older, dares become subtler—taking insidious forms—manifested in the shape of an odious phenomenon called *peer pressure.* All teenagers engage in dumb stuff at one time or another. But here's hoping that it's not as dumb as smoking pot for three hours and then staggering into a railroad train.

Parents

Some parents brag—to anyone within earshot—about their leniency with their children; unfortunately, these same parents often later regret having given their kids too much slack. Children appreciate borders and structure; they like hearing what the limits are, what they can—and cannot—get away with. Sure, teens violate these territories all the time, but that doesn't mean they loathe the adults who discipline them; in fact, the opposite is true. Teenagers respect authority figures who say what they mean—and mean what they say. Eventually, they look back on these people and count them among their saviors. Parents find that their unwillingness to impose restrictions on their small children leads to serious discipline problems in the teenage years. Teenagers will take whatever you give them, so designate some boundaries. Don't scoff at other parents who are stricter with their children than you are with yours. And don't call your children names that mock their maturity or manliness because they refuse to engage in risky behaviors. Years ago I heard of a father who had ridiculed his son because he was afraid to ride on roller coasters; the boy didn't go on a roller coaster until he was 16 years old. Later, as other boys goaded him about his hesitancy to walk along the cliffs overhanging a beach, thoughts of his father's derisive comments about his masculinity may have riddled his memory. Against his better judgment, the boy surrendered to his friends' disparagements, nervously trudging along the jagged cliffs of a North Carolina beach resort. His fear of heights and the imminent danger posed by the rocks 50 feet below did not prevail over his friends' taunts and ridicule.

Less than five minutes later, the boy slipped, his body thudding into the ground with a silent echo.

He died before help could arrive.

Protect your child; make sure that he associates with the right people. Peer pressure, after all, can be a *good* thing, *if good people are putting on good pressure for good reasons*. Lots of *goods* exist in that last sentence, but it can't be overstated: All teens are going to succumb to peer pressure at one time or another; it's, therefore, inherently incumbent upon parents to see that their children's peers are selected well—thus sheltering them as much as possible from unnecessary bad influences.

Teachers

Teachers are role models, so they need to be extremely careful about speaking to their students about any dumb stuff that they have personally engaged in. When teachers describe daredevil feats they accomplished in their youth or their past weekends of bungee jumping, scuba diving, motorcycle riding, or parachuting, it all sounds extremely interesting—even attractive—to teens. As adults we are entitled to those kinds of mature choices; but as adolescents, our choices— often poor and impulsive—are guided without wisdom. Boasting of potentially disastrous stunts has no purpose, other than to selfishly show off one's own bravado. Encouraging teenagers to make decisions that should be reserved for adults is tantamount to throwing a can of kerosene on the fires of immaturity and impulsivity.

Teachers need to warn young people about the *ugliness* of doing dumb stuff. Boys who act like buffoons in front of girls usually regret it sooner or later, wishing they could have those clownish moments back to repair the damage they've done to their reputations. Reminding high school kids that their moronic antics today may eventually become embarrassing tomorrow will not deter them in the present. But asking kids to look around and observe how most people are scoffing *at* them—and not laughing *with* them—has a slight chance of preventing at least a few toilet papering incidents or a couple of mindless, careless, high-speed drag races.

Teachers should role model maturity and dignity: dressing professionally, behaving responsibly, and thinking maturely. If teachers command respect from their students, many of those students will—at least, subconsciously—be determined to emulate the actions and lifestyles of those teachers, instead of burning a path that will attract ridicule and disrespect from others.

Teenagers

Phew! If you've hung in there this far, you already know that the two main reasons for teenagers doing dumb—sometimes *really dangerous*—stuff are directly linked to either peer pressure or alien immaturity. For both explanations I hereby offer the *ABCs for Resisting Dumb Stuff,* thereby significantly lessening your chances of succumbing to dumb, dastardly deeds of destruction (translated: doing stupid things that will really hurt you or kill you).

Allow yourself enough time to make decisions; don't *rush* into anything.

Before you do it, rethink it; reconsidering the deed could save your life.

Contact your parents and seek help when you feel trapped in an explosive situation.

Demand from your friends a reasonable justification for putting pressure on you.

Expect respect, only if you *earn* respect; doing dumb stuff deserves no respect at all.

Find other friends if the current ones are leading you into trouble.

Give no second chances to the people who have deliberately hurt you in the past.

Have no tolerance for those who ask you to do something illegal, immoral, or dangerous.

Intend to stay away from trouble that you don't need; follow through on your intentions.

Join organizations that less troubled teens belong to; *their* peer pressure can be *good*.

Kill time by acting *constructively;* excessive time on your hands may kill *you*.

Live as though there *is* a tomorrow, because there *will be* a tomorrow.

Mold the lives of children who are younger than you are by role modeling *responsibly*.

No *is* a cool word; saying *no* may save you from future heartaches.

Open the door to those you *respect,* even if they're not the life of the party.

Prepare for your future by acting as though you plan on *having* a future.

Quit acting on the spur of the moment; fatal choices often result.

Run—don't walk—away from the people in your life who would see you harmed.

Settle down; too much dumb stuff can happen when you're rattled or out of control.

Talk to an adult: a teacher, a counselor, or a coach, if you won't go to a parent.

Understanding yourself fully may never happen; don't fret about it.

Voice your concerns to a teacher, if you're bullied; don't keep this inside you.

Watch closely how some kids stay out of trouble; try *their* ways for a while.

Xerox into your brain that *dumb, awful* moment; this should help to prevent a repetition.

Yellow can be a practical color; don't let being *called* "yellow" influence you.

Zero in on all the great things you would miss out on if your dumb stuff killed you.

The *ABCs for Resisting Dumb Stuff* have power only if you allow yourself to look at it with an open mind. Some of you will get hurt because you *haven't thought things through;* or you will risk—and possibly lose—life and limb because you have been *led by your peers,* through either subtle coercion or overt bullying tactics. The ABCs encourages you to stand up for yourself, while holding on to your autonomy, pride, and self-respect. In the end, as with practically everything else in life, the choices are yours.

7

Athletes, Arrogance, and Angst

WHAT A HUNK!

In the 1961 motion picture *Splendor in the Grass,* a very young, perky Natalie Wood spends a great deal of time pursuing a very handsome, charismatic Warren Beatty. Bud, Beatty's character in the movie, has it all. He is the high school's star quarterback; the world is his oyster. Wild adulation from the girls and unabashed admiration from the boys come easily to Bud. Dressed in his football-player letterman's sweater, he needs only to exist to be popular.

Since the making of this movie, not a whole lot has changed.

Boys still long to excel at sports; girls still long for the boys who excel at sports.

The big-man-on-campus, high school football stud in the 1970s could be easily recognized: usually taller than the average; carrying an ample amount of solid weight; a face void of much emotion, wearing a dull gaze; and long, flowing locks conveniently tucked inside a protective helmet at game time.

A star football player of today can be easily recognized, too: usually taller than the average; carrying an ample amount of solid weight; a face void of much emotion, wearing a dull gaze; and long, flowing locks conveniently tucked inside a protective helmet at game time.

Hmm...

So, are there *any* major differences in student athletes after 35 years?

Four decades later numerous elements in society have changed, and high school athletes have changed, too. *Their* world is tougher because, well, the world is tougher. High school athletes today are bigger, stronger, more aggressive, and more talented than ever before; yet, paradoxically, they now are facing more difficulties than anyone ever thought imaginable.

During the 1980s, I had my most fun ever as a teacher. Coaching high school baseball was something I would have done for free. I had always longed to share my intricate knowledge of the sport that I loved more than anything else in the whole world; with teenage boys, I had the ideal audience. What a racket! What a life!

Soon, however, as with any other endeavor, some tough challenges were to rear their ugly heads. These kids faced pressures I had never encountered when I played high school baseball. It took no time at all for me to find out just how complicated their lives were; my position as head coach of the junior varsity baseball team left me privy to the nuts and bolts of student life I'd been shielded from in the classroom: locker room gossip; the personal lives of the players and their families; stresses brought on by college and pro recruiters; the attitudes of other students, teachers, and society in general toward the kids who played organized sports.

I discovered maybe *too* much about interscholastic sports:

the shortstop who swallowed his tongue and stopped breathing,

the catcher who charged toward the stands after he perceived a racist remark had been directed at him,

the scholarship-bound running back whose hatred for his father decimated his potential career and, eventually, his life,

the swimmer whose overexposure to water and weather elements in the wee hours of the morning at swim practice drove him into intensive care at the hospital,

the star quarterback whose father prohibited him from playing any more baseball if he didn't continue playing football (a sport that had almost crippled him),

the starting guard for the varsity basketball team (and student body president) whose decision to sit in the back of a pickup truck during a lunchtime jaunt to Taco Bell proved to be fatal,

the halfback who needed *five* years to graduate from high school but would only qualify for *four* years of playing football; he not only forfeited a scholarship ride to college—he surrendered the idea of going to college at all,

the second baseman who let out a long string of obscenities at an umpire, and the school district that called for the transfer of that player to another school,

the soccer player who impregnated his girlfriend and then captured the league's MVP honors (not connected to what he did to his girlfriend) for the season; as it turned out, he made another baby with a different girl three months later. Both of these girls attended his annual awards banquet, where he received an enthusiastic ovation from everyone, including rapturous, tearful applause from the two pregnant teenagers.

Struggle—even tragedy—in the world of high school sports is nothing new. We keep telling these kids that it's something they should expect as a rite of passage.

Student athletes see tangible rewards (parental adulation, hero worship, college, money, and sex) as their ultimate booty and accept the anticipated setbacks and inevitable struggles as the price of doing business.

In the spring of 1997, a student on my debate team came to me at lunch with the following request and subsequent proclamation:

"Mr. G....you need to help me."

"I'll try, David," I told him, trying to break off a piece of banana taffy with my front teeth.

"I'm doing a changeover."

"A *what?*"

"A changeover. You know. Changing my image and all that. I got up this morning, looked in the mirror, and said to myself, 'David, you gotta do something, man!'"

I nodded and held my breath. "What—what are you planning on doing—specifically?"

He answered with resolute confidence. "I'm going out for football."

David was the archetypical class geek. His lanky, frail body did not pose a promising challenge for a sudden gale of wind, let alone a charging 220-pound lineman.

I blinked at him.

"You don't like the idea?" he weakly inquired.

"Well, I, uh..."

The truth: I figured he'd be killed within a week.

"Look, Mr. G.," he pleaded. "I can't even get a date for the prom. I'm thinking of taking my sister!"

A better idea than going out for football, I thought.

"What's going out for football got to do with all this?" I asked, already knowing the answer.

"The chicks. The football players always get the chicks; I never get the chicks."

David never went out for football.

And David never got the chicks either.

Now, however, he probably gets all the women he wants. He's fresh from Berkeley's Bolt Hall and working for a prominent judge in San Jose, California.

Women of mature age tend to find money and prestige more than satisfactory compensation for some of the other characteristics of adolescent sex appeal.

The image of the warrior in battle heightens a teenager's sexual arousal. This is precisely why football players, some of whom are unable to articulate even two-syllable words, have had far more success in the sexual-conquests arena than, say, the Harvard-bound croquet player. Tapping that little ball softly through the wire wickets does not suggest nearly as much sweaty testosterone as a glistening, meaty lineman rushing toward—and then violently flattening—an opposing quarterback. Teenage girls in their short, pleated skirts do not jump up and down outside classrooms where speech tournaments are being conducted in order to lend support to the school's debate team.

I surveyed 100 male athletes in most of the major high school interscholastic sports, asking them why they participated. The results of that survey:

attracts the girls (17%)

scholarship for college (8%)

develops my skills (11%)

keeps me in shape/fit (14%)

love of the game/enjoyment (21%)

keeps me out of trouble (8%)

something to do with my time (4%)

meet people and make friends (11%)

my parent made me do it (4%)

other (2%)

A simple survey of a hundred male high school athletes may not offer definitive answers as to why teenage boys play organized sports; however, I found nothing particularly surprising about these results. It also isn't shocking that the number one concern athletes voiced about their athletic endeavors is the overall amount of time their sports consume. Daniel, a star wrestler, bemoaned, "I get up at 5:30 in the morning. I go to classes all day. I get home from wrestling practice at about 6:00 P.M., and sometimes, when there's a meet, I don't get home until around seven or seven-thirty. I eat my dinner, do my homework, and then go to bed; I get up the next morning and start all over again."

Daniel has no time for girls, movies, TV, pizza socials, video games, or even for his own family. When I asked him how he manages to complete his homework on time, he retorted, "I don't."

He carries a B average and a permanent scowl.

Why does Daniel do it?

He shrugged nonchalantly. "Everything I do—including wrestling and football—I do for my parents, especially my dad. My dad is so proud of me, I can feel him beaming after I win a match. I can feel his energy, even if he isn't actually there."

The survey did not uncover *that* truth—not exactly—but I accepted the veracity of Daniel's comments nonetheless: Pleasing their parents is right at the top of most teenagers' lists, even if they jump up and down shouting that just the opposite is true. Yes, some teenagers would travel to hell and play Old Maid with Satan himself (from what I've heard, some teens already have done something like this) just to tick off their parents, but most teenagers want nothing more than to make their parents proud of them. Sometimes the futility (real or imagined) of reaching this goal pushes kids in the opposite direction: Teens rebel; often they lash out directly at their parents.

Sometimes they just give up.

And other times, especially when it comes to sports, reported parental demands and expectations are so incredibly unreasonable, it's difficult to believe their validity. If not for seeing them firsthand, I would have scoffed at most of the horror stories about sports that come out of the high schools. I'd have passed them off as mere gossip—the worst form of sensationalism—because they're about teenagers, and stories about teenagers always seem to steal the limelight.

Angelo possessed a left pitching arm like no other I had ever seen. He consistently threw an 85 mph fastball and cut such a wicked slider into right-handed batters that the hitters usually came away from the encounter with a broken bat, if they were fortunate enough to make any contact at all. Since pitchers were allowed by league rules to pitch only every fifth day, Angelo spent a lot of time playing the outfield. I once watched in disbelief, along with many other astonished spectators, as he threw a runner out at home plate, after he fired a perfect strike all the way to the catcher, from medium deep centerfield!

A gifted, multitalented athlete, Angelo was also the starting quarterback on the varsity football team. He had the requisite concussions to show for it, too. And being violently knocked to the ground regularly by a rushing swarm of teenage goons is not exactly what's best for preserving healthy, intact bones. Angelo had discovered on repeated occasions the grim realities of a high school quarterback's brief stint at finding glory. His beaten and bruised body stood out in the locker room among the other baseball players' relatively unscathed bodies.

At lunchtime on the day of a baseball game, Angelo slipped into my classroom with a look of great consternation on his handsome face. Normally, he stood tall, straight, and sturdy, but today, his shoulders slumped forward, his face ashen.

"Coach," he began almost timidly.

"Yeah?" I perked up. I always liked it when my players paid a personal visit; it was usually with good news, and we often had a lot of fun talking about things unrelated to baseball or school.

"Coach," Angelo continued slowly, "I can't pitch today."

"Okaaay…" I tried handling this carefully; I waited, but he fumbled into silence.

"What's up?" I asked.

"It's my right knee. When I come off the rubber in my follow-through.... It's my knee."

"Then you'll play centerfield today. Don't worry about it," I said, hoping for the second best result. He could still bat, and if anybody tried to score from second base on a ground ball up the middle, I knew that Angelo would gun him down at the plate.

I thought that this fixed the immediate problem; it was the long-term problem that worried me. When would Angelo be able to pitch again? How badly had this boy been hurt?

"I can't play at all," he grimaced. "I can barely put any weight on the leg. My knee just buckles."

The perfect time to be blunt with him had arrived.

"Look, Angelo," I said, now standing at my desk, "it's football. You're a born *baseball* player. You're really gifted—more gifted than anyone I've ever coached—more talented than anybody your age I've ever met. But every time you get out there on the football field you jeopardize your future, not to mention your health and well-being."

He stood there and said nothing. I noticed that his eyes had begun to well tears.

"Coach," he finally began, "it's my dad. He says that I can't play baseball anymore—he won't let me play baseball anymore—if I don't play football, too. I gotta play football, coach."

I was shocked.

I shouldn't have been, though. This kind of thing happens all the time. Some people parent their kids mainly through the vicarious quests of their own youth. They attempt to recuperate personal failings or lost dreams at the cost of their children's rising stress levels, and even (as in the case of boys like Angelo) their physical health. Often the parents' enthusiasm for their sons' or daughters' participation in a sport surpasses the enthusiasm of even their sons or daughters.

The embarrassing behavior of parents sometimes falls off the dignity charts. I once had to tell a mother, "Look, I can't play your son today. Every time he plays, you're standing up and barking stupid instructions at him and yelling terrible comments at the umpires. . . . It's *my* job to bark stupid instructions and yell terrible comments at the umpires!"

Once a father squawked at his own son right after he had been called out on strikes: "You faggot! Take the bat off your goddam shoulders!"

Immediately following the game, I went to my principal and told him if this particular parent showed his face again at one of our games, I was calling my team off the field.

My principal then placed a call to the verbally abusive parent and informed him of my decision; the stubborn mule threatened to show up anyway. When reminded that the whole team, including his son, would forfeit the contest, the player's dad claimed he would file a lawsuit. My principal, one of the best high school administrators I'd ever worked for, calmly reiterated his decision. After the parent's display of immaturity and indecency, no amount of coaxing was going to change my principal's mind.

The dad never showed up at the games again; the incident went no further.

The immediate problem had been solved; however, what kinds of horrors had this 16-year-old boy consistently faced at home? His father found more importance in his son looking good in a single at bat than he did in the extreme mortification the boy would face because of his dad's ill-chosen words. The sad truth: Some fathers have such a driving intensity for their sons to succeed in sports that a terrific price is paid by their sons. It may begin well before the teenage years, but the last payment for athletic glory is usually made after the commencement of adulthood: fatigue, resentment, animosity, physical pain, and shattered dreams are not unusual. Dad is not around forever, and his son may have calculated that the price he paid to indulge his father was much too high for the pursuit of his father's dreams. Upon a cursory inspection, it seems as though there is an inordinate number of strained father-son relationships among professional athletes; the son's resentment of his father's narcissistic, obnoxious meddling may be a primary cause of the rift.

GIRLS HAVING FUN

The pressures that girls face in the world of sports are much different from those faced by boys: from parents, peers, colleges, and society at large; so the reasons for female involvement in athletics may—or may not—be surprising. I asked 100 girls the same question about why they played sports that I asked the boys. Here are the results of that survey:

attracts the boys (0%)

scholarship for college (25%)

develop my skills (13%)

keeps me in shape/fit (40%)

love of the game/enjoyment (7%)

keeps me out of trouble (1%)

something to do with my time (1%)

meet people and make friends (10%)

my parent made me do it (1%)

other (2%)

Readily drawn conclusions from the survey:

1. Girls play sports for different reasons than boys play sports.
2. Girls are cognizant of the connection between college and sports; perhaps, for girl athletes college is much more accessible. Data tell us that girls today have a much better chance of going to college than boys do. For whatever reasons, girls, too, value sports highly in their relationship to academia. Maybe the sheer numbers of girls attending college compel this analysis.
3. Girls clearly do not see their involvement in sports as a magnet for attracting boys. Not a single girl who took the survey presented this as a reason for playing her sport. Teenage girl athletes smartly concluded that smelly armpits, large muscles, and sweaty clothes do not send teenage boys into a sexual frenzy.

Female sports are competitive, demanding, and an overall benefit to the girls who are involved in them; yet, some girls decline to play because they would prefer to sail through their high school years without flicking even a single hair out of place or permitting a smidgen of makeup to run down their rosy cheeks. Others are saddled with the somewhat irrational worry of being thought of as too manly or—God forbid—a lesbian! Overall, however, most teenage athletes are capable of jumping right into the sports brew with much less trepidation than they would feel for finding the right dress for the senior prom.

In the mid-1990s, I had hardly noticed a tall blond girl who sat in the center row of my 11th-grade honors English class. I knew that she had a terrific reputation as the starting pitcher for the varsity girls' softball team. I occasionally heard glowing reviews from other students about her exploits on the field, but I did not pay exceptional attention to her. Finally, one day when I was in a particularly jocular mood, I challenged her to go outside the room and strike me out with her best stuff.

"Come on! See if you can blow them by me *underhand!*" I mocked.

She merely laughed at me.

And now I know why:

This girl went on to compete in the 2004 Olympics as a starting pitcher for the American softball team—the one that won the gold medal! Her quest had probably been motivated by potential fame and glory—and the love of her sport. Her charm and beauty sent out signals to young girls everywhere, giving them permission to deflect those unflattering stereotypes of the female teenage jock.

THE SPIRITED REDHEAD WITH FRECKLES

Student athletes pose an interesting dichotomy. On the one hand, they appear to be strong, stable, and secure; on the other hand, because of the stresses that they endure and the enormous amount of pressure that has been bestowed upon them, many of these kids are anything but strong, stable, and secure. Possibly flopping around on a deck of disorder, they begin to resent what so many others truly covet: adulation, adoration, hero worship; for these teenage warriors, it's as though they are living a lie.

The starting third baseman on one of my most successful baseball teams, a particularly vivacious young man with red hair and an abundance of freckles, appeared to have his act together. He brought a dry wit to the team, a personality trait that I especially appreciated, and radiated a youthful exuberance for life. His talent for playing the game was not extraordinary; he did, however, make contact with the ball often, and when we simply needed to avoid a strikeout, I could look to the redhead with freckles with hope. With his senior year well underway, early practices would begin right after the Christmas recess.

But after arriving at school on a seemingly ordinary morning, I found a note in my mailbox, asking me to see the principal immediately.

The lively, somewhat chubby third baseman had been out driving the night before. On a street near the school, he lost control of his small car and drove it into a ditch. Traveling at more than 90 mph, he'd been drinking beer and was not wearing a seatbelt.

The car crushed him, killing him instantly.

If you had asked me to explain this one, I couldn't.

But later the truth emerged. One very unhappy, impulsive boy inhabited the body of another boy, one we thought we all knew—the kid who was well adjusted, altruistic, and compliant. My redheaded third baseman had lived with an alcoholic mother and a philandering stepfather, and a baby was on the way. The freckle-faced redhead had been involved in heavy drinking for almost a year and once was arrested in eighth grade for selling marijuana to other students at his middle school. The ramshackle car that he had taken for a spontaneous joy ride that fatal night had been stolen from his stepfather.

Nobody had told me any of these things about my third baseman. His personality deceived almost everyone, and his parents—using their own form of fakery—had succeeded in blinding every one of us at the school. The only outlet for his depressed state, guilt, and lack of self-respect was baseball. High school baseball had given him some hope, some meaning in life beyond his destructive choices of recreation.

The sadness of this youngster may come across to some as no sadness at all— just another kid with a messed-up life (no excuse) who made a really bad choice (among other bad choices) and died in a thinly veiled suicide (luckily, he didn't also kill someone else). But I knew the redhead as a gregarious kid who good-naturedly chided other players for "throwing the ball like a girl" and taking too long to get to second base on a wild pitch. He sometimes made uneducated comments about baseball strategy, unwittingly revealing only a rudimentary knowledge of the sport. During a practice, he batted with only one hand, hitting a ball over the left-center field fence (a feat he never duplicated with both hands).

His home life, his criminal activities, his sadness . . .

I hadn't known anything about them.

Nobody else, except his family, had known anything about them either.

Here's some irony: During a eulogy at his funeral, one of his best friends (who was not on the baseball team) repeated one of the redhead's favorite jokes: one that had a punch line about *getting it right*. He then reflected on how the redhead *always* had to *get it right*. How the redhead—as though this were some sort of compliment—had been more concerned about getting it right with other people *than he was about getting it right with his own life*.

I don't remember the particulars of the joke exactly, but I do remember this: The kid who told the joke at the funeral temporarily forgot the punch line. He began the amusing story again, stammered, and finally said the joke . . . wrong.

MR. G.'S HOME-GROWN ADVICE

Parents

Back off. Avoid putting undue pressure on your kids to succeed in their pursuit of playing games. Of course, encourage your children to become involved in activities they might find beneficial or enjoyable; however, if they ultimately lose interest or don't wish to put in the effort, *leave them alone*. Your children's desires to participate in sports must be greater than *your* own desires for them to participate. An egregious error made by too many of you as parents is your attempt to project your own passions onto your children, even when your children may not share those passions or possess the innate talent to make *your* dreams become their reality.

You also have the responsibility to protect your kids, and this may require your refusing permission for them to participate in a sport—or any activity—that you conclude is unreasonably taxing or dangerous. Some parents, for instance, prohibit tackle football, because of its diverting, unrelenting practice schedule and a proclivity for serious injury. These parents have steered their boys in other directions, sometimes encouraging them to unleash their powerful physical talents in different sports or programs, such as wrestling or dance. One of my school's budding gridiron superstars was yanked by his father from the football program just before his 9th-grade year (a transfer from flag to tackle football) because his father deemed that the risks to his son far outweighed the advantages. Naturally, the kid squawked, and the coaches protested. But the father stood his ground, and his son went on to become starting center (with All-League honors) during his 10th-grade year for the varsity *basketball* team. Later, while he attended college, the same boy captured an amazing number of awards for gymnastics. Eventually, these star athletic qualities were useful in landing a six-figure salary as a show dancer at a major hotel in Las Vegas, where he would meet his future wife. Naturally, all stories do not end as Pollyannaish; however, ultimately, it's your obligation as a parent to use good judgment in permitting—or prohibiting—your child from engaging in *any* activity that *you* believe may damage him.

Finally, avoid sounding like the obnoxious idiot in the stands at the sporting event—the one we all make fun of all the time. Realize that when you're shouting instructions to your kids on the field, screaming obscenities at referees for making bad calls, or arguing with coaches for not giving your son enough playing time, no one—but *no one*—looks sillier than you do.

And you also look like a lousy parent.

Teachers

Cut the idol worship of the sports heroes in your classes. Give no more special favors to athletes who screw up their grades. They volunteered to carry the load, so awarding them unfairly because they can smack a baseball or dunk a basketball winds up doing them more harm than good. Some of these kids think they can get away with anything—and many of them do. You don't even have to dismiss them from your classes to make the afternoon games; it's up to you. If they're not passing your courses and displaying the sort of citizenship in your classrooms that is expected from your school's leaders, don't permit them to leave.

Once, another teacher asked me to change the grade of our school's star point guard (from an F to a C), so the kid would be eligible to play for the rest of the basketball season. Obviously, I was angered by this teacher's request and immediately rebuked her obnoxious encroachment on my professionalism. But mostly, my curiosity got the better of me: why would a math teacher be so concerned about the basketball team—to the degree that she would put her own reputation on the line? I conducted an informal investigation, one that ultimately led to ugly rumors of "questionable" conduct between the female teacher and the star hoopster. Yes, only rumors, but talk about special privileges for male athletes! Can't beat that kind!

Teenagers

You're doing a good thing, so chill out! It's only a *game*, dude! It's healthy, wealthy, and wise for you to play, but it's also absolutely ridiculous for you to take it so seriously. If you're not having fun, quit. If the physical strains or the sheer brutality of the sport are adversely affecting your health, quit. If the stresses and time restraints negatively impact other aspects of your life—your nonsports goals, your social life, your time with family—quit. And you're *not* a "quitter," if you've made a conscious, rational decision. Some renowned Americans and talented superstars have changed boats in the middle of the stream, simply because it was the *right* thing to do. (Abe Lincoln, Sandy Koufax, Oprah Winfrey, Bill O'Reilly, and Barack Obama immediately come to mind.) Remember, it's the only life you'll ever have; it's *your* future—not the future of your parents. And as you grow older, it becomes more difficult to create changes, because you've already invested so much of yourself. With your parents' guidance, you—and you *alone*—will make up your mind whether your venture has been worth it or not. I've already decided (for reasons previously alluded to) that my own son will be forbidden to play tackle football; so if you're still playing—*and like it*—consider yourself fortunate indeed.

Sports should be a friend that complements your life, not a leech that sucks the life out of you.

8

The Slime Who Hurt Our Kids

JEFF SPICOLI PLAYS FIRST BASE

The coach leaned back in his chair, his hair standing on end underneath his baseball cap. His players sat with their eyes fixed on him, their ears glued to every word he uttered. Usually, the coach lambasted them after a dreadful showing on the field, whether they won the game or not. This time, as the young high school players had been warned, his sermon would not be about how they had failed to make the routine plays or pick up signs from their third base coach; another topic, one of much greater importance, had stolen the limelight.

As the coach spoke, his eyes rose, as if to search for his words on the ceiling. But he knew the words he would use; he had calculated and auditioned every syllable the night before, as he lay in bed unable to sleep. And he had chosen not to curse today. He'd cussed on other occasions and regretted it each time. Besides, he didn't want any inappropriate language to distract from his message.

Finally, he looked down, meeting the eyes of each of his 19 players and his young assistant coach, who today sat among the rank and file. Russell was not much older than the high school players, so, perhaps, the coach's speech would have some relevance to him, as well. But the *ballplayers* were his concern of the moment, so the coach set his jaw and said in his sternest voice, "I'm not going to stand here and tell you that drugs can kill you. You already know that. Some of you guys think drugs are cool—and don't sit there and shake your heads, because you know who you are! Maybe not you, but you all know kids out there who think doing drugs is the raddest [a feeble attempt at Teenagese] thing you can do. Even those kids—if they manage to survive—in 5 or 10 years are going to realize what fools they were for taking drugs or thinking drugs were cool. I'm not going to lecture you about your drug habits; I'm not going to beg you to stop, because you already know you should. But here's what I want to understand: *How do students at this school get such easy access to drugs and booze?* I want you to flat-out tell me. I won't say a word about who said what. And nobody else sitting in this room is gonna blab either. Get it? What's said here stays here. Get it? So . . . *where are the drugs coming from?* It's bad . . ." The coach paused, focused on one or two random teenage targets, and added, ". . . as some of you already know."

For a moment the room stood still, and then one of the leaders of the team spoke up; he said, "We're not using, Coach."

"Speak for yourself, Bryce," the coach snapped. "Some of you are. I'm not sure exactly who, so I won't make any accusations. The question is—again—where are you getting it from?"

Nobody uttered a word.

"All right," the coach continued, now through his teeth. "I guess you're worried if you give me the information, someone will squeal on you. So here's what you're going do: You're going to write the information down on a piece of paper. Don't use your name; just put the truth. Nobody's going to get accused or arrested without a thorough investigation. And nobody will know which of you left their paper blank—or who named names and places."

"They're comin' from everywhere!" a player blurted.

The coach shook his head. "No. Not good enough. I need specifics."

"But why?" another player wanted to know.

"Because I am going to get 'em. I'm going to the police, and I'm going to get rid of these slime. These suppliers are not your friends. Do you think a friend—presumably someone who cares about you, loves you, and wants what's best for you—would help you to do something that would destroy your life? To do something that would contribute to the possibility of your dying? Some of these vermin stand outside elementary schools and sell LSD to fifth graders! *Fifth graders!* And you think these cockroaches are your *friends?* It makes me sick—and I've had it! Once I find out who they are, I'm doing something about it. It might not work; it might not get rid of this—this—blight on our planet, but at least I'm gonna try. Now who are they?"

The severity of the teenage drug problem in America has fluctuated. In 1989, as I delivered that impassioned plea (that eventually took me nowhere) to my baseball team, the drug crisis had been at an all-time high (no pun intended). I'd noticed that some of my students—and baseball players—looked like Jeff Spicoli from *Fast Times at Ridgemont High.* I couldn't use even seemingly innocent words like *joint, smoke, token,* or *pot* without getting snickers and hoots and howls. Everything went back to the drug culture; everything emanated from the drug culture. The drug culture ruled the roost, and the roost had failed to fight back.

When five teenagers (four boys and one girl) crept into the group interview session, they seemed almost lethargic; after we became immersed in our discussion, however, their energy levels soared. They even volunteered to speak freely, without hesitation. Whether they were users, I had no information. In truth, if I had evidence a student was currently involved with drugs or alcohol—on or off campus—I had a moral and *legal* duty to report him to an administrator. And I informed them of this obligation around 60,000 times before we began our conversation.

Some of that interview:

Boy One:	You can get drugs from anywhere.
Boy Two:	Sometimes they're hard to find, depending on what you're looking for.
Me:	What's easy to get?
Boy Two:	(a huge smile) You're askin' the wrong people, dude!
Me:	No, no. I'm not asking you what drugs you get; just—you know—what are some drugs that other kids look for that are hard to get?
Boy One:	Nothing's *that* hard to get.
Boy Three:	Well, ecstasy. From what I hear, ecstasy was really easy to get in the nineties up until a few years ago. The clubs are lookin' out for it now, and if somebody does have it to sell, it's really expensive. If they want it, mostly the rich kids can get it. Also, I've heard about kids who use over-the-counter antihistamines by mixing 'em with beer; it gives 'em a good buzz.
Boy Four:	Crystal meth is the thing now. Adults get it pretty easy; parents even—but mostly older siblings. Lots of people are into meth. And marijuana.
Boy Two:	It's always been the thing: pot.
Girl:	None of my friends smoke [pot]. Sometimes when they go to a party, they'll just . . . they'll try and relax, so they smoke a joint. But they're not really users.
Me:	I'm confused. You said they don't use—they don't smoke pot—and then you said that when they go to parties, they . . . smoke pot?
Girl:	(giggles) Nooo! Only sometimes. Like, only every once in a while. They're not, like, regular smokers. They're not potheads.
Boy Four:	I see a lot of pot now. I didn't see it at all in middle school. Now I see it—mostly at parties. The thing that's worse than

	pot—I mean, a lot worse, because you see it more—is alcohol. You see alcohol everywhere.
Me:	What kind? What are they drinking?
Boy Four:	Mostly beer.
Boy One:	Wine.
Boy Three:	Wine coolers.
Boy Two:	(laughs) Beer!
Girl:	Everything. It depends....Mixed drinks make you sick. Lots of kids get really sick by mixing.
Boy One:	Sometimes there's drugs and hard stuff—booze.
Girl:	Yeah. Some kids say they would never do drugs—never touch drugs—but I don't know why not—all the booze they drink. It's gotta be worse for you than a joint every so often....
Boy Two:	Some kids get to drinking at home. Their parents let 'em drink beer and wine and maybe worse. But then they sneak it into school. They usually don't get caught. I mean, there were some kids in my classes last year who were drunk, but nobody said anything or did anything, even the teachers. I don't think the teachers knew they were drunk, though.
Girl:	Or high. Lots of students come to school high on pot—usually it's pot. They're funny sometimes; the teachers can't figure out what to do with them. Most of the teachers figure they're just ADHD or having a bad day, but sometimes it's just because they're high.
Boy One:	Then a bunch of girls on the soccer team got expelled for showing up at school all wasted on a late-start [teachers' meetings] day. It's also, like, the major reason for cutting school. They usually skip school to go smoke or drink or whatever. Most of the time it's, like, a miniparty or something. It's, like, most of the parents aren't even home, so they use their houses to drink or smoke.
Me:	When you say smoke...?
Boy One:	Weed. Nobody—well, I shouldn't say nobody—but almost nobody smokes cigarettes.
Girl:	(angrily) That's not true!

Boy One:	Yes, it is true. Just look around. You don't see that many kids smokin' cigarettes.
Girl:	Of course, you don't see it here at school. But you see it a lot.
Boy Four:	I agree with [Boy One]. The reason you think so much smoking is goin' on is that you hang with the smokers. You're probably a smoker—I mean, I don't know, but...[1]

Data tell us that teen smoking is down considerably, although the rate of decrease is smaller than it is for adult smokers. Whereas the aggregate of cigarette smokers in the United States has been cut in half since 1961, the number of teenagers who smoke cigarettes has diminished about a third. Teenage girls smoke more than boys do, and in 2004 the number of girls who smoked increased slightly.[2] What I find perplexing is that while teenagers rage against cigarettes (which is a good thing), they ignore an even worse—far worse— problem in America: alcoholism. When smoking cigarettes was cool, à la James Dean, nary a bad word was uttered about smoking. Now that drinking has grown to be *cool*, à la the sexy beer commercials on television, hardly anyone dares to criticize beer-swirling, six-pack–chugging drunks at parties: Puffing on your cigarette—*Die, smoker, die!* Downing your fifth vodka gimlet—*Alllllll riiiiight!*

Match point to the trendsetters.

After the group of five finished their discussion, I thanked them for talking about a problem that many of their peers refuse to even recognize. And one of them apologized to me for not being able to think of any solutions.

IT'S AN ALBATROSS

People make excuses for drug abusers and drunks—even when those drug abusers and drunks are minors. Society has shown compassion for kids whose hands are caught in the cookie (drugs) jar; sometimes drug pushers get winks of understanding, because a lot of those pushers technically are still children. Some kids turn to artificial, brain-numbing substances in order to escape the pain and stresses of their lives. But should that be an excuse for their poor decisions? There's an enormous difference between *understanding* our kids' destructive behaviors and *excusing* their destructive behaviors. *Understanding* means, "I know why you did this; it doesn't mean that I agree with you or approve, but at least I know why you did it." That's entirely different from *excusing*, which means, "Now that I know why you did this, I absolve you of all responsibility for your destructive behaviors; it wasn't your fault."

See the difference? *Understanding* informs; *excusing* absolves of any responsibility. So without *excusing* anyone from her self-inflicted, destructive behaviors—without relieving anyone from taking *responsibility* for her awful choices in her young life—just why does a teenager use brain-numbing, artificial substances?

From over the past 37 years, straight from the horses' mouths:

A girl about marijuana:	It feels good. I like to feel good. I don't do it a lot, but when I do, it feels good.
A boy about marijuana:	Getting high is better than getting wasted [drunk]; it makes me forget all my problems.
A boy about alcohol:	What's wrong with a drink or two? My parents do it. My dad drinks beer—like a six-pack—every day.
A boy about drugs:	Why not? As long as you don't get caught. It's my right to do what I want to myself, and it's not doing nothing [*sic*] bad to me.
A boy about drugs:	I hate me [when I take drugs].
A girl about drugs:	I don't know; it's none of your business.
A boy about marijuana:	It makes me forget my problems...and it feels good.
A girl about marijuana:	I feel relaxed; it makes me more relaxed.
A girl about alcohol:	I can have more fun. And then the next day I can say—well, people will think—it was the booze that made me all crazy and not the real me.
A boy about drugs:	It's the thing to do; like, everybody's doing it....It makes more people have more fun at the same time. You can go all crazy together and nobody's gonna criticize you.
A boy about drugs:	I hate my mother; this drives her crazy...
A girl about drugs:	I just—can't help it. I can't. You think I can, but you're wrong.
A boy about alcohol:	You lose your inhibitions. I like it when girls let down their guard; they're a lot nicer to me. I think that's why some girls get drunk, especially at parties. It gives them the courage to do what they wouldn't do if they weren't drunk.
A boy about drugs:	It's just cool. People do it; they can stop when they want to. You shouldn't get carried away or addicted, but some drugs make you cooler, and everybody knows it...so don't give me all that shit about how terrible of a person you are for using drugs. It just depends. It just does. It's not all the same. For some people, there's a cool thing goin' on.

Most teens won't talk candidly to adults about this topic. They fear others will find out about their—or their friends'—involvement with drugs. They worry about what their peers may think of them. Many teens don't want *me* to find out what they're doing; they know that I would report them. Some teenagers just refuse to talk about the subject, and many serious drug users are in denial about their addictions.

And it always comes back to Rick (chapter 6). Rick's the boy who exchanged his life for absolutely nothing when he got sucked into a freight train one Saturday night in 1994. Rick had been smoking marijuana with friends—the main reason he unintentionally challenged the roaring train. Rick, one of the most promising young acting talents and sharpest young minds I've ever met, was dead, due mostly to his chronic use of marijuana.

About two months before he died, I'd spent a few private moments with Rick. Now out of high school, sometimes he judged for our speech team at local tournaments. At one such event, Rick was taking his small truck to get some food for our competitors, and I asked to go with him.

He drove this gray tin box. As we motored toward Carl's Junior, I asked him, "Where'd you get this thing?"

He flashed his handsome, charming smile. "This thing? You mean my truck?"

"Yeah, Rick."

He watched the road and not me, as he drove. "My dad gave it to me. He still lives in Sacramento. The last time I flew up there to visit him, he told me to drive this home. Pretty cool."

"Pretty cool, if you're 19," I thought to myself. But I said, "This thing is a deathtrap, Rick."

He shrugged without shrugging. "Yeah, well, if I got hit by a diesel truck, it wouldn't matter what I was driving, would it?"

At least he didn't say "hit by a train."

I wanted a congenial lunch. "Have you seen your dad much lately?"

He remained stoic. "Nah. Maybe every few months; my dad's busy."

I remembered how Rick urgently had flown to Sacramento last April, interrupting the rehearsals for a show we were working on together. His father had had a heart attack, and Rick seemed to be the only one who cared whether he lived or died.

And then he laughed—that condescending tone that had endlessly irritated me in the past. His dismissive attitude had not changed in the few months I had not spoken with him. Same old Rick: anything for a laugh, but if you don't like who I am or what I do or how I lead my life, you can go to straight to hell.

"Are you thinking of going to college? You'd be a sure success, if you apply yourself."

"But I can't."

"Can't what?"

"I can't apply myself." He temporarily removed his eyes from the road in order to look at me. "You know that, Mr. G.!" he scoffed. "God, you were so ignorant! Maybe you still are! A great teacher, but so naive!"

"Rick, what are you talking about?"

"You're as bad as my dad," he sneered. "My dad thinks I should go to school because I'm smart. He's looks right past the reason I can't go to college—or maybe he just chooses not to see it. I don't know. And you did the same thing, Mr. G. Those times I missed the Saturday morning buses for speech tournaments because I supposedly overslept? Yeah, right."

A wave of apprehension flooded my body. "What?" I asked involuntarily.

"All the drugs. . . . I loved school, and I loved speech. And I loved you, too, Mr. G. But I loved the drugs more. And I still do." He actually conveyed all of this to me while grinning. "Now, don't get me wrong. I'm not doing anything that bad—mostly pot—and I don't drive under the influence. But I like it. I'm not sure if I could stop, even if I wanted to—which I don't. . . . I have some right now, if you'd like?"

His grin turned devious, as he reached for his glove compartment.

Perhaps my next comment was not the coolest or the most level-headed, but it was how I felt at the time, having been deceived—even used—by Rick in the past.

"Rick, if you show me any drugs—if I can even *see* any drugs—I'm going to ask you to leave the tournament, and I'm going to report you to the police. Obviously, you're technically an adult now, and you can make your own decisions about stuff like this, but I don't want you judging for our school anymore."

He said nothing; his face had transformed from smile to frown, and I swear that I detected a small tear falling on his cheek.

I never ate lunch that afternoon.

And I didn't hear Rick's name mentioned again, until the April afternoon I played that awful message on my answering machine: *Rick was killed in an accident.* And for certain, drugs—mainly marijuana—had been the catalyst for Rick's totter into a charging, thunderous freight train.

MR. G.'S HOME-GROWN ADVICE

My personal attitude about drugs, much like my philosophy about AIDS and other sexually transmitted diseases, has gotten me into some difficulty with students, parents, and other teachers.

I believe that AIDS and drug abuse, unlike most other afflictions, such as cancer or heart disease, are *choices*. Everyone knows sex without a condom makes us more likely to catch a disease. Everyone knows using illegal drugs is bad for our health. No one is dragged into unprotected sex. And no one gets a marijuana cigarette stuffed down his throat. When choices are involved, I have less sympathy for the so-called afflicted. Other people—you know the type—always see themselves as victims of *something*. And these are the same people who claim that *I* lack compassion. The truth, however, is something very different: Studying our options before we act affords the best types of prevention; in order to do this, however, we must—and I can't ever emphasize this enough—*we must understand that we ultimately are the ones in control of our lives, of our choices, and—in the end—of our attitudes*.

I'm not an expert on drug abuse, but I am an expert on teenagers. Given my reputation for pontificating in the classroom, the following ideas may not surprise some of you; however, if you have never taken a class from me or do not know me personally, you may be in for a bit of shock.

Parents

As usual, you are the first line of defense. And this is a hill you *should* risk dying on; winning our first battles with this scourge can carve out the path to winning the entire war.

Role modeling substance abuse is the surest guarantee your kids will abuse something too. Stop smoking cigarettes around small children. If you don't contain your smoking—especially around children—you will be seen as an adult with a child's lack of self-control. I realize that cigarettes and drugs are not equivalent in their destructive capacities, but role modeling self-control is powerful on any level.

Be extremely alert as to whom your kids are hanging out with, especially in middle school and high school. Links to drugs are made through chains of acquaintances; peer pressures rule during those years, not parent influences. And the real culprit is a lack of self-discipline. If only teenagers controlled most of their impulses as easily as they controlled the knobs on their iPods!

By the time they're teenagers, they already know that drugs are bad—perhaps deadly. The challenge for teenagers is to understand that something deadly actually has the potential to *kill* them. Too often, adolescents don't put two and two together. "If it's in some way attractive, it can't possibility hurt me! Hope springs eternal! Look on the bright side!" It's rarely: "You know what? This stuff is bad. It's torn apart families, cost society billions of dollars, and even killed other kids my age. Hmmm...It could do the same thing to me!"

Constantly remind your children of their own mortality, of the fragility of their lives. Once they accept the fact that they, too, can experience a fatal consequence of bad stuff goin' down, they should be able to connect the dots: "It can happen to me, too!"

Remember, parents: teaching your kids to say *no* to anything is useless, unless they have good role models, adults who have demonstrated their own capacity for restraint. Show them that no matter how much you may want something—an object, an award, a lifestyle—sometimes you just can't have it. Your swearing off coveted desserts or your third glass of wine provides a powerful image for your kids.

No can save lives.

By the way: Your inklings about your children's involvement with drugs or other vices *that can kill them* have the power to throw out all the rules about privacy and autonomy. Diaries, journals, text message records, and the like are all fair game now. Of course, do not intrude if you have no reason to suspect. But mere *suspicion* would compel me to work double time to find out the truth about my kids, no matter what I had to do. Their lives may hang in the balance; they can bitch and moan and complain about my snooping into their stuff until doomsday. My first obligation is to protect my children, whether they like it or not. And—oh!—those store-bought, handy-dandy drug tests might surprise the Flaming Hot Cheetos right out of your kids, which is exactly what you should want if you thought there was even a slim chance they were up to no good.

Finally, I've heard of cases in which drug pushers have stood outside elementary schools and sold LSD-laced Donald Duck stickers to fifth graders, who compliantly shelled over their lunch money to these creeps. As a parent, I intend to lobby for the death penalty for any adult who sells drugs to children. I will not rest until I have given my best to make sure these slime have been exterminated.

Won't you join me?

Teachers

You decry drug abuse all the time; don't contradict your own messages and set yourself up for ridicule by virtue of your hypocrisy. Nothing says *hypocrite* like making drug jokes in class, or implying that Mary is such a pathetic, little *victim* because she became sick on ecstasy at a rave party. Nothing projects *weak* faster than a teacher who fails to tell the truth about drug pushers: "These cretins are not the friends of teens." Nothing says *irresponsible* better than a teacher who fails to focus on the dramatic harm done to the drug abuser and the evil deeds of the drug dealer.

Most of my own students who have used drugs have been rather successful in covering up their involvement. They are aware of my utter disdain for the drug culture and know that I will fink on someone if I have proof the student is using. Several years ago, however, a rather brazen student wrote an essay on this topic: "After being beaten, bruised, and battered, how did you bounce back?" Here are some of his thoughts:

> I'm always beaten, bruised, and battered. The hard part is the bouncing back. . . . I guess you could say that I bounced back from my parents' divorce and my really bad grades in school during my freshman year. . . . I have tried to bounce back from drugs, but I'm still stuck on pot. Pot gives me the strength to bounce back from lots of other things that hurt. . . . I choose not to bounce back from pot, because I don't look at this as something that I need to recover from. We should recover from things that hurt us. Pot doesn't hurt me. It makes me better.

After I handed Greg's essay to his guidance counselor, his parents were asked to come in for a conference. Since there had been no evidence of Greg's possessing drugs or selling drugs at school, the school itself would not take any disciplinary action.

But Greg had his own way of disciplining me for "ratting him out." His mother removed him from my class (as though I had been the real culprit here, rather than the guy who tried to save her son from his continuing vice). Greg's friends refused to talk to me anymore (which was probably the only positive result of all this), and several of my students no longer wished to communicate honestly with me in their essays (their way of shielding themselves from a turncoat English teacher). But I had to turn Greg in. He needed help—and fast. Drugs blight the face of America, and our children don't handle drugs very well. Adults must intercede, making themselves a reservoir of solutions.

A no-brainer for teachers: Graphically point out the harms of drugs. The physical and mental anguish of addictions is always tough to talk about, but minimizing or ignoring it does damage. Teens focus on their rationalizations for drug use ("My teacher doesn't think it's so bad"), rather than how they plan to meet head-on the various challenges that lie ahead of them.

Teenagers

Ultimately, the ball is in your court (and this is true, even if you don't play tennis or basketball)! The decisions you make now, the wisdom you unfurl now, the strength you muster now, will affect the rest of your life. They may even determine how long the rest of your life will last! So begin by reading—or rereading—the ABCs for resisting dares and peer pressure (from chapter 6).

I'll wait...

Welcome back. Now, consider these 15 reasons that drugs really, really, really stink (sorry—*suck*):

1. You die.
2. You get really sick.
3. You lose the right friends.
4. You get stuck with the wrong friends.
5. Your "business" contacts stink up the joint.
6. You waste a lot of your time, and you also sleep way *too* much (forever, if you're not careful).
7. You flush tons of money down the toilet and may wind up broke.
8. You get beat up.
9. You get fired.
10. You get fined or go to jail.
11. You do not pass Go; you do not collect $200.
12. You retain a crummy reputation for the rest of your miserable life.
13. You have a lot of explaining to do to your own children.
14. You make babies who inherit your genetically altered gunk.
15. You get written up in books in chapters about losers.

There are zillions of books designed to help you with the drug quagmire. One of the best books for helping teens is *The O'Reilly Factor for Kids* (HarperCollins, 2005) by Bill O'Reilly. Read it. Some kids have informed me that there are some pretty decent DVDs available on this topic—much better than those antiquated, boring old videotapes that you have seen in your health classes.

My play, *Out—Out, Brief Candle*, produced by Phantom Projects, will rattle you like nothing else you have ever seen on stage. Ask your school administrators to bring it to your school. Go to Phantom's Web site for information that may favorably change—or save—the lives of people you claim to love: http://www.phantomprojects.com.

The whole drug scene sickens me. Here we are, living in the greatest country in the history of civilization: We have the most modern of all conveniences, the most progressive of all technologies. Our medical breakthroughs have made it possible for people to live longer with a better quality of life than ever before. Human beings have more things to do, places to visit, and ideas to dream; yet, despite our many blessings, a large segment of our population still finds it necessary to numb their brains. Personal pain somehow has managed to reach such intense levels that enormous numbers of people—many of them teenagers—require the deadening of their senses as their primary method for coping.

Kids in particular should find this state of affairs troubling. Children have their whole lives ahead of them. In essence, one part of the adolescent population (the druggie constituency) is saying to the other part of the adolescent population (the nondruggie constituency): "This is what you have to look forward to. Sure, you have every luxury, every modern convenience, every opportunity at your fingertips, but you will, nonetheless, find it necessary to induce a state of mental and emotional numbness in order to struggle through your lives."

But why?

We live once. And only once. After that: What?

Life is too important to mess with it in such a disrespectful, cavalier way. I beg you not to take better care of your car or your skateboard than you take care of your life. And cooking your brain on drugs like you're frying an egg on the stove is not the way to do it.

At a recent "Back-to-School Night" activity, a parent introduced herself as a former student of mine and the mother of one of my current students. She pulled me aside and said, "You don't know how worried I was about coming to see you here tonight, Mr. G. I thought you might remember me. I was on your speech squad [in 1978], but I didn't do much because I was drugged out most of the time. I'm pretty sure you knew then—and I was afraid that you would remember now. And I didn't want to embarrass Robbie [her child]. But I also wanted to tell you a success story. Right after high school, I met a man. We started dating, but he eventually told me that if I didn't get off drugs—it was mostly pot, but, yeah, worse stuff, too—he would break up with me. Well, that was plenty of incentive, and I've been clean ever since!"

Wow! What a "Back-to-School Night" that was!

Frankly, I didn't recollect this woman or anything that she told me about her past. I vaguely remembered her name. Her husband seemed familiar, but I recalled him as being kind of goofy. No matter. Stories about young people who managed to elude the severely life-altering—and sometimes fatal—consequences of drug use are always good to hear.

It reminds me of why I have dedicated my life to teaching teenagers.

9

When *Party* Became a Verb

A PARTY BY ANY OTHER PART OF SPEECH

"You gonna party this weekend, Mr. G.?"

"I gonna what?"

"Party."

"I gonna party? Let's see.... Am I going to *a* party?"

"Yeah."

"Am I going to *a* party, or am I gonna *party?*"

"Whatever. What's the difference?"

There is a huge difference: the *party* I attend versus the *to party* milieu teens have shared since around 1970. In yesteryear, parties were a pleasant distraction; today, parties have become an avocation.

If you can remember attending *this* party when you were 16, you are now around 800 years old: Boys and girls dance *with each other.* During even the fast dances, there is some contact. The touching of each other's genitals is not permitted. A boy shows up with a suitcase full of old and current 45s (small enamel records) that he's brought from home and designates himself "The Record Guy." He's the unofficial D.J.: "Hey, Bill!" One of his friends shouts to him, "Run around Sue" [by Dion and the Belmonts]! "No!" Another guy clamors, "Put on a slow one!" So Bill finds a copy of "Where or When" by Dion and the Belmonts, and the party temporarily lapses into a quiet, romantic atmosphere. The teens are decked in clean attire, dressing in what they would wear to church or school. The food consists of fast party snacks; the beverages are nonalcoholic, with punch and soda on prominent display. Every so often one of the adult chaperones makes her way through the kitchen, politely making small talk with the teen guests and asking them if they're having a good time. She then disappears for a while, only to come back, intermittently repeating her responsibility as the watchful eye of the party.

Fast forward about 25 years to 1988.

If you can remember attending *this* party when you were 16, you are not *that* old, but you are still old enough to be *considered* old by anyone younger than you are: Boys and girls dance *near* each other. Sometimes during the fast dances, it's hard to tell who is dancing with whom. But that's okay, because it's acceptable to dance even with *yourself*. The touching of each other's genitals is not permitted (unless you are auditioning for the film *Dirty Dancing*). Nobody shows up with his own records. But a guy walks in with a huge suitcase of tape cassettes, a microphone, and some oversized amplifiers. He's the unofficial D.J.: One teen shouts, "Hey, dude! Put on some Pet Shop Boys!" And another teen snickers, "Pet Shop Boys? Slayer, man!" he pleads, still stuck in the seventies. A pretty, blond girl, sitting in the corner of the room by herself, secretly wishes the D.J. would spin something like "All Out of Love" by Air Supply. But at this party, Air Supply would be archaic. The mood here continues to be anything but romantic. The teens are decked in T-shirts and jeans and shorts, some of which have not been washed for days. The food—if any—consists of fast party snacks; the beverages are mostly beer, wine, and some nonalcoholic choices like cola. This party boasts of no adult chaperones; the homeowners are visiting Las Vegas for the weekend. Upon their return, they will find signs that their house had been used for a raucous teen celebration and a refuse for vomit and other body secretions. But they will choose to ignore these signs. Wishful thinking that their son or daughter had stayed home alone and watched movie tapes all weekend rules over their powers of observation and common sense.

Fast forward to 2008.

If you have just attended *this* party, you are still in high school (or—shudder—middle school!): Boys and girls dance *near* each other. Sometimes during the fast dances, it is difficult to ascertain who is dancing with whom, but no one cares because it is acceptable to dance with even *yourself*. The touching of each other's genitals is permitted—even encouraged (the film *Dirty Dancing* means very little to you, because so many films of this genre have been released since 1988 with so much *dirtier* dancing). Nobody shows up with his own records or music; in fact, the requirements for dancing or having fun at parties involve no music at all. But a guy walks in with a huge suitcase full of compact discs, a microphone, and some oversized amplifiers; he's the official D.J.: "Hey, dude! Put on some Led Zeppelin!" one teenager shouts. Mired in the late sixties and early seventies, this teen is ignored by the throngs because they haven't *heard* of Led Zeppelin. The kids who *have* heard of Led Zeppelin want to beat him up; in fact, he has been beaten up before just for yelling "Led Zeppelin!" at a party. A pretty blond girl, sitting in the corner of the room by herself, secretly wishes the D.J. would spin something by Faith Hill, but that will never happen at this party. The ambiance here is anything but romantic. The teenagers are decked in T-shirts and jeans and shorts, some of which have not been washed for days. The food—if any—consists of fast party snacks; the beverages are beer, wine coolers, and some nonalcoholic choices like cola. A couple of boys are smoking pot in the den. Drugs are common, the most prevalent marijuana; other drugs abound. Cocaine and heroin are used more covertly, but crystal meth and ecstasy make their presence known. Couples engaged in a wide assortment of sexual activities occupy a few of the bedrooms; even the master bedroom has been invaded. This party boasts of no adult chaperones; the homeowners are visiting Las Vegas for the weekend. Upon their return, they will find signs that their house has been used for a raucous teen celebration and a refuse for vomit and other body secretions. But they will choose to ignore those signs. Wishful thinking that their son or daughter had stayed home alone and watched DVDs all weekend rules over their powers of observation and common sense.

Some have billed this evolution of teenage parties as *progressive*. But progress toward what: pregnancy? drug addiction? rape and other uncivilized behaviors? Teenage parties have always boasted of a sexual element, but as society has changed, the degree of the sexual component has intensified.

"IT'S MY PARTY—AND I'LL DIE IF I WANT TO!"

Randy goes to parties almost every weekend; I asked to talk to him because he ran with a popular crowd that attended a large number of parties. What follows is a portion of the interview with Randy and some comments offered by other teenagers during class discussions on the topic of parties:

Me: So, you've been to a lot of parties?

Randy: Oh, yeah.

Me: How many?

Randy: Like what do you mean?

Me: How many a month?

Randy: On average, three. But sometimes I go to two or three a weekend.

Me: Are formal invitations handed out?

Randy: (a slight laugh) Noo...

Me: So, you just show up?

Randy: Sometimes party fliers are spread around school or at the mall or even at Carl's Junior. Sometimes you just know that so-and-so is having a party...

Me: ... 'Cause their parents are out of town?

Randy: Sometimes. Or sometimes the parents leave the house on purpose so their kid can have the party he wants. And other times the parents charge a fee for the party, like five dollars or ten dollars, which covers everything. Kids usually don't collect the money at the door; it's a bouncer they hired. These parties sometimes get pretty big, and a big bouncer—they need a bouncer. Lots of stuff goes down.

Me: Let me get this straight: *Parents* sometimes know what's going on—and they even profit from it? They take money from the kids?

Randy: Well, it's not just high school kids who are there. Usually it's a lot more older people, like college age or older.

Me: Right.

Randy: It's not just teens.

Me: But they profit off teenagers?

Randy: Uh-huh.

Me: Whew! Okay. So, there's usually booze there?

Randy: Sure.

Me: And drugs?

Randy: Usually just pot. But I've seen other drugs. Yeah. But usually just pot. At least, at the parties I go to. I don't drink or use drugs, though; I have to tell you that.

Me: The booze. Who buys it? The kids can't.

Randy: Some of them have fake IDs. Also they know which places will sell to kids. And like I told you, lots of times the parents or big brothers or sisters will buy. Or some of the older people who go to parties. It's legal or easy for them to get alcohol.

Me: Have you seen situations when the police have come and broken the party up and made arrests?

Randy: (shrugs) Oh, yeah. Sure.

Me: The police came and arrested adults, too?

Randy: Unless a kid is rowdy or drunk, it's only the adults who get arrested. I don't know what comes of that; I really don't. But I do know situations where there have been fights—or like at this one party a guy had a gun—and then the cops started to cuff people.

Me: Did *you* ever get busted?

Randy: (a sheepish grin) Not from a party. Not at a party. No.

Me: Then what for?

Randy: (throws his hands up) No way, dude!

Me: Okay, but you've been to some parties that have turned violent?

Randy: Sure.

Me: And people have been hurt there?

Randy: Well, most of the parties I went to where there was some kinda violence, it was just a lot of punching and kicking—and sometimes the chicks really got into it, too! I've heard of parties where girls got wasted and some guys did 'em [raped them]. But so far I haven't seen it. So, yeah, I've been lucky."

Before I pull all this together with a witty, semi-intelligent commentary endowed with the requisite tasteless, inappropriate jokes, I recall a conversation I had recently with Marcie, a statuesque blond who asked to speak with me privately after class. We'd just had a discussion on underage drinking. Marcie's face, normally deadpan and apathetic, now breathed concern. "Mr. G., you need to help me with a problem."

"Sure," I shrugged. It was lunchtime; my mind was on the turkey sandwich in the refrigerator. "You look worried."

"I am," she said, sitting down in front of my desk. "I have a problem, and I need to know what to do."

I said nothing. The far reaches of my mind sadly watched my sandwich floating into oblivion.

She got to the point. "My friend's mother sets up some of these parties I go to. She charges us, like, ten dollars and provides the booze and food and all that. It's really getting bad, Mr. G. A lot of kids are going—and some of them come from, like, L.A. and Whittier…"

Pondering what would be safe to say next, she stopped. And then: "I know this is really bad. Lately some eighth graders have been coming to the parties at her house…."

I leveled with her. "You gotta stop it," I interrupted her.

"How?" she cried. "I can't stop it."

"Yes, you can."

"How?"

"Here's the deal, Marcie: Give me the name of the woman behind these parties. Give me the names of any other adults involved. That's all. No one will ever know that you told me."

"What are you going to do with her name?" she asked me with pensive eyes.

"I'm going straight to the police with it."

I saw Marcie blanch at my directness, so I calmly asked her, "Marcie, if a kid leaves one of these parties and is killed in an accident—or if somebody ODs at a party—how would you feel?"

"Terrible," she answered, barely audible.

"That's because you know you can prevent it. Adults shouldn't be throwing parties where their goal is to make money on teenagers—especially when it has to do with booze and drugs and sex." I smiled at what I had just said. "I know. That all sounds like lots of fun, but you know how destructive it can be; if you didn't, you wouldn't have stopped to speak with me."

She said nothing.

I continued. "I'm saving you the trouble of going to the police—which is what you should have done a long time ago. Just tell me her name. That's all. You'll be done with it."

She waited; without looking at me, she said, "I want to think about it."

"Okay," I nodded, but she could see my disappointment. "Let me know."

Marcie suddenly perked up a bit. "How 'bout, if we do this: If you hear from me, if I come to you, I'll tell you her name. If you never hear from me about this again, well, I decided not to rat her out."

Better than nothing.

But nothing is what I eventually received. Two weeks later she was transferred to another school for excessive violations of the dress code. Marcie never spoke to me again; plainly, she had decided not to snitch.

Teenagers have never invited me to a party. For one thing, I'm not cool enough; for another thing—and the most obvious—I'm way too old. For the clincher: I'm a teacher. In years past, I had chaperoned some parties that were sponsored by my speech and debate teams, but these parties were not the real deal. The speech kids were—and still are—known as the geeks of the school, and the reputation of their parties had legitimized this designation. Nobody was having sex there. Nobody was even kissing there. Hardly anybody even danced there—but when they did, they revived ancient American dances of the past, like the Charleston. Sometimes the speech kids played charades or board games like Clue (*very* uncool), or sang old fogey songs from the sixties (*more* uncool). Worse, they sat around and *talked,* complaining about experiences at speech tournaments. And to top everything off, there was always an adult chaperone present: *me.* How square was *that?* Picture a schoolteacher hanging around a party of teenagers, while he chuckled and cajoled with one of the kid's *parents!* Yikes!

So I have never been to a *real* teenager party.

I've tried, though. The teenagers in and around my high school were extraordinarily cooperative when it came to group discussions, personal interviews, and surveys for this book; however, when I flippantly commented that I would love to be a fly on the wall at one of their parties, not one of the kids so much as cracked a smile. Just as well. My—wholly inappropriate—presence at this sort of party could have gotten me into legal and professional trouble. It would have been like a newspaper photographer snapping his camera on a monk as he protested the Vietnam War by setting himself on fire. The chance of stopping something ugly from happening is overcome by the opportunity for reporting on it.

Very bad.

Lately, my students have told me about an alarming new trend at their parties: violence. Consider these brief accounts from three different students:

> Saturday night, me and my friends were going to this party—and there were cars lined up for blocks with people trying to get in. Suddenly, there was this really loud explosion. All of these people started to run in the opposite direction of the house, screaming. Come to find out that somebody had set off an AK-47 and got his hand blown off.

> I partied three times Saturday night, and the cops busted up all of 'em. At one, three guys got in a fight over—I don't know what. Then we went to another party, and the neighbors called the cops. People at the party were throwing beer bottles over the fence into their yard. I guess somebody broke one of their windows with a bottle. . . . At the last party, a bunch of people jumped this guy—who nobody wanted to be there—and they messed him up pretty bad. The cops had to call the paramedics.

> This guy I know took a gun to a party. He started pointing it around, and people started screaming and freakin' out. Well, the gun was empty—it didn't have no bullets—but it still scared everybody. I guess he was trying to be funny or shocking or something. But it didn't work out too good for him. He got the shit beat outta him.

I've been to many parties—including dozens of them when I was a teenager—and *not once* have I seen someone shot or beaten. Not once have people from a party been forced to flee for fear of losing their lives. Not once have I seen a bouncer at a party. Not once have I paid admission to get into a party. Not once have drugs or alcohol been used by minors and then traced to adult suppliers. Yet, many teenagers now tell me this is how they have a good time on the weekends.

"Hey, dude! You gonna party this weekend?"

Hear the call *to party:* This verbal (infinitive) suggests booze, babes, and boys. These—combined with the potentially lethal ingredients of swollen tempers, enlarged egos, numbed brains, and out-of-control testosterone—foreshadow danger. As a matter of habit, the cry *to party* has replaced *going to a party*, and—perhaps coincidentally—this seemingly innocuous alteration in syntax has spelled more trouble for America's teenagers.

MR. G.'S HOME-GROWN ADVICE

Stick-in-the-mud, deadbeat, killjoy, no fun, old-fart teacher—yes—but I *still* don't want our kids to travel through some of the most impressionable days of their lives without the excitement of attending parties. These kinds of social interactions were a vital part of my own maturation process. But there's a balance. Parties don't have to regress to the clumsy, mundane climate of the 1950s; yet, they don't have to perpetuate the hedonistic, dangerous lifestyles of today.

Parents

If you leave your homes in the hands of your teenage children while you leave town overnight, you're asking for it. Even the best kids—whatever that means—are sometimes tempted to entertain friends and strangers. True, this does not necessarily suggest that your kids will pump up the volume and invite 150 libido-throbbing drunken adolescents to celebrate in your house. But they *may*. More likely, your teenagers will stay home, watch movies, play video games, and talk on their cell phones. Their new freedoms will scare them, paralyze them with "What do I do next?" anxiety. However—and this is a very big *however*—otherwise trust-worthy teenagers may wind up hosting the kids from hell in *your* kitchen, bed-room, and living room, as your prized sofa contracts all sorts of weird blemishes, tears, and stains it never had before.

In many states if someone consumes—even without your consent—alcohol in your home and then smashes into someone on the street, *you are liable!* Lawsuits don't care whether you personally poured the beer or not. Many courts figure homeowners inherited those responsibilities the minute they signed the title deed. Anything that originates in your kitchen or living room does not end there. Heaven forbid you should come home one morning to discover that a 16-year-old who drank wine coolers in your living room was killed an hour later, after los-ing control of his car. Some families have been ruined financially by this kind of negligence; yet, it can be avoided: *Stay home and monitor what happens inside your own house*. Teenagers do not have adult judgment; your nice teens are sometimes *too* nice and don't resist the pressures for catering to the whims of their peers, and then your house becomes a petri dish for unmentionable, unpardonable—and sometimes absolutely disgusting—disasters.

Jay Boyarsky, a former student/debater of mine (who reminds me often that I gave him a D in English), is now a prominent deputy district attorney in Palo Alto, California. One of his most recent (and noteworthy) cases revolved around the prosecution of a married couple for throwing an underage drinking party for their teenage daughter. Boyarsky writes, "Two young girls were found [by the police] vomiting inside the house, suffering from alcohol poisoning.... [I needed to] send a message to the community about the harms of underage drinking."[1] The parents, both college-educated professionals, were home during the party. They were sentenced to probation, payment of fines, and attending alcohol counseling.[2] Boyarsky has told me of his sense of personal satisfaction when he strikes back at the adults who hurt our kids. Protecting children is the forte of my former speech star.

Adults who sponsor underage drinking parties, supply liquor or drugs to minors, or permit illegal or immoral activities should be arrested and thrown to the wolves in the legal system. One of the underlying premises of this book is that parents are as much to blame for messing up their kids as anyone else—perhaps, *more* than anyone else. Naturally, there are wonderful, pragmatic, conscientious, hardworking, responsible parents out there; these folks are blessings. But parents who aid and abet the destruction of their children through negligence, manipulation, and permissiveness negatively affect others around them.

As for parties:

Don't let your kids go. Tell them *no*. The consequences for going *anywhere* without your permission should be grave.

Always find out where your teens are headed and make sure they are well chaperoned when they arrive. Phone the adult in charge and talk to her about the activities that are happening under her supervision.

Occasionally, canvas the party. From afar, check who's going in and who's coming out. If you have an inkling that there are illicit activities going on—or behaviors you forbid of your children—go inside and check; in fact, I recommend that you occasionally pop in on your child's activities—party, sleepover, study session—anyway. The worst harm that comes from this: you embarrass your child. Oh, well. After a few of these surprise visits, you will know whether you can trust her.

Frequent heart-to-heart talks about the kinds of friends we should keep and instructions for how to behave in social situations help a lot. Kids who are brought up to respect authority, obey their parents, and embrace decency usually don't *want* "to party" that much. Even these teenagers, however, *should never be left alone* while you are out of town. Especially when there is a cabinet full of liquor beckoning, even good kids can mess up—and they do it *all the time*.

Afterward, ask your child about the party. Did she like it? Who was there? What kinds of things did she do? What did she have to eat and drink? Listen to her answers very, very carefully. Don't pass judgment unless you need to; but don't be afraid to pass judgment—if you must.

Teachers

As a teacher, you can't control your students' social hours; however, you *can* provide healthy, attractive ideas and models for adolescent communal interchanges. Sometimes I see a gleam in a teenager's eyes that says to me: "I wish it were like that now." And if I have to embellish my descriptions of the parties we had "back then," I do it; emulation is one of the finest forms of flattery, and it's especially nice when you know you have improved someone's life by sharing your past (even though those so-called good old days probably weren't *that* good).

Anything a teacher says in her classroom that encourages her students to make healthy, moral choices is valuable; for every so often an attentive teenager finds her teacher's wisdom compelling, and she wisely decides *not* to attend the party. Yes, the apparent futility of trying to lead 16-year-olds to safety and health does tempt me to give up. But I don't. And I won't. No one seems to want to save the children anymore, so now a teacher's job description has been enlarged to include the salvation of kids' lives.

Teenagers

It's time for a lesson in critical thinking.

Uh-oh. Zzzzzzz...

Before you doze off for the duration of this chapter on parties, you should understand that what you read here may save your life; that is, if you take it seriously.

Take out a sheet of paper and draw a line down the middle, making two columns. (I'm serious! This could potentially save you a lot of grief!) At the top of the first column, write the word *costs*. At the top of the second column, write the word *gains*. In the *costs* column make a list of all the terrible things about attending teen parties, such as drunkenness, drugs, violence, conflicts with parents, tarnished reputation, risk of pregnancy, STDs, and so on. In the *gains* column, make a list of all the good things about teenager parties, such as uh, well, fun—a lot of fun—and, uh...

Well, you get the idea, right?

We call this *cost versus gains analysis*. When we use our heads to make important decisions, we have been truthful with ourselves. Making a list of the *bad* things about doing something and then another list of the *good* things about doing something can provide us with more clarity for making our decisions because we can see right before our eyes (brains) what we must do and why.

What it takes is *courage* to do the right thing.

Of course, in doing cost versus gains analysis on parties, the conclusion as to what we must (not) do is obvious. So how do we muster the courage to go with our *brains*, instead of our *hearts*?

Vera had the best answer I have heard to this question.

Vera is gorgeous: Long, brown hair, parted in the middle, flows down the center of her back. Her hazel eyes gleam with life; and a perfect, smooth complexion, along with a trim, curvaceous body broadcasts to everyone that she takes good care of herself. Her congenial nature attracts many friends—both girls and boys—though especially boys flock to her as though they were tiny particles of steel and she a magnet.

But Vera doesn't go to parties.

Ever.

"I try to not put myself into places where I can get into trouble—and around people who aren't good for me," she says. "You hear about girls getting drunk and then used by two or three boys at a time.... If I think about it enough, it becomes clear what I should do.... With all the wonderful people in the world and things to do and places to go, I've discovered I don't need all the trouble the party scene would give me."

"But aren't you tempted?" I ask Vera.

She shrugs. "Sure! But my whole life—I have a whole life of resisting temptations every day. Each day I'm alive there are things I want to do that I shouldn't, and there are things that I don't want to do that I should. Sometimes I think if I had been Eve in the Garden of Eden, we wouldn't be in this mess right now!"

And then Vera flashes a dazzling, personable smile that would be a welcome sight around teenagers or adults: "The thing is, I honestly don't think I would have been all that smart in the Garden of Eden; most teenagers wouldn't have been. The key for me is, because of the temptation there, I wouldn't have put myself in the Garden of Eden in the first place."

10

Snitchin' Ain't Bitchin'

WELCOME TO SING-SING HIGH SCHOOL

In January 2007, I asked the following question of several classes of 11th graders: "If you knew that your best friend, who is 15, was sneaking out at night to have sex with her 20-year-old boyfriend, would you tell her parents?"

We'll get to their interesting (gag me!) responses a little later.

Teenagers have the prison felon's mentality when it comes to snitching. Nothing is worse than snitching. Nothing. One student—not using hyperbole—bragged that he would not tell anyone, even if he knew his friend was on the verge of attempting suicide!

It's the same way in *prison*. Of course, convicted felons didn't wind up in their predicaments because they had an admirable grasp of right and wrong, along with a commendable record of self-control. When a particular moral concept, one that transcends religious or moral holiness, houses its hardcore followers in the state and federal prison systems, one should take a solid look at the mentality that lies behind that concept.

A convicted felon stated his sanctimonious position on the act of snitching, ratting someone out, tattling, or narking: "When you wind up here, you hit the low spot in your life. And, yeah, lots of guys are used to it—to being here—but when it comes right down to it, you've pretty much lost everything you have, even your dignity. So what you do is show your pride by not being weak. Weak is telling everything you know about someone to a cop. If you land a guy in the pen because you ratted him out, then you're considered lower than the dudes in prison who have done some really ugly stuff."[1]

The only standard of morality—even if it is a twisted, demented morality—that prisoners have retained is their ability to protect their fellow felons by withholding vital information that they have, and others want.

Transposed to the lives of modern teenagers, we must stretch a bit to see anything sensible or decent about ethics like these; *except*—in a manner of speaking—young people today also have a sense of powerlessness, feeling as though nothing in their lives is under their control. They maintain that by remaining mute about the questionable antics of their friends, they can "protect" them from the tentacles of authority. As with prisoners, they may have information about someone else that others sorely desire. But to surrender this sensitive, secret information could cause a major chain reaction of punishments and paybacks. This power affords a teenager an opportunity to regain some dignity, respect, and control. And if he relinquishes this dignity, respect, and control, he has forfeited his last chance for moral parity with those who had the gumption to remain silent.

And the other kids will hate his guts.

Here's a question I posed to a class of 11th graders: "Would you tell a parent or a teacher if one of your friends was using cocaine or driving drunk?"

Those who responded with *no* had their share of excuses:

Because you don't want to get your friend in trouble.

Other kids will hate you for doing it.

No one else will trust you.

Their parents probably couldn't do anything about it anyway.

It would depend on how much he would get in trouble with his parents.

It would be the end of our friendship.

What if his parents aren't cool?

I wouldn't want him to snitch on me.

That's gross; it's the lowest thing you can do.

You just don't do that.

Then my friends would rat on me.

I have secrets I don't want out there either.

Who am I to judge?

If these answers frustrate you, join the club. The prisoner's mentality (on snitching) is one thing—inmates don't have ownership over much else—but the idea of a teenager going about his daily business with such misplaced loyalty can be mind-boggling. For some teenagers, their loyalty becomes their protector; they know that they, too, have dark secrets. To see others getting caught through the testimony of one of their peers is to lose a sense of personal safety. *That boy could have snitched on me!*

But here's some good news: One of the advantages of working with kids—instead of hardened adult felons—is that most kids figure they still have a lot of living to do, and they may actually *care* whether they live or die; also, teenagers, as they grow and become more mature, tend to be open to more learned ideas. And, certainly, molding the goodness in young people is an attractive alternative to dumping them behind bars.

Sometimes students snitch in order to help their friends, as long as their anonymity is fairly assured. This note was put on my desk: "Help me, Mr. G.! My best friend [uses name] constantly gets hit by her boyfriend. She tries to cover up the bruises with makeup, but it's pretty obvious she's getting smacked around. She won't tell her mother, and she won't leave him because she says that she loves him. This guy is a real jerk. And I know she's having sex with him. She's on the pill, but her mother doesn't know about that either. I like her mother, and I think it would help if I told her. But I'm sure if I did that, my friend wouldn't want me around anymore."

Several insidious problems lurk in this note:

- The friend's boyfriend is beating her. We don't know how old he is, although we can assume the girl is a teenager, presumably in high school. He could be an adult—an adult male who is beating a minor. No matter: the girl is in physical danger.
- The girl won't help herself. She won't alert her mother to what's going on, and she won't leave the boy. The normalness of this situation disgusts me; I have seen it far too often.
- A teenager is taking birth control pills without the awareness of a parent; obviously, she's sexually active.
- Her mother, apparently her only parent, is oblivious to clear physical signs of abuse.
- Another absent father impacts a troubled female teen's life.
- The writer of the note obsesses about the wrath of a friend and the potential for losing her, implying the overall importance of this loss over that of saving her friend from further harm.
- The girl portrays her mother as powerless.

Assuming the note writer is not stupid—as in lacking the intelligence to know the gravity of her friend's situation—the only answer as to why she balked at getting help for her friend lies in her fear of how others will perceive her. To her credit, however, the note writer eventually sought help from someone: in this case, a teacher. Ultimately, a guidance counselor took over, a restraining order was procured, and the boy was expelled from school. Rumor had it, though, that the girl continued to see her abusive boyfriend anyway.

ON THOSE LITTLE ROMPS IN THE HAY: MUM IS THE WORD

Sometimes the kids come in with a concern, wanting to swear me to secrecy, all the while knowing I am not committed to keeping secrets. I have always told my students or athletes or actors that when they reveal information about themselves to me, beware: if I think my snitching may save them—or someone else—from a perilous plight, all is fair game. They know this. They understand this. Which is why I usually have interpreted my students' confessions or stories about others as pleas for help. They know I don't share their concepts of loyalty or allegiance and am perfectly willing to "rat someone out," if I judge the ratting to be in their best interests. I am, after all, a teacher—a professional ratter-outer—and my loyalties are quite different from theirs. My open door policy is not a confessional; it's a place for them to go for help.

I recently read a news story in the *Orange County Register* that caused me some unwelcome gastric juices. The content was so horrifying—and mystifying—that I shared it with all my English classes. I asked them for their explanations of rather dubious behaviors and decisions reported in the story.

An 11-year-old girl had been abducted and taken to Mexico by the live-in boyfriend of her mother. The 35-year-old boyfriend had been molesting the 11-year-old for quite a few weeks, apparently right under the noses of everybody in the house.

A 15-year-old half sister of the 11-year-old caught the 11-year-old and the mother's boyfriend doing some heavy kissing on the front porch of their Santa Ana, California, home. The 15-year-old had the fortitude, the wherewithal, to go immediately to their mother and report the sordid details; 15 or not, inexperienced in the forbidden act of snitching or not, she refused to watch her little sister serve as a victim of this live-in predator, even if he was her mother's boyfriend.

Good move! Very proud!

Right?

Unfortunately, the story didn't end there. The mother refused to heed her older daughter's information. She shook her head in denial and said something like, "This can't be right. He would never do anything like that. He's a nice man who has helped us all out so much. You are just jealous of your little sister—you are jealous of everything! This is your way of getting back at her!"

And then she temporarily ostracized her 15-year-old daughter. The rest of the family concurred; the older daughter should have not been a snitch.

A week later, the boyfriend and the 11-year-old disappeared.[2] Rumors surfaced that he had kidnapped her and taken her across the border. When some of the family members challenged the term *kidnapping*, rational individuals reminded them that an 11-year-old doesn't have to be forcibly taken to be kidnapped; she doesn't have to be stuffed screaming into the trunk of a car.

The mother still carries a grudge against her older daughter and has banned her from the house. The rest of the family, instead of actively searching for the scum who abducted the 11-year-old, has vilified the 15-year-old daughter.

Three observations:

1. The mother defended her 35-year-old boyfriend, a man who molested and eventually kidnapped her daughter! She had denied truth in the *face* of truth. How many children are forced to suffer the consequences of disgusting, selfish, obnoxious stepparents, boyfriends, girlfriends, studs, and honeys like these? Actual data are fleeting, but anecdotal evidence demands further awareness and concern.

2. A pedophile was given amazingly easy access to an 11-year-old. The family either looked the other way or did not look at all. Too busy—or in denial—to check on the welfare of her children, the mother did nothing to ward off the events that would inevitably occur. Once again, we spotlight another home without a father—a man to protect his daughter.

3. The snitch became the villain! The older daughter should have been heralded as the only courageous person in the house; yet, the family targeted *her*, because she "ratted out" the 11-year-old. The man was 35. The girl was *11!* A 15-year-old who was bold enough to do the right thing and risk the fury of this twisted family should be the real hero here.

When I read this story to my students, almost all of the kids decried the mother's unwillingness to recognize the evil in the man she had let into her home. They all applauded the older daughter's decision to spill the beans to their mother, understanding that she was the sole chance to save the 11-year-old from the creep in her home.

Interestingly, when faced with another dilemma and somewhat similar circumstances, these same students concluded differently.

I asked them this: "If you knew your 15-year-old friend was sneaking out of the house at night to meet her 20-year-old boyfriend—probably for sex—would you tell her parents?"

The given: all of the students would first *talk* to the friend. The assumption: the friend would not listen, that the sexual companionship of an adult male trumps any desire to heed her friend's warnings.

Houston, we've got a problem!

To wit: the buck *doesn't* stop here. Only *16* of the 150 kids who answered this question would have told the parents that their daughter was sneaking out to have sex with a man.

Perhaps, the question I should have asked is, "What is the *right* thing to do?" rather than "What would *you* do?" But the fact remains: Only 16 of 150 teenagers saw themselves as friends who would seek help from the girl's parents. Here are their verbatim comments:

Her parents are the reason she does this in the first place; they're no help.

No way. Rattin' somebody out is wrong, especially if she's your friend.

Snitchin' is wrong.

Rattin' people out is the lowest thing you can do.

I would have to ask myself, what would I want her to do if the shoe was on the other foot; I wouldn't want her to snitch on me.

I will not be a low-life narc.

This is a tough one, but I told my friend that I would always be there for her no matter what. This is the "no matter what" part.

No way. Never!

She would get in more trouble with her parents. That would be worse than what's going on in her life now.

Her parents might beat her.

It would ruin our friendship.

She would never trust me again.

How could I ever expect anybody else to be a friend of mine?

I would talk to the boy and tell him to get lost.

No. And everybody else would consider anybody who did (snitch) a scum.

The friend should go to someone else, like a counselor or a teacher, not her parents.

If I were that girl, and my friend didn't tell my parents, later on I would consider her a pretty crappy friend, because she thought of herself first.

When push came to shove, only a small fraction of the kids said they would have gotten help for their friend from the most obvious source—her parents. One girl commented, "It's easy to say what you would do when you're given a situation in class. But what about real life? I think it's a lot different then." A boy said,

"I'd go right to the guy she's sneaking out with and punch his lights out." Looking at the boy who said it—about three feet tall and 40 pounds of bones—I had to laugh out loud. His bravado came easily with the knowledge he would probably never have to put his chin where his mouth is. Thinly disguised, his words veiled his hesitancy to defend snitching on someone, even if it eventually would serve to help his friend.

The stigma of snitching on a friend carries greater intimidation than being accused of withholding vital information that could save that friend. The selfishness of this philosophy eludes most teenagers; they don't see it that way. As with most *thought* that permeates the teenage brain, *emotions* rule. And with emotions come colossal rationalizations.

ROLLING THE DICE ON SUICIDE

With reference to the question about the 15-year-old who sneaks out to have sex, John came up with the most ringing comment. He made no bones about saying, "Look, even if I knew she was going to *kill* herself, I wouldn't snitch."

"Did I hear you right, John?" I asked, knowing that I had.

"She might not; in fact, people threaten suicide all the time to get attention, but then they don't do it."

"But what if *she* did, John? What if she did kill herself, and you *knew* she was going to? How would you feel then?"

"Awful."

"So, then?"

"So," John sighed, with the hazy thinking that characterizes kids his age on issues such as these, "I guess I made a mistake. But the odds are she wouldn't kill herself, and then she woulda been really pissed at *me*. A lot of people would be really pissed at me!"

Fortunately, another student spoke up, one who would not have ratted out her friend on the sex issue. But the suicide comment by John was too much for her to sit passively: "You can't think that way," she shouted. "If she kills herself, that's it. You woulda had a chance to fix it, and you didn't. That would really, really suck!"

"You're a hypocrite!" John snapped at the girl. "You wouldn't say anything in the other situation. Same thing."

"No, it's not the same thing!" The girl cried. "It's not! The girl who's sneaking out at night isn't doing that much wrong. But the girl who's saying she's gonna kill herself, well, that's like totally serious! They're not the same!"

"They are!"

"They're *not*!"

I happen to agree with John here: John's equating of sneaking out to have sex with threats of suicide is fair only to the extent that both girls are involved in acts that potentially are very harmful to them. The parent is the first line of defense against these sorts of behaviors, so both girls' parents should be informed; even so, the severity of each of the acts is not comparable, since one would result in death, and the other—though still of grave consequences—would probably not kill the girl. John's basic premise, however, is right on: If your friend is about to do something that would hurt her—and she won't listen to reason—it's the responsibility of the person who knows about it to inform the individuals who might be able to thwart it; in most cases, these are the parents.

Isn't that obvious? I would think so, but there are certain perspectives on the whole snitching, loyalty, family/bloodline thing that boggle my mind. All the time I watch these crazy events unfold, and I'm truly flabbergasted.

Don't get me wrong: Family loyalty is a good thing. One of the beauties of family is that we get through the rough times with support we cannot depend on from strangers. Here's the rub, however: When blind loyalty to family wins over morality, what we are left with are Hitleresque views of right and wrong that are based on *blood*, not ethics or virtues. The Nazis were loyal to Hitler, but the party had obliterated the line between right and wrong. On another level, when a boy knows his father is selling cocaine to high school kids and keeps it a secret, the boy's *loyalty* has become his determinate virtue. "Dad is, well, Dad. You don't snitch on Dad. And why don't you snitch on Dad? Easy. Dad is . . . well, Dad."

I asked my students the following question: "If you alone knew that your brother had robbed a bank and was likely to rob another one, would you tell the police?"

By this time the prevailing answers should not be surprising:

I couldn't; he's my brother.

Only if he killed someone. Did he kill someone?

My parents would hate me.

My brother would hate me. He might even kill me; so, no.

I was brought up that you are always there for people in your family; they come first.

I would tell on him. He might do it again, and I could prevent it. I would turn him in.

Robbing a bank is wrong. I would have to let someone else know.

I would go to our father first. The next time, they can rob the bank together!

I would talk to my brother and let him turn himself in.

I wouldn't let the police know, but I would talk him out of doing it again.

Including the ludicrousness of the last two responses, the students were divided:

would tell the police (11%)

would tell someone other than the police (21%)

would not tell anyone (54%)

something else (14%)

When I analyzed the responses to the survey, as well as those anecdotal examples via class and group discussions, I felt ambivalence: On the one hand, the results depressed me, because so much blind loyalty seems to spit in the face of courage and morality; on the other hand, almost *half* of the respondents indicated they would not allow sleeping dogs to lie; that, if compelled, they *would* stir up the pot; they *would* risk alienating other family members who thought a bank robber—or even a murderer—should be protected, simply because he is blood kin.

I tell my students that Ted Kaczynski, the Unibomber, was apprehended only because his *brother* had snitched on him. For years the FBI had tried to locate the man who had anonymously mailed lethal letter bombs, killing several innocent people. No one could find Kaczynski, until his brother came forward. His brother told the FBI that he would consent to (snitching) on his brother, if the government promised not to seek the death penalty. Although the FBI was unwilling to plea bargain on the Unibomber's life, the brother finally gave them the information they required to locate this deranged environmentalist, who had been living in a cabin in the mountains of Montana.

Snitchin' is not bitchin'—when your sister has eaten the last cookie and you run to your mommy and whine about it—but sometimes tattling is the only way to suit a morality that is less superficial than the amoral attachments we adhere to through honoring our bloodlines (or even the adolescent bonds we share with our peers).

MR. G.'S HOME-GROWN ADVICE

Parents

I play a game that has made my own kids think about the concept of snitching and doing the right thing. Our game has to do with a fictional "person" in our lives by the name of Mr. Washcloth, who is nothing more than a handheld washcloth I use like a puppet while I give my little boy and girl their evening baths.

Oh, yeah. Mr. Washcloth can talk; he has a very high-pitched voice (like Mickey Mouse), and too much of Mr. Washcloth is annoying, even to my children. But sometimes Mr. Washcloth comes in morally handy:

Mr. Washcloth:	I have a secret; tell your daddy to close his ears.
Little Girl:	Daddy, close your ears.

Since Daddy is holding Mr. Washcloth with his right hand, he covers his left ear with his hand; now, of course, he can't hear anything that Mr. Washcloth says.

Mr. Washcloth:	(very high pitched, squeaky) Tonight, just before your daddy goes to bed, I'm going to put a *spider* in his pillowcase! Then the spider is going to crawl out and bite your daddy *on the nose!*
Little Boy:	(knowing that Daddy's nose presents a rather sizeable target for the spider) Wow!
Mr. Washcloth:	Remember, don't tell your daddy!

The children sit with frozen smiles; they literally don't know what to do.

Later—maybe the next night during the bath and in Mr. Washcloth's absence—the following scene occurs:

Daddy:	(acting bewildered) Do you know what happened last night?

Both of the children shake their heads.

Daddy:	Well, I was lying in bed and felt like something was tickling my face. I turned on the light, and there was a big black spider on the sheet! I don't know how it got there! I don't ever remember seeing a spider in my bed before! Do you have any idea how a spider got in my bed?
Little Boy:	No, Daddy.
Little Girl:	Well, maybe he just crawled up on the bed.
Daddy:	Yeah, maybe. Good thing I got him before he bit me!

And then I explain to my flustered children that they should always tell someone a secret, *if someone may otherwise get hurt.* I make them feel guilty by commenting, "I'm sure glad *you* didn't know anything, because neither one of you warned me, and I could have gotten very sick from that spider!"

I don't claim to be a perfect parent or a final moral authority—far from it—but I know when it comes to issues like these, we have to work on kids while they're young. What to do about a badly behaving friend will be a constant challenge in your children's lives. Your kids need guidance, so they're prepared when those inevitable conflicts over snitching and moral virtue arise.

About 15 years ago, a small brunette by the name of Candace—known as Candy—sought my advice concerning her drunken friend. To the best of Candy's knowledge, her friend's parents were aware of their daughter's plight, but they had not gotten her any help. Candy wanted to know what she should do, considering her friend's drinking was not only damaging their relationship, but also—by association—harming Candy's reputation. Benjamin Franklin warned, "He that lieth down with dogs shall rise up with fleas."[3] And even if he didn't really catch fleas, everyone will think he caught them anyway.

"Should I just dump her, Mr. G.?" Candy queried. "I mean, she's my friend; I can't just give up on her."

My advice to Candace was threefold. First, she should speak with her friend's parents to confirm that they know their daughter is a drunk; second, Candy should make some suggestions to her friend—like going to AA meetings or rehab—for getting help. If these ideas don't work, or her friend refuses to try them, only the following option is left: third, Candy levels with her friend—"It's either the bottle or me; you stop drinking, or I'm outta here."

"But, Mr. G.," Candy pleaded aghast, "I can't just abandon her like that! She needs me! She's my friend!"

I shrugged. "Oh, really? Doesn't friendship work both ways? Maybe you're *her* friend, but is she *yours*? This is a win-win situation for you, Candy. If she chooses the bottle, you'll know the bottle was more important to her than you were. But if she chooses *you*, you will have helped her to recover. See? Win-win."

Teenagers don't agree this is a win-win situation; it puts them in peril of being tossed away like garbage by *their* friends. Friends, after all, are people you stand by, no matter what; even Hitler's friends did that. Never mind that saving your friend's life should be the priority. As long as she isn't mad at *you*, well, you must have done the right thing by not snitching on her! (*Please catch the sarcasm!*)

Parents must clarify issues of loyalty and allegiance. Children should know loyalty is good, but only *if the thing or person to whom they are loyal is also good.* (The Nazis, after all, were blindly obedient to Hitler.) Parents must also preach to their kids about blood and morality. I am comfortable with a child who chooses to do the right thing, even if he has to fink on his mother; I'm not impressed by loyalty to blood, simply because it's blood. That kind of loyalty would have meant an uncontained Unibomber.

Teachers

One of the values we impress upon our students is that of loyalty; unfortunately, loyalty comes in all shapes and sizes. Point out historical examples of how blind loyalty led to human misery: Hitler, Pol Pot, Saddam Hussein, and, to a lesser degree, Nixon. Loyalty that hurts innocents is immoral; loyalty that protects good people, good ideas, and good causes is a virtue. Teenagers are capable of knowing the difference between the two.

One way that I attempt to debunk the calamity of unconditional loyalty is by censuring men and women in my own profession who deserve criticism. It's a common belief that we should protect our own. After all, doctors protect doctors. Lawyers shield lawyers. And, yes, teachers protect teachers.

But why?

The most credible criticism of someone—I believe the most effective—happens when teachers are not afraid to refute, chastise, and berate other teachers. Obviously, doing this sort of thing all the time becomes obnoxious and unproductive. But when it's done sparingly and for good cause, it not only works to make the profession better, it also teaches impressionable young souls that we shouldn't have blind loyalty to a person or group—even our own flesh and blood—simply because they are *ours*.

I tell my students: "If I found out that my own son, when he became an adult, committed a murder, I would be among the first to go to the police and tell them all I that knew."

My students gasp. The hairs that stand up on the backs of their heads when they hear such dogma are pointing upward for a very good reason: the better part of them knows that I am right. Thanks to the courage of the parents of a teenage boy in North Carolina in April 2008, a high school and dozens of lives may have been saved. When bomb-making instructions addressed to their son arrived in the mail, Mom and Dad thought it was peculiar enough to alert the police. Blowing up the high school in a sick commemoration of the anniversary of the violence at Columbine just may be going too far! Loyalty to one's child is a good thing, but if what has been reported about this boy is true, he needs to be locked away for a very long time. Thankfully, his parents saw this truth early on and, in a refreshingly bold act, did the right thing.

Teenagers

Here comes another list. My advice about snitching and loyalty is summed up in 10 declarations:

1. Right now—this very minute—decide for yourself what kind of a person you want to be. *Do you want to be someone who does the right thing, or*

do you want to be someone who wants everybody to like you? If you choose the latter, there's no need to read this chapter any further. Seriously. Stop now and go to another chapter. Maybe that part of the book will do you some good; this part won't. I mean it; save your time.

2. Write down the five most important qualities you want in a true friend.

3. Using that list as the criteria, make another list, this time of your friends who fit those criteria. *These are your true friends.* They probably won't count beyond the fingers of one hand; but if they do go over to the second hand, redo the qualities you wrote in #2.

4. Carefully study that list of *true friends*. Politely ditch your other friends. Don't be abrupt or abrasive, but you need to find a way to get these people out of your life. They're draining your energy; they're a distraction from the time and vigor you should be giving to your *true* friends.

5. Run this list by your parents. They don't have to agree with every name on it; they probably won't. But getting your parents' approval of your friends will make your existence a whole lot easier, later gaining you much more freedom.

6. Consider some values that you hold dear. When one of these values is challenged because of your friend's behavior, talk to that friend. If you're silent about it, that *silence* may be construed as validation for his bad behavior. And it makes you complicit; for example, if you found out that your friend drove while he was drunk, don't laugh or shrug it off. Don't treat him the same way you would treat him if he had eaten five cheeseburgers during lunch. Driving drunk is an *awful* thing to do; eating five cheeseburgers is merely a *stupid* thing to do.

7. Tell your friend what you really think of this sort of behavior, and—here's the hard part—that next time you will inform his parents. If he threatens you or accuses you of not being loyal, remind him that you will take this action because you're his friend and not just some idiot who wants to stand by and watch him destroy himself.

8. Allow your friend's reactions. You will always be there for him, *if he decides to do the right thing.* Remind him of that.

9. Frequently reiterate to yourself that nothing is more important than goodness, and you will not compromise your integrity in order to protect even a family member if he is doing—or about to do—something wrong.

10. Have the following discussion with those who are closest to you: "Someday I will tell my children: If I find out you are involved with something

illegal—drugs, public drunkenness, shoplifting, driving like a fool—I will pick up the telephone and call the police. Good laws require enforcement on everybody who breaks them. My children will not be an exception simply because they are my children."

The prison mentality: snitchin' is not bitchin.' Snitching has inherited a bad rap; it's become more forbidden than even the most dreadful crimes that put people behind bars in the first place. In prison, anything goes. Bad people are heroes; good people are defiled. Prisoners have already demonstrated they make terrible decisions. But 30-some years of working with teenagers has taught me that teens will make the right decisions if we hand them solid reasons and show them unmistakable paths to righteousness. Consider my student who would have rather chanced his friend's suicide than snitched on her: Clearly, this kid had never been handed those solid reasons or shown those unmistakable paths.

11

Hard-Bodied, Soft-Headed, and Stone Dead

SWAGGER AND STRUT

Hector's nights began around 9:00 P.M.; they ended about 3:00 A.M. Sometimes his nights didn't end at all. It was not uncommon for Hector—especially on weekends—to slip into his small stucco home in the wee hours of the morning, just as the sun made its slow ascent in the east. On the weekends Hector began his day around noon; on school mornings, however, he hardly got any sleep at all.

Hector belonged to a local gang.

Well-groomed, always chipper, and somewhat interested in his summer school class, Hector didn't fit the profile of a typical gang member: He managed to usually get his homework completed, and he was always polite when he spoke to me in person. I never heard him curse in my classroom; I never saw him in conflict with another student, not even a verbal disagreement. Once he expressed in a writing assignment that his Latino background made a difference to him—he was especially proud of it—but I never saw him put down others for *any* reason. Perhaps, Hector's conduct around teachers was a pretense for adults in positions of authority; or more likely, that was just Hector: courteous, quiet, reserved, respectful.

I am not going to dissect the gang culture; others do a much better job analyzing gangs than I can. But I will offer some hard-hitting controversial advice that emanates from my intimate—but limited—personal experiences in this arena. One may not teach high school for nearly four decades and escape the gang scene entirely.

Gangs have not infiltrated my school; to be sure, there are some gangs present, but they are not cohesive, and they stand out like a sore thumb. Many hooligans who attend my school find that most of their fellow gang members go to other schools. For this reason alone, it's difficult to maintain a spirit of unity within a single gang.

Gang members move with a macho swagger that easily identifies them. Another self-designed method for recognizing gang members is their attire: They wear baggy black pants that are usually off dress code. Often they're covered in chains and spikes. But instead of appearing menacing, that look lifts them right off the prints of a really dreadful B movie. Most of the gangs at my high school are composed of Latino boys; however, a few white and Asian gangs roam the campus. It's sad that gangs are segregated by race, but this is still the case; race and ethnic makeup divide gangs in teenage America.

Few in number and impotent because of their lack of harmony, gangs on my campus do not reside on the same tier as gangs in some other cities in America. Gangs in areas that closely surround my school, however, embrace lawlessness, hate, and violence. Of the gang members who have not yet dropped out, many in bordering cities go to the other high schools in my district, with some of them conveniently bussed to my school.

Maybe the words *hate* or *hateful* are not fair when describing a teenager who belongs to a gang. During the times I've made personal contact with these kids— even in my limited capacity—I haven't seen hate in them. What I've observed over the years is a misdirected machismo, finely crafted down to the last detail, precise over a period of time: how to walk, how to talk, how to stand, even how to sit. Body language is of paramount importance; mere facial expressions and eye contact generate enough hostility to ignite major physical conflict.

And then even more kids will die.

A SMORGASBORD

I asked students about gangs; they wrote anonymously:

Kids in gangs are looking for family. They probably don't have a family of their own.

Gangs are disgusting. The kids who join gangs are disgusting. And, no, I don't really care about any solutions, because I don't really care about these disgusting people.

It's weird because my mother was the one who encouraged me to hang out with gang kids. She thought they could protect me from other bad kids. I never joined a gang, but some of my friends are gang kids....Do I feel protected around them? Not really.

The cops should just shoot to kill....It's not right what's going on out there, with all the innocent people dying....If I was [sic] a cop, I would shoot these gang members and ask questions later.

The police make it worse. They get kids all worked up. Gang kids like to go against what people tell them to do; so if you're a cop and you tell them one thing, they will do something else, usually bad. This is how things get out of control.

All the gangs aren't Mexicans. There are white gangs in my school, and nobody ever talks about them.

If you can make more money selling drugs, why would you even want to get another job?

Some of the kids who are into gangs at my school sell drugs; they make so much money. If you offer them after-school sports and clubs and things like that, they'll just laugh at you. They make real money doing what they do.

My three brothers are in gangs. I'm the only one who stayed out. I finally caught on that I needed to get an education, if I wanted to make something of my life.

My brother was in a gang.... He was killed at a party last year.

I didn't want to have to jump in; that's the part that scared me.

Gangs are for losers. You always know who the losers are. They're wearing gang clothes and gang insignias.

Many years ago I received this essay from a student:

I was walking home from school; I was in the sixth grade. I still lived in Chicago in a really bad part of town, known for all the violence and drive-by shootings, so I was pretty much used to being on my toes, always looking around to make sure that somebody wasn't about to attack me. About fifty feet ahead of me on the street corner, was a bus stop. I happened to notice two girls sitting there on a bench; I guessed they were waiting for the bus. I didn't think anything of it, until a blue car—an old model of something—pulled in next to them. At first I figured they were guys trying to pick up on the girls, because one of the girls went over to the passenger's side of the car and seemed to be talking through the window to a boy. The other girl stayed on the bench. The girl near the car began to laugh, when I heard a loud pop—like a balloon bursting—and she fell down to the sidewalk. She crumpled like a puppet [marionette] being cut off the string. I froze; I didn't believe what I was seeing. The girl on the bench began to scream. She just stayed there screaming and screaming. I looked at the girl who was screaming even after the car drove off with the tires screeching on the street. To this day I wonder why the girl standing near the car was laughing just before the guy killed her.

MR. G.'S HOME-GROWN ADVICE

Based on my years of experience interacting with the youth of America, I have reached some personal conclusions about gangs. Here are my 10 suggestions for diminishing the youth gang problem in the United States:

1. Encourage kids not to breed until they have matured and are no longer part of gangs. Generally speaking, we want our children to look forward to their futures, a time when they *will be ready* to have children of their own. Sometimes when I walk across our campus and gaze at the hordes of teenagers, I think to myself: "Oh, my God! One of these days, these kids are going to breed!" I shudder; I can feel the blood rushing through my veins as it makes its way to the clot forming somewhere near my brain. The truth is, some children should be told that having babies is not a wise thing for them to do—especially now. Some children should be reminded that not all people—young or old—are cut out to have children. Kids who come from gang-infested neighborhoods with a family history of violence don't come from an environment for raising healthy children—not while they themselves are children. And not when they still possess the gang mentality and intend to pass it along to their kids.

2. Point out the advantages of putting newborn babies up for adoption. For every American newborn who entered the world in 1988, there were 12 married couples who would adopt that baby, regardless of his race, gender, or health condition.[1] Although this compelling statistic comes from the late 1980s, there is no reason to believe that things have changed much. Married couples today must still deal with a three- to five-year waiting period in order to adopt a baby, and I personally know of adoption scenarios that have taken over seven years. There is a shortage of newborns. What better gift could be given to a baby than a life in a home with a loving, married mother and father? I may have a personal stake in this discourse: I was adopted by a saintly married couple at just three days old after having been dumped in a trash bin right outside the front door of a Buffalo police station. Okay, not really. But I was adopted and know the beauty of being loved by parents who really wanted me and whose goal was to turn me into a kind, decent human being—and not whose goal was to cultivate a generational breeding ground for hate, revenge, and murder. Gang bangers beget gang bangers. The cycle can

be broken through the courage to put these babies up for adoption and campaign for decent people to adopt them. Emotions, tantrums, and personal desires aside, what is best for the child: to be sucked into a sink, *or...* be raised by a single, struggling mother, often just a child herself, *or...* be placed in a loving home with a committed man and woman who are married to each other?

A no-brainer.

Society does not grant the adoption option enough status—and that's a pity.

3. Social services agencies could use more teeth. And guts. Abuse of children should never be tolerated. It's unpardonable for social service agencies to stand by knowingly and watch kids suffer the consequences of physical or sexual abuse. It's indefensible for us to watch young males—and sometimes females—living unashamedly in a gang environment, headed for gang lives of their own. *Who protects children anymore?* Parents? They're supposed to, but cases of abuse and neglect have skyrocketed in the last decade.[2] Teachers? They ultimately don't have any power. The courts? *The courts!* The courts favor blood ties in awarding custody— especially if it's the mother—even if she's a drug addict who hasn't been able to walk straight since the Chicago Cubs last won the World Series. But social service agencies are *designed to protect children*. Let's put out a call for social workers who love children, believe that kids thrive in a safe, secure environment, and have a spine that makes itself known.

4. The role of the church should expand. Churches and temples across America wield awesome power. Reaching out to the people who need their moral and social guidance, however, is not enough. In cahoots with the community, churches must convince parents and children that it has something special to offer them. The *Wall Street Journal* reported that boys without their fathers in their homes are almost three times more likely to wind up in prison.[3] I would speculate that data are not the same for boys who regularly attended church or synagogue; in fact, I will leave it up to you: *What percentage of young men who are in prison for violent crimes were avid churchgoers at the time they committed those crimes?* Hmm...

5. Fathers must stay. The importance of a father in the life of his son cannot be overstated. My mother's cries of "Wait 'til your father gets home" drove a chill up my spine. Her blocking the door to prevent me from leaving the house would not have provided the deterrent effect of my father's chilly glare. Boys who have strong, positive, law-abiding male

leadership and companionship in their homes will not crave it from somewhere else; turning to testosterone-laden gang leaders will be the furthest thing from their minds.

6. The community should get its act together. Okay, it's not a panacea, but anything constructive that diverts kids' attention in their spare time from activities that will hurt them is advantageous. People poke fun at Big Brother mentor programs, community gymnasiums, and after-school basketball. They contend that handing a budding gangsta a ball at four o'clock in the afternoon isn't going to prevent him from hangin' at night with his "homies." And for the most part, they're probably right. But unless we create diversion tactics that keep kids off the streets, we're doomed to lose this fight. The hardcore kids will do *their* thing, no matter what *our* thing is. The borderline teens, however, still have a fighting chance (no pun intended).

7. Uncle Sam wants them! Well, not really, but it's an extremely good place for them to go. Historically, the U.S. military—no matter which branch—has been the most efficient fighting machine in the world. Boys enter the military *boys*, and they leave it *men*. Basic training alone changes a boy into a man. Former students have appeared at my doorstep, and I hardly recognize them. They had left school as gawky teenagers, and then six months of basic training in the Marines or Army matured them into handsome, *disciplined* warriors. Young men on the threshold of gang life had decided to thwart that lifestyle by doing a stint in the military, and it shaped them into men—literally saving their lives.

8. Schools must prepare students for practical alternatives. The prospect of going to college does not bode well for everyone. Some children are not bent for higher education (and maybe they were never meant to have *any* kind of formal education either). What some kids require is the understanding that they will *not* be better off in college. People are different; some teens are good with motors and wrenches and wood and computers and wires and shovels: A student of mine, Ozzie, struggled with our complex analysis of Henry David Thoreau, but when it came to figuring out why my car wouldn't start—and hadn't started for three days—Ozzie performed miracles (for free)! Ozzies fill our classrooms everywhere, and if they don't find their niches because their parents and their schools have misguided them, gang acceptance can look mighty good.

9. An enhanced law enforcement presence would act as a deterrent. Already proven: when there are more police on patrol in a community,

crime goes down. Mayor Giuliani's "Broken Windows" policy for fighting crime worked wonders in New York City during the nineties. A huge part of that success was due to the increased presence of the police. Gang members despise it when there are police around, and they usually take their lawlessness elsewhere. Gangs thirst for communities that allow thugs to get away with murder. Leaders have lamented the absence of police in most urban centers across the United States; some have called it a national crisis. The more cynical among the population have pointed out the alleged irony of placing hundreds of thousands of troops around the globe to fight terrorism, while local terrorism thrives in our neighborhoods at home. Given the data that tell us 50 percent of gang members in Los Angeles do not live in this country legally,[4] it would be wise to tighten security at the border. We need more law enforcement personnel. Places that have lots of men with guns fixed in their holsters tend to have a much lower incidence of wailing mothers in the backyards of their homes, standing over their fallen five-year-olds who have just been shot dead at their birthday parties by wayward bullets.

10. Make the penalties more severe. Boys and men in gangs fear practically nothing. For them, the dignity and pride in the—albeit twisted—codes of honor that permeate gangs have trumped the worry of being injured or killed in a gang lifestyle. As a result, the fear of going to prison has eluded most of them; in fact, going to the right prison for the right reasons has become a badge of honor. Real *punishment*—not rehabilitation—may be the answer. The prospect of being taken off the streets forever, of never seeing their home turf again, of losing relationships with their "homies" and families may be enough of an incentive to disengage these thugs from their gangs. Various special interests groups like the American Civil Liberties Union defend the rights of young people to assemble in mobs—anywhere that their hearts desire. The men and women who constitute the memberships of these organizations have never spent time on a high school campus and witnessed the hollow eyes of kids who belong to gangs. They have never attended the funeral of a boy who stood on a street corner eating pizza when a bullet from a passing car ripped into his young body. They have never felt the fear of a 14-year-old who was threatened with relentless beatings until he consented to be "jumped" into a gang. I am repulsed by academically and politically motivated talking heads who have never been close enough to the real action to understand that their philosophical rhetoric mutes in the ears of those who know the true ugliness of youth gangs.

The thing that I most remember about Hector: his sense of humor. He was a little guy with a big heart, and he flourished when he made other people laugh. I shake my head now when I reflect on the absurdity of Hector's paradoxical existence: the Hector stepping into the night and forcing violent confrontations with other teenagers versus the Hector showing up in the morning for my summer school class and cracking jokes about his old Mexican grandfather, whose old-fashioned values and methods for handling problems seemed so refreshingly contradictory to the calamity of modern urban warfare.

But that *was* Hector.

Hector was murdered at a party near the end of the very summer I had taught him about Sandburg, Steinbeck, and Salinger. Uninvited guests had shown up at a large gathering of teenagers and picked out Hector to silence. His loud, extroverted conduct drew attention to his small stature, and the teenage gang member who fired the bullets that tore through Hector's brain fled the scene before anyone could stop him.

Was Hector's murder related to his gang involvement? I don't know; my guess is that the perpetual cycle of gang violence had claimed yet another victim that warm night in August. Retribution in the guise of justice is a top priority for gangs; that's why it never stops. Sometimes boys are instructed to kill other boys, without being told why. And once again loyalty wins out over morality.

Years later, and nobody at the school remembers Hector. Sadly, as Hector's body lay cold and rotting in a grave without a headstone, his name will remain tucked away somewhere in crepe-edged files—a place in which the powerless and faceless are guaranteed eternal anonymity.

12

Sex, Oral Sex, and "Hey, Everybody's Doing It!"

THESE DEADLY HANDS

By the time my daughter is 12 I'll be sitting on the front porch, shotgun cradled in my arms, ready to blast away at the first pimple-faced male adolescent who comes within 10 feet of our house.

Reason and logic (let alone mercy and understanding) play absolutely no role in the life of a father and daughter when it comes to dating, love, and—um—sex. Just the sight of the word *sex* on the same line with the word *daughter*, and my fingers begin to jitter on the keyboard. My Little Sweetie Pie, my Darling Angel, my Precious Honey Bunny will not be allowed to have sex with anyone until she's 45 years old, even if I've already been dead for 20 years. In fact, she will not—although my wife voices some disagreement here—be allowed to *date* a boy until she's 30. If I'm caught off guard (without my shotgun), my fists alone will turn her escorts' faces into something resembling cookie dough.

I'm probably using a *little* hyperbole here, but there's something about fathers and daughters that doesn't foster a father's rational thought process after his daughter has noticed, uh, boys.

Or worse: after boys have (gulp!) noticed his daughter.

We'll begin our discussion of, uh, sex with a snippet from my own teenage past: my first date with my high school sweetheart. She was, uh, 14, and (although gorgeous, talented, intelligent) only a, uh, freshman. I, after all, was a big, bad *junior*. But I didn't think this was a mismatch; she didn't think this was a mismatch. Her father, however, thought this was a *big* mismatch.

Cindy lived on the second story of a modest apartment building. The outside stairway I used to reach her apartment consisted of 10 easy steps. That night I planned for us to go miniature golfing and then have cheeseburgers, figuring I would have Cindy home about midnight. I wasn't an aggressive boy, although

I hoped I would work up the nerve to give her a quick good-night kiss at her front door. But as I walked up those eerie steps, I found that her front door did not exactly glow a gracious welcome: Cindy's father stood there, his eyes already staring through my face.

"Oh!" I intelligently mumbled upon noticing his lurking presence in the half-darkness of the evening.

He said nothing; then again, my "Oh!" did not exactly inspire him to engage in David Mamet dialogue.

I stuck out my hand in order to shake his.

He simply glared at me—his bugging eyes were all I saw—and pounded me in a soft voice meant only for my ears: "Here's the deal, son. It's now seven-thirty. You will have Cindy back here safe and sound no later than *ten*-thirty. And I want you to know something: My hands are registered as lethal weapons with the L.A. County Sheriff's Department; I'm a black belt in karate. Do you get my drift here? Are you following what I'm sayin'?"

I gulped, humiliated that the gulp was so noticeable. "Yes—yes, sir," I stammered.

The rest of the night, terrified, I kept looking at the clock in the car. What if I ran out of gas (no cell phones to call from then)? What if Cindy and I were enjoying each other's company so much I lost track of time? I mean, endless possibilities could lead me to a gruesome, horrifying death.

We did make it home on time that night, as we had begun our exclusive two-year relationship. During that time we never had sex, we never broke curfew, and we never got caught necking (*necking?*) in front of Cindy's apartment building. And oddly, I respected Cindy's dad almost as much as I feared him. *Almost*. It was then that I decided the kind of father I would be around my future daughter's boyfriends: Mussolini.

Dads make powerful differences in the lives of their daughters. Teenage girls who live without their fathers (mom's boyfriends and stepfathers notwithstanding) have a greater probability of being promiscuous than girls who have grown up in a home with a loving father. A statistical correlation between fatherless females and early sexual activity clearly exists.[1]

When I lurked in the caverns of adolescence, every boy in the school knew which girls would put out. Girls who did sexual favors for boys were labeled with names that the most gallant, chivalrous boys never repeated in mixed company; amazingly, especially by today's standards, some boys fought for the honor of girls they didn't know. They weren't hesitant to punch another boy in the nose if that boy had tarnished a girl's reputation, even if the truth about her had been told. Bringing down a girl—any girl—was not tolerated by many boys.

Today something very disturbing is evolving: Teenage girls have relinquished their power to boys. Someone has forgotten to tell American girls that women really *do* have control over their own bodies; that pregnancy only results when girls *allow* boys to penetrate them. Yeah, "it takes two to tango," but if the girl wants to stop, the dance should be over.

"MY OWN BODY!"

The April evening had begun to wind down, just as the sun was setting beautifully in the cloud-sprinkled western sky. I'd been at school too long that day, but the state speech tournament was looming, and the competitive speakers and debaters required lots of extra tutoring. I was anxious to go home, but just as I closed the locks on my briefcase, one of the most outstanding female speakers, Maxine, tugged gently on the back of my T-shirt. Normally, Maxine's blue eyes sparkled with wit, humor, and passion. With a slightly turned-up nose, her girlish face made her look 5 years younger than her 17 years. Her body, however, clearly reflected a young woman growing into adulthood. Around five feet two inches tall, Maxine had no shortage of boyfriends during the four years she competed on the speech team.

Today Maxine looked distressed. Although I didn't notice it until later, she also was scared. "Mr. G.," she whispered, "I need to speak with you."

Maxine liked to talk with me; we shared a special bond: her love for hockey, and my love for hockey—the Los Angeles Kings mainly—had embellished many of our other conversations. I knew a lot about Maxine's family, her past digressions and indiscretions, and her wild streak. Talented in acting and speaking, that wild streak, thankfully, remained contained...most of the time.

So, as we had done on numerous other occasions, we talked. Our conversation took place more than 30 years ago, but I remember it as though it were this morning.

I found it appropriate to make small talk with Maxine, and I sometimes teased her mercilessly. "Are you gonna chicken out?" I smiled.

"What?" For some reason she wasn't in the mood to goof off.

I'd caught on to her foul frame of mind, but I stupidly barged ahead. "You've had so much success with that DI [dramatic interpretation] piece, it's about time you hit a bad luck streak. And right before the State Championships. Is that what's—?"

"I'm pregnant."

I hoped she had tried merely to distract me from my obnoxious tangent about her dramatic interpretation; however, I finally recognized her utter seriousness.

The fear on her face now readied me for other roles I had often filled during my career: guidance counselor, confidant, surrogate parent.

But my next few words did not exactly transmit mentor expertise: "Huh? W—what happened?"

I knew she was fighting her tears, saving the downpour for later. "Billy Mitchell."

The way Maxine had uttered Billy's name implied I had tacit understanding of her predicament. Billy Mitchell played left field on my baseball team; he didn't play often, and frankly, he wasn't that good. Billy smirked constantly, making him one of the least likable players on the team. One thing about Billy Mitchell, however: he was good looking. Today's girls would refer to Billy as a *hottie;* in those days Billy was known as *rad*.

"Billy?" I winced.

"At a party about three weeks ago," she managed to say.

"But you didn't even *like* Billy. You told me so. You always ..." I didn't know how to finish.

"We went out to the car to talk; I'd been drinking. One thing led to another ..." she tried to say matter-of-factly, figuring I would fill in the rest myself: Billy was *rad*. Billy couldn't be resisted.

"What are you going to do?" I asked.

She started to cry. "I don't know. That's why I'm asking you—telling you about this."

"You've told your parents?" I asked, but suddenly knew the answer.

She shook her head.

"They would help you," I said, confident I was right.

Again, Maxine shook me off, trying to thwart her sobs.

"You have to tell them," I gently implored her.

"I can't, Mr. G.! They'd be so disappointed in me!"

I wanted to say, "Yeah, they'll be disappointed; they might even be devastated. And they should be. Look at what you've done!" Instead I said, "There're options; your parents can help you, Maxine."

"I already know what I'm going to do."

Of all the things she could have said, that is exactly what I hoped she would *not* say.

The decision to abort a child should not be made flippantly. Not that Maxine had been flippant, but her parents could offer mature advice and counseling, as well as love and consultation—if Maxine would let them know what was happening.

Not in a million years was Maxine ready for my recommendation. "Have you considered adoption?"

"What?" she cried. The concept seemed foreign to her.

"You put the child in a two-parent, married family. That's what's best for your baby. You're not ready to raise a child, Maxine." I tried my best to sound soft, understanding—not what I felt like inside.

She wailed, "I'm *not* ready! That's the point, Mr. G.! That's why I'm gonna have an abortion!"

Teens and sex aren't a good mix. Their bodies crave sex, but everything else about them is unaccommodating to the consequences of sex. Depending upon the study—and always varying with the publisher of the study—teenagers have sex quite often. *Newsweek* reported that more than 70 percent of males under the age of 18 and 55 percent of the females have had sexual intercourse at least once. The rates for oral sex are not as high, but they embody the word *frightening* with this fact: 11-, 12-, and 13-year olds are engaging in oral sexual activity; this time, however, middle school girls are involved at a bewildering rate of 34 percent, and the boys at 35 percent. To hear these kids talk, the girls are hardly ever on the receiving end of oral sex: Fellatio accounts for more than 90 percent of oral sex among middle school kids.[2]

Maxine had dismissed my suggestion for adoption, so I recommended the next best thing: "I'm going to take you to see Mrs. Elldridge [her guidance counselor]. She'll contact your parents." I saw her panicked expression. "*But* only if you let her," I quickly added.

Weird: without parent permission, I couldn't dispense an Advil at a speech tournament to Maxine; for her to receive *any* medicine, one of her parents had to sign a medical emergency form. Without this release signature, even the paramedics couldn't treat her while she bled on the side of the road. But getting an abortion? I *legally* could have driven Maxine to the abortion clinic, waited for her, and then taken her home without her parents ever knowing about it!

"Will you come with me?" she asked, her face a mass of tears.

"What?" I flinched, knowing full well what she was asking.

"I can't go alone. And it will cost about $250; I'll pay you back."

If I agreed with what she had decided to do, and if I loaned her the money for the abortion, what would this mean to my career? Would I—*could* I—get fired for it? And morally, what grounds did I have to stand on? No matter; I wasn't going to finance an abortion, especially not for a *child*.

"Maxine," I drew in air slowly, "I'm not going to an abortion clinic with you; I'm not going to give you the money to have an abortion. You'll see Mrs. Elldridge, and she can—"

"I don't *like* Mrs. Elldridge!"

"That's—"

"I don't *trust* Mrs. Elldridge!"

And with that, I knew my conversation with Maxine had ended.

Like almost everyone else, in the past 30 years, I have grown up. My maturity level today is gargantuan compared to what it was then, and many of my views on social issues have changed; also, concepts of appropriateness for a teacher-student relationship have evolved (in a more appropriate direction) over those many years. Three decades ago my reaction to Maxine's quagmire had been hugely different from what it would be today. Today, I would immediately sympathize with this child's plight, hug her—and then pull out the cell phone and call her mother. Then I did not call her mother. I *did* call Mrs. Elldridge, who—and this is *true*—offered to finance her abortion! What's even weirder is that I harbored the abortion secret throughout the duration of the state speech tournament that weekend—with Maxine's mother on hand as one of our official chaperones! How many times I yearned to say to her, "Mrs. Toma, here's a little tidbit of news: Your daughter is pregnant, and she's having an abortion on Tuesday morning!"

But I didn't. Much to my everlasting remorse, I didn't inform Maxine's mother of her daughter's intent to abort her child. This, perhaps, has been the single most regrettable, mortifying personal decision in my entire teaching career. If I had it to do over again, I most assuredly would do it differently. Thirty years is a long time ago. But now, as I relate this story, I cringe with embarrassment.

Another decision I had made, however, turned out to be wiser.

One afternoon after a class of ninth graders had left my room, I found a folded-up piece of paper on the carpet. In a girl's handwriting, the words on the paper said the following (and please skip this part if you're easily offended):

Hey! How's it goin? I was with Den Saturday night. I know whatchar thinking but I really luv it when he slams me against the wall and fucks the shit outta me! If you haven't tried it don't knock it cuz it rocks!!!!! Suz

I made three copies of the note: one for the principal, one for Suzie's guidance counselor, and one for Suzie's (soon to be bedridden over this incident) mother. Rather than phoning—we didn't have e-mail in those days—I found my way to Suzie's home and spoke with her mother in person. While I was sure that sexual interaction among teens happened as a fact of life, I was new to the fold when it came to finding notes like this one. Although I had no idea how her mother would react, I needed to make sure she saw the note and understood the danger it suggested. Even if Suzie's note simply had been teenage bravado about sex, her parents needed to deal with that situation, too. Obviously, this was a troubled little girl, only 14, who wrote in mind-boggling graphics about experiences—real or imagined—that 14-year-old girls should not be spending *any* part of their days even thinking about.

Suzie's mother cried when she saw the note. As she spoke with me that afternoon, her hands trembled. She explained that Suzie's father had bolted from the family when Suzie was four and her brother eight. Suzie's brother had hopes of finishing continuation school soon, so he didn't have time to keep an eye on his little sister. And evidently neither did Suzie's mother, who held a clerical job at an electric company during the day and managed a fast-food joint at night.

Whether the events described in the note were real or perceived, the combination of circumstances in this 14-year-old life presented a combustible environment, ripe with all sorts of motives and opportunities for sexual experimentation: the absence of a father, a working mother with no time for her daughter, a derelict for a big brother, an empty house for the majority of the day and night, and minimal—if any—moral training. Girls like Suzie, budding young women who too anxiously cast aside their armor of innocence, *beg* for a male to pay—what *they* see as loving, passionate—attention to them. Emotionally unhealthy young women like Suzie are inspired to become willing sex objects and participants, because they see this as an outlet for embracing the most passionate, *loving* male attention they believe they will ever obtain.

WHEN SEX GOES BAD

Most people do not quiver with delight over the prospects of their teenage children having sex; however, some adults—even parents—don't seem to care very much. When I reflect on this—and I do reflect, pontificate, articulate, and sermonize endlessly—I sometimes get the nagging feeling that I'm missing something. Why am I so—is this the word?—*obsessed* with this issue? What are the harms of kids having sex? *Are* there harms? And then I sigh, knowing that my passions have not been wasted. Having been around teenagers for 37 years in the intimate settings I have described, I'm aware of the truth: Kids having sex is bad—*very bad*—for the teenagers themselves, their parents, other people who care about them, and *society in general:*

1. Pregnancy Happens. Actually, pregnancy doesn't *happen*. For a male and a female who indulge in an activity that has a primary outcome called *pregnancy*, pregnancy is a choice. "I got pregnant by accident" just doesn't cut it. An *accident* is when a 16-year-old is so worried about her mascara that the rearview mirror in her car becomes a vanity device that distracts her from noticing the pole in front of her. Bam! Now, *that* is an accident. Getting pregnant is a *choice*.

2. Parenthood Obliterates Our Freedoms. The worst age—the most awful time—for a woman to have a baby is when she's 16 or younger. During her early teens, a female's body is not biologically developed for pregnancy or delivery; and, unfortunately, it's also the most inappropriate time of life for mothering a baby. Sixteen-year-olds should be tossing french fries at each other, not burping infants. Everything changes during parenthood. *Everything*. The most tenacious and capable adults often pronounce parenthood as the toughest experience of their entire lives! A girl who gets pregnant in her teenage years might as well kiss college and career good-bye (at least, she *should*, considering her baby is going to need a doting, full-time mother for a very long time). Parenting is a new life, a totally foreign experience for anyone who does it.

3. Having an Abortion Engenders Eternal Trauma. Women who have chosen abortion usually do not walk away from their experience with a slight shrug of their shoulders and then calmly go on with their lives. Some women—albeit a minority—will never have another child due to complications from their abortions. Some women die. Many women who have abortions live the rest of their lives wondering: "shoulda, woulda, coulda—why *didn't* I?"

4. Bad Reputations Really Suck. This is especially true when a major feature of the bad reputation is *sucking*. Sure, boys can get away with smutty, skanky behavior, while girls can't—at least, they couldn't up until recently. And one of the reasons: jerky, inconsiderate, drooling, frothing, salivating boys are a common part of the teenage landscape; in other words, it's *expected*. Girls, on the other hand, are made of sugar and spice and everything nice—or so they say; regardless, girls who slut around become the prime targets of the gossip mongers, and their reputations are sullied. And nobody respectable cares too much for the boys who bed-hop around either, especially if they kiss and tell. Come to think of it, just about every teenager—girl or boy—shuns these especially obnoxious braggarts. Having another notch in your belt ain't all it's been cracked up to be.

5. An STD Is Not Something You Dump in the Carburetor. Sexually transmitted diseases can *kill* you. It is known that AIDS still kills, even though fatal cases have decreased in the past few years. Other diseases, herpes, gonorrhea, syphilis—and scores of others I can't even pronounce—rear their ugly heads, too. Nobody with a lifelong sexually transmitted disease attracts eager sex partners. Ask yourself this question: How enthusiastic are *you* about marrying a man or a woman with herpes or genital

warts, knowing that you could never *ever* have unprotected sex with him? Sounds *very* attractive, no? Even so-called safe sex is risky, because some STDs are transferred through skin-to-skin contact—and pills don't cover skin.[3] Condoms don't cover all parts of the penis either, especially *some* penises.

6. Parents—Particularly Fathers—*Die* When Their Kids Have Sex. Yeah. No lie. If teenagers would keep their sexual escapades a complete secret from their parents for their entire lives, fathers might survive; however, this is rarely the case. Even *suspecting* that their children are engaged in sex is enough to *kill* parents. And this is particularly bad for fathers. Fathers know what guys are thinking about their daughters! The *thinking* is awful enough, but throw in the *actual* sexual contact and the father's mind runs rampant with frothing animosity toward the boy. As I skimmed through the TV channels a couple of years ago, I became half-amused, but fully horrified, wondering about the fathers of some of the girls on sex-based reality shows: Watching the girls' antics on *The Real World* and *Elimidate*, I thought to myself, "These girls must have fathers who are watching! How many fathers are now writhing on the floor in pain, or simply lying there dead, after having suffered a heart attack?" Some of those girls stuck their tongues into the mouths of boys they'd known for all of 20 minutes! What father could survive that kind of…? What's the word: *humiliation? mortification? resentment? disappointment? wrath? horror? rage?* Pick one. Or several. It won't change the answer. When it comes to their boys, fathers maintain a somewhat different stance on their sons' sexual escapades. Also protective of their boys, most fathers transfer their own sense of gallantry—even though they may not have had it as teenagers—to their male offspring. Contrary to opinion in some circles, a lot of fathers definitely do *not* think it is cool to hear that their sons are having sex, especially if their boys are underage: no notches, no kudos, just plain *wrong*—and a debasing way to treat a lady.

7. Big Investments Receive Little Return. Much of American society has assigned little stigma to teenage boys who have sex. Society figures this is simply something boys are going to do, because there is such an enormous drive to do it. When boys have sex, they often do so without depth of feeling, without investment of emotion. It feels good. It's risky. It's a sign the girl cares. All three of these are definite pluses *for the boy*. Girls, on the other hand, invest more when they have sex: Girls give more of themselves—even *all* of themselves—in their sexual escapades. For girls, the risk is not that they will get caught doing something daring,

adult, and naughty; the risk comes in the form of a question: "What will eventually happen to her investment?" If you invest little and lose it, it's no big deal. If you invest *all* and lose it, a crisis ensues, usually of great emotional proportions. I tell my students, "Every romantic relationship you will ever have in your lives will end. Except one. And even half of all marriages end in divorce." People who manage to stay together until they die have beaten the odds. But even for them, *all* of their previous relationships had broken up. The return that a girl receives on her sexual investment may not have been worth it; and that is always— always—tough to take. A girl becomes more jaded about sex every time one of her investments tanks.

8. And Just How *Many* Guys Have You Done? If you're a girl, you need to think about the inevitability of having to answer this question; most husbands or fiancés or boyfriends will get around to asking it. You can respond with indignity and tell him it's none of his damn business (even if it's your husband), or you can stand there like a statue, blushing in silence. When wives (and girlfriends) get around to asking this question about girls—and they will—they sometimes expect that the answer will not please them. And they are usually not surprised by the answer. How refreshing it would be to say to your spouse, "I saved myself for you. You have all of me now." When my students write that they are not going to have sex "until they meet someone special or know that they are in love," I ask them how many times they have *already* thought they were in love or had met someone special. Usually, during an uneasy silence, they squirm. For some of them, my question is answered by quite a long laundry list. And most of the girls find it quite embarrassing. By the time they're 30, if they have not married and settled down, how many sexual interludes will have been in their pasts? Eventually, how will they respond to their (future) husbands' curiosities about their sexual histories?

9. The Youth Culture Confirms It: In the Muddy Gutter. Most teenagers are tired of hearing about how bad they are. How immoral. How selfish. I know that I hated hearing all of this negativity about my generation when I was a teenager. Some kids always try doing the right thing, because doing the wrong thing plagues them; their deterrent is their conscience. Pregnancy, STDs, and emotional turmoil don't enter the folds of their daily concerns, because they already know they won't be having indiscriminate sex—even discriminate sex—with anyone. Why? They hate what it says about their collective reputations, and they don't intend to

exacerbate the problem. Usually, it's adults who embrace this mature philosophy, but many teens wish to be known as responsible individuals, trustworthy people, and they know that when their group is branded otherwise, it reflects upon them, too. Other teenagers who tarnish the image of even the "good kids" (by virtue of association) repulse them; right or wrong, guilt by association is a reality. These teenagers clearly view engaging in sex, oral sex, or "friends with benefits" as a form of hypocrisy. Philosophically driven, they remain celibate.

10. Wrong Is, Well, *Wrong*. Teenagers do not possess an objective sense of right and wrong—many people don't. And the answer to whether teenagers should be having sex does not come from an objective source, unless we look to the Christian Bible. There are numerous sanctions against unmarried sex in the New Testament but none in the Hebrew Bible (the Old Testament). Conviction that having sex out of wedlock is wrong, or babies making babies is wrong, has to be taught from an early age. There is, however, a pragmatic way for teenagers to view this: "This is one pain in my life that I don't need! Gag me [uh, here probably not the wisest choice of antiquated teenage slang]! What! With school problems, family problems, job problems, friend problems, problem-problems, why add the unnecessary burden of sex problems!" Sex problems push the regular drama of relationship problems up a *huge* notch. Who needs that!

Sometimes we simply have to accept that some things are...simply because, well, they *are:* Two and two are four. The sun rises in the east. A teenager who engages in sex is doing something reckless. Intercourse for kids is not kosher. Having unmarried oral sex is degrading, especially for teenage girls. All arguments waged in *verbal* intercourse do not require recognition that they must have *two* sides, as most assuredly, *sexual* intercourse—with all its consequences—looms on the horizon.

MR. G.'S HOME-GROWN ADVICE

Condescending attitudes frost me, especially when they revolve around teenagers and sex. Occasionally, someone throws a wink and a nod that says the winker and nodder is willing to play my "little game" for a while—even humor me, if she must—but she wonders what insights I have on this topic that she *doesn't* have. Granted, I am not the last word on teenage sex; and if I decide that I'm wrong about something—it would not be the first time—I'm willing to confess my mistakes. There are so many subjects that I know absolutely *nothing* about—computers, auto mechanics, and carpentry, to name just a few—so when others patronize me about topics I'm an expert on, I get a tad miffed. Nobody else has listened to more teenagers than I have; nobody else has studied teenagers longer and collected more empirical data; and nobody else has read more heartfelt, personal, gut-wrenching essays from teenagers. I know I hold powerful expertise on certain topics about teens—not the least of which is sex.

Parents

Your role modeling matters more when it comes to sexual attitudes and appetites than it does in any other aspect of properly bringing up your children.

Young children are naive about sex; what they know in their early years comes from *you*. The manner in which *you* behave formulates your kids' views of marriage, parenting, and family. Parents who shack up (live together without the sanctity of marriage) are more likely than married parents to raise children who will do the same. Girls who don't live with their fathers are more prone to promiscuity than are girls who grow up in homes with the presence of their fathers.[4] In sex-related issues, here is where your role modeling matters most:

promiscuity

marriage

kindness to a spouse or boyfriend

courtship

public displays of affection

sexual deviancies

nudity

body image

potential for commitment

healthy attitudes about sex

appropriate attire

This is a lot to worry about—no? Yet, this is what you parents show your children, what you demonstrate, what you communicate, *simply by living your lives!*

Fathers must demonstrate to their sons the proper way to treat women. Mothers must illustrate to their daughters what it means to demand respect from a man—not just *hope* (which carries no power) that he gives that respect to you.

I tell my students about the second date with my (now) wife: I leaned over to kiss her good-night; she then gently pushed my head back and said softly, "I like you, and I want you to kiss me, but I'm warning you right now that I'm not going to do anything that has even the slightest chance of getting me pregnant. I don't intend to have babies until I'm married."

She was saying, "These are the rules; take it or leave it, dude."

I reluctantly accepted her dating terms—and she wasn't just testing me either! I had to abide by these rules for the *three years* before our marriage. Talk about tough! Whew! She drove a hard bargain! But I knew exactly where I stood with her when it came to sex. And believe it or not, I truly respected her candor. I also respected *her*. Her clarity set the tone for our relationship, one that has always been based on trust and honesty. What's more, she knew from the very beginning that I was interested in her for more than just a hot fling.

The controversial, nationally syndicated talk show host and best-selling author Dr. Laura Schlessinger contends that, generally, women hold most of the power in a relationship. Unless the guy is a jerk (and that's a *big* "unless"), it is *she* who clasps the key to happiness.[5] A guy will do anything for the woman he cares about; he wants her approval...and her body. But a man also wants to please his woman. It's ingrained. If a guy is unwilling to swim shark-infested waters to fetch a glass of lemonade for his woman, she should reevaluate the status of their relationship.

Mothers should not only preach this concept to their daughters, they must *show* their daughters this theory in *action*. A mother who allows men to take advantage of her or abuse her will find her daughter behaving in an identical way.

Our sons and daughters are *watching* us.

Religious education and participation in rituals of worship provide vehicles for healthier attitudes about sex. Studies show—not surprisingly—that kids who belong to churches or temples are far less likely to indulge in early sexual activity.[6] *Children who are brought up in religious homes are more likely to have better self-discipline.* Being religious can sometimes be a total bummer for teenagers: It means there are some really terrific things they *want* to do but can't, and there are some awful things they *don't* want to do but must. Someone trained in self-control is less likely to lose that control in matters that most impact her life: drugs, crime, food, and sex. Religious teens do not refrain from sex because "God is gonna get 'em"; they remain virgins because they've been taught it's the *right* thing for them to do. Of course, nonreligious households can—and do—raise wonderfully moral and respectful children; a religious home, however, makes the attainment of these goals that much easier.

Finally, a thought about parents, sex, and the Forbidden Fruit Theory: The supposition goes, if we make a behavior out to be bad, unconscionable, *forbidden* by the masses, then people—especially teenagers—will want even more to do that behavior. The story goes, "Eve ate the apple in the Garden of Eden *because* the Serpent had forbidden her to do so. Had the Serpent not been so petulant about Eve's upcoming indulgence, she probably would have just smiled, apologized, and devoured some foul-tasting plant agents. But every time the Serpent said, 'No! No! No!' Eve probably thought, 'Oh, yeah! Oh, yeah! Oh, yeah! I *gotta* have one of them apples!' And so she bit into one."

This story demonstrates how having a positive attitude with your kids about sex can make a difference. Sex is not terrible; it's wonderful! With a loving couple, in the context of marriage—the only legitimate relationship *commitment* we have in America—sex is totally groovy! Kids should be advised that sex is something to look forward to—not something to do just because their hearts are calling them, their loins are urging them, their friends are daring them, or their boyfriends are blackmailing them. If you speak candidly to your children about sex, they will have better chances of sliding relatively unscathed through very tough times in their lives.

Kids have to know where *you* stand—what *you* expect; if you leave it up to *them* to decide, you're asking for a heap of trouble.

Teachers

Teachers have few options when it comes to discussing these issues with their students. I have been in the unique position of having written several popular plays about promoting self-control for teenagers. Old-fashioned or traditional attitudes about sex are not exactly the craze in America; people laugh at you when you promote values like abstinence until marriage. Today, even suggesting a degree of selectivity in sex partners incites caustic laughter. Teenagers, however, will listen to teachers they respect; they will at least *consider* any subject that rolls off these teachers' lips. I believe—and I say this with the utmost sincerity—teachers *must* present alternative views about sex. These are unconventional ideas that most kids are not receiving these days. The official doctrine calls for discussing sex, but treating it only as a health or science issue. A conspicuous appendage to these lessons about sexual reproduction is the promotion of condom use. Never mind that those condoms are not 100 percent effective; most teachers are using terms such as *protection* and *safe sex*. Condoms do not fully protect anyone from pregnancy or STDs, nor are they *safe*. But the official line of the public schools is for teachers to handle sex within the parameters of birth control. Mentioning abstinence is known as an unrealistic or prudish approach to teaching; and in all public schools in America, pushing abstinence on teenagers has been prohibited or compromised with the promotion of the condoms approach.

Teachers don't have to tolerate these absurdities. Surely, a system unwilling to dispense Tylenol to teenagers, but one that arranges for condoms and abortions, can do better; the amorality of this approach booms in its lack of subtlety. Teenagers are bombarded with sex from every nook and cranny of the media. In some instances parents are doing little to control what their kids watch or read in their own homes. The influence of the church is diminishing, with high school kids who embrace serious religiosity looked down upon as squares—throwbacks to the Stone Age.

Good teachers must work to buck these trends.

Here's an academic justification: Sexual activity is a threat to the learning process, because it has become a serious distraction. Not that 16-year-old boys require much else to distract them when it comes to sex, but with all the hype, and, well, *skin* around them, they don't exactly have their minds glued to the policies of President Grover *Cleavage* Alexander. Girls, in particular, suffer emotional setbacks after bad sexual experiences, and these setbacks make learning about participles and infinitives much less stimulating than figuring out horrifying ways to exercise one's sexual freedom. Our youth culture is entrenched in a morass of sexual thoughts, emotions, and behaviors; sex, and all that goes with it, is consuming that culture. A huge segment of our adolescents thinks that Clinton and Lewinsky never really had *sex*—and that it's quite proper for 14-year-old girls to place boys' penises in their mouths, because at least they can't get pregnant that way. And, hey, do you want a "friend with benefits"?—someone to "hook up" with and share a mutual *lack* of trust, awe, and admiration? They're there for the asking!

We teachers must talk with our students about sex in terms of dignity, appropriateness, emotional investment, misogyny, and self-respect. These topics transcend health and science, for all of society has an enormous stake in the eventual direction our teenagers will take. Deciding what we should do with our own bodies is not only about whether to have an abortion; the decision to engage in sex is a conscious *choice*.

Teenagers

You're tired of being nagged at and preached to about sex. No doubt, much of what we old farts tell you goes in one ear and out the other; however, you're reading this book, presumably for *some* enlightenment, so I ask only three favors for your respectful consideration:

1. Ask yourself these questions: Where do I want to be in 10 years? What dreams, ambitions, and goals would I like to be working toward? What good things in life do I wish for myself? Now: think about how having a baby or a devastating, lifelong disease would impact your ability to actually live your answers to those questions.

2. Reflect on how you would want your own daughter—or son—to behave when it comes to sex. Would you like *your* daughter to give some guy a blow job? Would you like *your* son screwing almost every girl in the city and taking no responsibility for what happens after that? Do this: If you're a boy, treat every girl as you would want a boy to treat *your own daughter*; if you're a girl, do nothing with a boy that you would not like *your own daughter* to do with boys. Just the thought of this should scare the pants off you! Whoops! On second thought . . .

3. Reread the earlier part of this chapter that offers 10 reasons why it's bad for teenagers to have sex. Please don't blow them off; assume they're the *truth*, and go from there. Then go back to chapter 6 and reread the ABCs for dealing with peer pressure—*again*.

Oh, yeah.

Back to Maxine and her abortion.

The only good part of this story is—and I'm grasping at straws here—Maxine *did* get around to telling her mother that she had scheduled an abortion for Tuesday morning. But whatever her mother did—however she reacted—she did not change her daughter's mind.

Maxine aborted her baby.

In a culture that sometimes equates sucking a baby out its mother's womb with the yanking of a decayed tooth, sad stories like this one go by us with less fanfare than the reporting of the morning baseball scores. The truth is, sex comes not without serious—perhaps, lifelong—consequences. One can only hope that those *few seconds* of sexual intercourse were so incredibly wonderful, so special—among the most fantastic five seconds you've ever spent!

Considering the enormous costs, I hope that orgasm turned out to be the most pleasurable five seconds of your life!

13

Devouring Junk

WHAT'S IN A SONG?

"Sixty Minute Man," by the Dominos, dominated the charts in 1951, shaping the course of rock-'n'-roll. The critics—along with much of Middle America—panned the record for its dastardly implications of some rather impressive sexual performance skills. For most of those critics, a *real* "sixty *second* man" would have been out of the realm of sexual feasibility.

In the movie version of *Grease*, the number "Greased Lightning" had to be drastically changed, because the original stage play contained more sexual innuendo than the MPAA allowed under a PG rating; for example, there were references to using plastic wraps as condoms. So that the song could be performed, the movie ignores blatant references to condoms, but Danny briefly rubs plastic wrap over his crotch.

Phil Spector's "To Know Him Is to Love Him," by his first band, the Teddy Bears, soared to the *Billboard Magazine* Top 10 in 1957. Curmudgeons thought the song alluded to an easy girl who would have sex with any boy she knew.

"Whip It," by seventies group Devo, had been described as an attack on President Carter—*and* as a salute to masturbation and sadomasochism. Also, there is an allusion to inhaling nitrous oxide from whipped cream cans (taken from the name *whippet*, the nitrous chargers for whipped cream dispensers). The words clearly summon images that guide us right past political discourse and straight into sexual intercourse.

Eminem's lyrics have been generously sprinkled with scorn and ridicule of his wife Kim. Their relationship troubles received public scrutiny, were the subject of celebrity gossip, and spilled over into public feuding. "Kim," the popular track on a lucrative CD, has Eminem shouting verbal abuse at her; it ends with the sound of her throat being cut, while Eminem shouts, "*Bleed, bitch, bleed! Bleeeed!!!*"[1]

American music critics and others have labeled these songs *suggestive*.

Suggestive, of course, implies something bad; nobody labels music or books or movies or magazines or photographs *suggestive*, unless the person's implying sexual arousal. So self-anointed moral authorities, with the intent of preserving the welfare of our nation's young people, have proclaimed it their solemn duty to defend American teenagers from, well, even themselves.

A touchy subject—for of all the topics that have come up for discussions in my classroom, the impact of American media and pop culture on teenagers has fused the most dynamite. It's no secret that the media—particularly certain forms—have a powerful impact on America's youth: denigrating their ideas, deteriorating their language skills, diminishing their values, and dumping on their thinking ability. In a nutshell: American media significantly hurt our children. Out-of-control *uncensored* (especially by parents) media are worse. Parents have seemingly handed Hollywood and New York carte blanche to exploit our young people, and the entertainment industry has responded by taking advantage of a golden opportunity.

By the way, I'm not interested in debating this subject. Studies and experts' analyses are relatively unimportant to my argument. I mainly contribute anecdotal examples and my *own* expertise. And you know what? There are some truths studies cannot defy; there are some realities surveys cannot contradict. Common sense and logic prevail, especially when they clash with the hired guns who have done so-called *fair* market research.

Every time I observe that something has clearly changed about the way my students are dressing or wearing their hair, I figure it has to do with their music. But I'm not always right about this. A good example is a "new" style of hair for boys these days. As one kid told me, "For boys, nothing's trendy—or everything's trendy."

Huh? What did that *mean?*

"Yeah?" I challenged somewhat belligerently, mainly because I didn't want to see my theory about trends and styles demolished before I had the chance to present it. "Then why is it déjà vu every time I look at my classes and see the hair—the long hair—that flip page style I saw *everybody* wearing when I first started teaching 37 years ago? Huh? Why?"

"Calm down, Mr. G.," the student smiled. "You don't need to get all haired out by it."

Haired out by it?

Seriously. Was that a pun or outdated slang?

I'd already gone through this 30 years ago and didn't consider myself ready—or willing—to go through it again. But he was right: working up my blood pressure over practically nothing wouldn't be good for anyone.

But when it came right down to it: Why did it bother me even *slightly?*

"You know what it is, Mr. G.," he said with a sneer I desperately wanted to wipe off his 16-year-old face. "What it is—the seventies have been recycled, and you can't stand it."

I thought about that. Why would I care if the seventies had been recycled? Whatever that means.

"That Seventies Show."

I heard his words, but I still searched my head for answers to my sudden irrational resentment of long hair on boys.

"Huh?" I asked, picking up the intellectual tenor of the dialogue.

"That Seventies Show with Ashton Kutcher. It's brought back a lot of style from the 1970s."

A faddish television program could not have possibly reintroduced one of the worst generations for boys' hairstyles in the history of the United States of America!

Could it?

But my student had been right all along. After some further investigation with an expert (I talked it over with my wife), I now knew at least one television series that had impacted today's teenagers' dress and style trends—as if what happened 35 years ago wasn't bad enough!

The media have the potential to alter an entire generation of American teenagers. From the way they dress to how they talk to how they wear their hair, teenagers jump on bandwagons, which are driven by the covers of *Seventeen* or an appearance of Zac Efron on MTV.

Speaking of which: if a *single* element of American culture can be given the credit—or the blame—for changing youth culture in the most radical, far-sweeping ways, it would be Music Television. Hands down. No contest. But until 1981 nobody ever *watched* music. Music had been a product for the *auditory* sensors, with concerts as the sole purview of our visual receptors—and only if we were fortunate enough to have a seat that didn't require a telescope to see the stage. Before 1981, musicians didn't have to look like Christina Aguilera to sell their recordings; ugly singers sold their music, too.

Have you ever seen Bob Dylan?

Television and music now combine for a powerfully pernicious effect on American culture. And MTV persuades teenagers to buy *music* via the music *trends:* the clothes, the hair, the tummies, the sex, and the swagger. They promise to change America in almost every cultural facet.

Finally, I certainly don't want this chapter to be about rap music, but rap music is all that comes to mind when I see boys on my campus tuning out the rest of the world with an iPod in their ears. My imagination scares me: "Fuck you. Fuck you. Yo, bitch! Bitch. Ho! Bitch! Yo, ho! You motherfucker! Eat shit and die!" These are my random words, not those of the rappers who are truly embedded in the ears of 13-year-old boys all over America. But what these kids *actually* hear is far more explicit. Many teens have become so accustomed to a constant string of profanities, they have accepted them as commonplace. Now young people, loudly and publicly, speak words once forbidden in the public sphere, and sometimes without realizing they are cussing.

Responses by my students to my favorite challenges to rap music:

Not all rap music is like that.

Some rap is good. Have you heard Tupac (Shakur who was gunned down on the Las Vegas Strip at the MGM Hotel in the spring of 1996)?

We don't know what they're saying.

We could stop cussing, if we wanted to. We don't want to.

If your parents teach you right from wrong, it won't affect you.

It's not that bad.

Old people will never get used to it.

It's just an act. It's like a character in a movie.... It's not how they really are.

Women like it, too.

It's the modern music.

When you guys were young, your parents told you how terrible your music was.

If your head's screwed on right, you will do the right thing no matter what music you hear.

It's art.

I don't listen to the words; I just like the beat.

When I asked these kids why they didn't buy the music with the same beat (rap), instead of the music with the same beat but the misogynistic, profane lyrics (gangsta rap), some of them looked at me as though I had sported a checkered blazer or just arrived from Pluto. One student challenged, "It's not the same beat; it's just that you *think* you hear the same beat. Do you even *listen* to it?"

Which, I must admit, I don't very often; however, when I *have* heard rap music, I noticed the pounding, pulsating beat exists in songs with kindness—and the pounding, pulsating beat exists in songs with murder and rape. So if the beat were the same in all rap, why not support those rappers who don't suggest that women be abused, used, and deposited in garbage reservoirs? I mean, if the *beat* were truly the thing...

Over a period of time, junk takes its toll: If a kid eats potato chips, candy, and cookies all day, his body will deteriorate. This is a given; *nobody* disputes this. So when a kid devours junk *music* all day, why is it not also a given that his *soul* will deteriorate? A constant input of *fuck* and worse (compound words that will put hair on your chest!) into his young soul cannot be good for a 15-year-old boy. The amount of respect he develops for women, and the degree of modesty he cherishes for himself, are siphoned from the music he has chosen to embrace. And with the absence of fathers—and *the* Father—in so many American homes, how can we expect the souls of our young men to be nurtured?

That vacuum will be filled by *something*.

And music—*the bad kind*—often is the *something*.

So here are my responses to students' defense of rap music:

Not all rap music is like that.

Correct. The good rap, the nonmalignant kind, does not attract wrath or concern; it's silly to bring that up.

Some rap is good. Have you heard Tupac?

Yes, Tupac Shakur made his mark with his sentimental stuff. But he also reveled in his vile stuff; his murder probably had something to do with it. We like the *good* Tupac.

We don't even know what they're saying.

Yes, you do. You know the music you like is being vilified for its moral shortcomings. Playing ignorant with others is not a way to make those criticisms disappear.

We could stop cussing, if we wanted to. We don't want to.

Right on both counts. You *could* stop swearing if you wanted to; and, yes, you do not want to. A steady diet of media junk makes it easier for you to have those positions.

If your parents teach you right from wrong, it won't affect you.

This is the most popular comeback to my classroom media tirades. But the media are a *method* for teaching kids values. When bad media are used, bad values are propagated. When parents take it upon themselves to ban harmful music in the home, they teach their children values; they have made it clear what is acceptable and what isn't. Part of teaching kids right and wrong comes with the sorts of media that parents allow in the home. Learning right and wrong becomes an improbability when parents use harmful music to inseminate their children with the *wrong*.

It's not that bad.

Not that bad? Young women regularly and unceremoniously are referred to as *bitches, pussies,* and *cunts* by the so-called artists. Teenage boys often discharge other obscenities and variations of *fuck* in their everyday conversational language, sometimes unaware that they even said those words. So, yes, it's "that bad."

Old people will never get used to it.

Is that a promise?

It's just an act. It's like a character in a movie. . . . It's not how they really are.

But teenagers fully know these so-called artists are not playing *roles*. Many of them lead the kinds of lives they communicate in their messages; consequently, it's become rather impossible to distinguish the rapper from the actual person. Very often what we get are dreadful men with dreadful points of view.

Women like it, too.

I've always wondered about these women; then again, some women allow themselves to be used for eye fodder in porno magazines.

It's the modern music.

Sorry. Not even an old, almost-ready-to-retire teacher buys this sweeping, unfair generalization. How many genres of music are there? Whenever my students report on their favorite kinds of music, they mention no fewer than a dozen different genres.

When you guys were young, your parents told you how terrible your music was.

Yes, my parents reeled in horror when Elvis Presley gyrated his hips during his first appearance on the *Ed Sullivan Show*. I also remember the Beatles' live debut about seven years later on that same program, and my mother commenting to my father, "Look at their hair; look how long it is! They look like *girls!* They won't last!" Not to sound presumptuous, but an actual comparison between Elvis's swiveling hips and Eminem's *kill bitches* anthems won't be taken seriously by anyone with an IQ of 12 or higher.

If your head's screwed on right, you'll do the right thing no matter what music you listen to.

If your head were screwed on right, you wouldn't be glorifying these sounds and enabling the people who recorded them.

It's art.

Jesus in Urine was defended as *art* in a 1992 New York exhibit. Art? Go figure.

I don't listen to the words; I just like the beat.

Most rap has the *same* beat; there are enough rap songs with the very same—or close enough—beat to "like the beat" without endorsing misogyny.

The rapid changes—and deterioration—in music have had a more deleterious effect on teenagers than any other segment of our population. I've been in the trenches with these kids; I know what's happening to them and why. While it's true that parents of every generation have censured their kids for their romance with junky music, times have changed; the worth of junk has depreciated. Before the last two decades, teenagers had already surrounded themselves with music that had too many calories, too much fat, and not enough vitamins; teenagers today indulge in music that is spiked with poison.

LIGHTS! CAMERA! TRACTION!

Every Monday I begin my classes by asking for a recap of my students' weekends: "So? What's going on? Anything exciting? Anybody see good movies over the weekend?" I ask, desiring that they share part of their world with me.

Occasionally, a kid peppers us with events I wish she hadn't mentioned. More often, however, students simply tell me about movies they saw over the weekend:

"Yeah, I seen [*sic*] *Disturbia*."

"*And*," I ask, hoping for more than one syllable.

"It was good."

"Why? What did you like about it?"

"It was, like—good."

Which of course gets us nowhere academically, but at least the kids have the opportunity to talk about things that interest them, even if their reviews do not threaten the jobs of professional movie critics.

Students often tell me of seeing films with R ratings. Since I provide them with a list of movies they may review for extra credit, and some of those movies on the list are rated R, this doesn't disturb me; however, I make certain the R-rated films on my list are not exploitive. *Ordinary People* is on the list; its content is not raunchy, although the swearing singularly assured its *Restricted* rating. The profanities are absolutely essential to this beautiful, tender film's theme. On the other hand, my favorite movie of all time is not on the list: *Sideways* contains too much, uh, material that some students and parents may consider obscene and, therefore, objectionable. Still, when students boast of seeing movies like *Hostel*, they immediately pique my curiosity: My first question is usually something like, "Which parent did you see that with?"

Here's the deal: children under the age of 17, by regulation of the industry itself, have been forbidden from certain movies. The Motion Picture Association of America came up with this system in 1968, and since then the majority of Americans—including parents—have found it satisfactory. Ultimately, protecting our children is our paramount goal; society has said that *adults*—mainly parents—should be shielding *children* from certain motion pictures.

But the industry itself also has volunteered for that responsibility; so I asked my teenage students how they got in to see some violent, women-hating, exploitive R-rated films; here are some of their disillusioning answers:

They just let me in.

I got someone outside to buy my ticket for me.

My parents bought my ticket and then left.

My older brother went in with me and then sneaked into another movie.

I sneaked into the movie without buying a ticket for anything.

I watched one movie and then went over to another one (the R-rated one).

I went with a bunch of friends; most of them were over 17, so they let me in, too.

Bought a ticket for one and then snuck into the one I wanted to see.

I showed a fake ID.

They didn't check for an ID, and they didn't ask about my age.

None of these revelations is particularly surprising. Disappointing, however, is the refusal of the industry—the theater chains themselves—to enforce their own rules. The obvious motive for their lax enforcement is money; they don't even try to hide it. It's kind of like the liquor store owner who looks the other way when a teenager tries to purchase a six-pack of beer: "Ah, what's the harm? What's the big deal?"

The tangible harm is that Americans are becoming increasingly fed up with Hollywood's vulture approach to our children. Whenever and wherever they can make more money—with no attempt to apologize for what they are doing—the film industry indulges, signifying that *they do not care about protecting kids*. True, parents shoulder the greater responsibility here. But when parents depend on movie chains to keep their kids from sneaking over to R-rated movies and the chains do not respond reliably, the trust between the parents and the film industry is breached. A responsible parent might legitimately ask, "How can I depend on you if you do not do your job? I drop my 15-year-old off to see *Enchanted*, and she winds up seeing *Saw IV*. What gives here?"

While parents—and certainly teens—share the blame, the "what gives here?" inquiry may be answered by observing an apparently mounting number of adults who are calling for more restrictions and government intrusions into the creative process of filmmaking. One parent complained to me, "Even if I personally put the DVD in—and I know what movie my kids are about to watch—I still have to preview the coming attractions or make sure my kids skip them altogether." Americans have lost their patience with Hollywood; many seem to be saying, "All right, you won't help to protect our kids from this garbage; then we won't *allow* you to make this garbage!"

And what this ultimately means is that *nobody* will be able to watch this "garbage" in the future—even adults—because the government will censor it, or the studios simply won't make it. Isn't this too high a price for the benefits of giving curious, hell-bent teenagers a knowing wink and nod, as they mischievously slither into the wrong theater auditorium?

THE VAST WASTELAND HAS BECOME VASTER

Nowhere is a steady diet of junk more ubiquitous than television.

Thirty years ago when my students talked about their favorite television programs, they almost always mentioned *Happy Days* and *Laverne and Shirley*. Admittedly, these icons did not exactly qualify as the filet mignon of American television; however, when today's teenagers report on *their* cool shows, they speak of television programs that I have no idea are television programs.

Everybody knows about reality television. Just as the words *shame, humiliation, dignity, self-respect, self-control,* and *class* have flown from the vocabularies of America's young people, Hollywood moguls are able to convince an under-20-something crowd to do *anything* for a camera.[2] I watched a short, vivacious brunette jab her tongue down the throat of a boy she had just met on one of those MTV dating "hook-up" shows and moaned to myself, "Somewhere—*somewhere*—she has a father who is watching her right now."

But in the age of *Girls Gone Wild,* much of what the feminist movement had fought for and won has drifted off in an ocean of narcissistic fulfillments. My students, of course, don't see it this way (though I do help them to open their eyes). I remind them that if they maintained a steady, never-ending diet of junk food, their parents would nag them mercilessly about the harm this junk may do to their bodies; this is also true of what junk *media* can do to their souls. But few parents today pester their kids about *soul* pollution.

Once I made the mistake of asking my students, "Who has a television in their bedroom?" And most of them raised their hands. When I watched television as a child, I saw the same programs as my mother and father; we watched them together in the living room. The idea of having a television set in my bedroom was ludicrous. Back then kids viewed television on a 12-inch black-and-white box with a fuzzy picture and a rolling horizontal line. Most areas of the country were limited to three or four channels. The Federal Communications Commission did not allow words like *pregnant* or *breast* to be broadcast, and even *married* couples on television slept in separate beds. Nobody ever had sex on television—or even kissed that much; in fact, I learned about kissing for the first time at a sixth-grade party, when a hefty Gretta Stern grabbed me around the neck and pulled, almost landing me in permanent traction.

So looking back, even though not much was happening on television 50 years ago, our kids were wild about it—far more passionate about TV than they are today. The world stopped—well, the United States of America stopped—on Wednesday nights at 8:00 P.M., as the familiar driving theme music from the *Adventures of Superman* hit the airwaves. True, the quantity of our selections was dismal—a bummer. But allowing a young kid to lock the door of his bedroom with a remote control in his hands and 317 uncensored cable TV channels at his beck and call is—shall I say it?—gross negligence.

"Come on, Mr. G. Don't you trust me?"

No.

VIRTUAL SLAUGHTER

I called Bryan's name, but at first he didn't raise his head. Normally, I simply stride over to the offending student and kick under the bottom of his desk, usually enough to awaken him. But this time, my kick lacked enough impact. After a second jolt, Bryan lifted his head, his eyes slits; he didn't know where he was.

I had recently phoned Bryan's mother and informed her that Bryan couldn't stay awake in his zero period class; Bryan's excuse: "I was up 'til four playing games, man!"

Up 'til four doing *homework?* Nope. But, *Up 'til four playing video games, man!* And from the looks of Bryan on a daily basis, he probably repeated this behavior nightly. Bryan, of South Korean descent but very Americanized, had chosen to forgo his sleep, putting his health in harm's way, so he could sit in front of a video terminal in the solitude of night, playing—Lord knows—games, until he finally lapsed into two hours of unconsciousness.

I figured Bryan's mother would help. Most Asian American parents are grateful when teachers call them about their children's indiscretions, especially when it affects their grades—especially before it digs them so far into an abyss they have practically no chance of passing the course.

My brief conversation with Bryan's mother:

"Your son can't stay awake in my class. He sleeps with his head up! And he looks awful—like death warmed over."

After a long pause: "Yes, we are working on the problem."

I wanted to say: "Well, how about throwing his butt into his bedroom about nine o'clock and telling him if he so much as turns on a computer or television or video terminal, you will send four frothing pit bulls in there to tear him to pieces! How about that?"

But I said, "He needs to stay away from distractions."

She responded weakly, "I'll see what I can do."

Which didn't turn out to be very much: Bryan wandered into class three more days, looking as though he needed about a thousand volts of electricity to get his morning started. Believe me, if I could have pushed a magical button on the fantasy charge panel at my make-believe electrically wired desk, I would have *zapped* him; in fact, I would have zapped him twice! No, make that *three* times! I would have zinged *three* zealous zaps into this slouchy sleeper!

I'd had quite enough. "Bryan," I chided him in front of his English class. "You're done, dude."

He was too exhausted, too sleepy, to comprehend the seriousness of my admonition.

Extending my left hand, I pointed at the door and said in my most authoritative teacher voice. "Get out! You can sleep on the grass [there was none]! You can sleep out there until hell freezes over [whatever that means]!"

Bryan stumbled out of the room, too near a state of being comatose to be embarrassed. I swore to myself at that precise moment, "Any student who played video games past 6:30 in the evening would flunk my class, even if he scored all As on tests and did every scrap of his daily homework and brought me six Jack-in-the-Box tacos every day for a week!" A given: this was irrational—too emotional—motivated by my concern for Bryan's health and a hatred for games like *Blood Slayer*.

Actually, I lied about the Jack-in-the-Box tacos; they would have brought his grade up.

The *Oxford American Dictionary* defines *junk* as "useless, of little value; worthless writing, talk or ideas." Teenagers come daily into my classroom, usually during or after lunch, eating cheeseburgers, french fries, stale candy bars, or Doritos. Even when they're not eating at that precise moment, I know they've probably devoured some junk food in, like, the last 10 seconds. Adults eat unhealthy foods, too; and we all have a multitude of excuses for doing so. Increasingly, the health police have paid a lot more attention to our diets, having banned trans fats in certain communities. At my school the kids can't even get a delicious, chocolaty Three Musketeers Bar anymore!

Very often, thoughts drop down from inside my head and out my mouth faster than gumballs rolling out the long chute of a 25-cent candy machine; sometimes, I wind up producing a comment I regretted at the moment I made it—but applauded myself for much later: In a lively class discussion about my perceived evils in some part of the media—probably television this time—I clenched my teeth and said firmly, "I would rather that my daughter were addicted to cigarette smoking than television viewing."

I could hear the class gasp. I wondered to myself: "Did I say something incredibly stupid again?"

A stern, dark-haired girl immediately panted, "You would rather she *smoked cigarettes* than watched TV?"

Whoops! I had better clarify. "Look, when it comes right down to it, I would prefer she be addicted to neither. But if I were forced to pick one—which is unlikely—but if I were forced to pick one, I would pick cigarettes. Yeah. I hate cigarettes. I don't allow people to smoke in my home or car, but if *forced*…" I repeated it for the third or fourth time; I lost track.

"Don't you know that cigarettes can kill her?" another girl blurted out accusingly, implying that I wouldn't mind if a foreign substance killed my daughter.

"Here's the deal," I sighed, desperately attempting to recover some professional demeanor before this throng of audacious adolescents. "I can summarize my thoughts this way: If forced to pick one—I'm more concerned about my child's *soul* pollution than I am about her *body* pollution." And then I added arrogantly, "Unfortunately, some of you don't have a clue as to what I'm talking about, because you don't know what a soul *is*."

I shouldn't have said that. But I was angry. Too much of my time in the classroom—and in those other school duties I've performed over the years—has been spent dealing with the saddest products of society's ills. Why do *I* have to be the one to say to these kids, "Wouldn't it be a nice thing if we spent as much time looking in the mirror at our *characters*, as we did looking at our faces and bodies; if we worried as much about how people perceived our *souls*, as we did about how people perceived our sex organs?"?

Modern music, movies, television, and video games spend practically no time at all addressing the character of today's young people. Frankly, on a list of things Hollywood and Madison Avenue worry about, the well-being and the humanity of our children don't rate near the top 10.

During the eighties one of my competitive speech students wrote an oration about the brutality of horror films. In those days movies like *Halloween*, *Friday the Thirteenth*, and *Nightmare on Elm Street* reigned supreme. His idea excited me; I thought it was a winner. And for the first time he seemed genuinely enthusiastic about an oratory topic.

And then I read his speech.

Jerry's oration did not *condemn* the gruesome qualities of those films; Jerry actually condoned—*praised*—those movies! Even his few criticisms were aimed at the filmmakers for not introducing even *more* gore and misogyny into the genre. Initially—until I came to my senses and remembered I was supposed to be the teacher—Jerry practiced his final polished speech before me. I do not have a verbatim copy today, but I vividly remember some passages:

> Some people are critical, but the way I see it, the best parts of these mov-
> ies are the nude scenes, always-pretty girls who are undressing in a locker
> room, having sex with a guy, or getting ready for a bath. This is when the
> killer strikes. You have the best of all possible worlds here: babes, nudity,
> sex, and grizzly [*sic*] murders.

Need I clarify what I meant about *finally coming to my senses*? This part of the speech alone—the section I most recollect—disqualified Jerry from receiving my permission to compete in the tournament. (Yes, as the teacher in charge, I had that power.) The poor bugger didn't even try to defend his speech by describing it as satire! Teenagers flocked to horror movies in droves. From his perspective, Jerry was totally right. What *is* more exhilarating to a teenage male than watching "babes, nudity, sex, and grizzly murders"? We nagging, spoilsport adults, however, may have to remind boys like Jerry—and his parents—that these commodities do not always have a healthy effect on an average teenage boy's psychological well-being. Regular ol' sex and violence meshed together soon wears thin, and actions of greater intensity and larger proportion soon inject themselves into the moral-ity equation, especially when it comes to boys' attitudes toward girls. Murder may not be a legal option today for releasing male testosterone—thank God—but eventually this may change.

My students constantly boast of seeing torture movies like *Saw* and *Hostel*. I have no idea why these films ever get made (not exactly true: *money*), but they have certainly raised the bar. *Hostel,* for example, did not lack excuses for its mayhem, and it basked in the wealth of its box office receipts. The movie's rating may have kept out a few teens who would have otherwise patronized it, but don't bet on it. At least from anecdotal examples, I know of teenagers who saw it—and many of them repeatedly. How did they circumvent the industry's R rating? Just reread the comments from the kids earlier in this chapter; they tell you how to see *any* film out there—no matter your age, your maturity level, or your propen-sity for doing violence. The ratings be damned!

Jerry and teenagers like him who feast on slasher movies scare me. Their desensitization to violence against women constructs a harrowing scenario; after all, when they see the atrocities that happen to women in torture movies—the horrible ways they die, usually nude or in sexual situations—what's so terrible about a good, old-fashioned punch in the mouth or even a rape?

Big deal! At least nobody killed her!

MR. G.'S HOME-GROWN ADVICE

In these "Home-Grown Advice" sections, I like to present ideas that have some practical value; much of that pragmatism comes from suggestions (for parents, teachers, and teens) about taking control. When it comes to media, however, control is largely in the hands of the *teenager* alone. No matter what parents and teachers say or do, the kids will access media as they wish. My three best ideas for each of these groups—parents, teachers, and teens—are based on that premise.

Parents

With or without you, the media are going to help shape who your teenage children are and what they will become. No ranting or raving or fits of denial are going to change that fact, so they aren't allowed. Tough bananas!—or whatever.

1. Take control of the television set. Monitor what your children watch from toddlerhood to teenagedom. Limit the duration of your kids' TV watching. And by all means: *do not allow your kids—no matter what their ages—to have a television set in the privacy of their own bedrooms!* And those TV trays that encourage even more TV watching during family dinnertime: get rid of them! *Talk* to your kids at dinner: I know, a scary concept, but after you muster a little courage, it's one you might actually *enjoy*.

2. Supplement their media hamburgers with prime cuts. Your kids are going to chow down on junk no matter how much you scream and yell, so give them lots of choice offerings to go with the junk: elevating music, uplifting films, educating television (or skip the TV altogether). Let them have *theirs*, but give them some of *yours*, too. And ban the poisonous stuff—the music and movies that rot the soul—from your home.

3. Always talk with your children about what they have watched on television, seen in the movies, heard on their iPods, or strategized with their joy sticks. Ask them questions. Make suggestions. Allow them to voice their opinions and concerns. Most important of all: bring to light the moral and ethical issues that are raised by those media.

You take these three courses of action, and you're providing what your kids need—and, surprisingly, *desire*—more than any other parental behaviors related to the media: your loving *guidance*.

Teachers

Not necessarily your place to change your students' relationships with media, your charge is less, but still vital.

1. Familiarize your students with gourmet media: Play powerful music for them; show them dynamic films; introduce them to classic television. Guide them to Web sites that analyze, scrutinize, compare, and contrast all realms of media. Enlighten them about what goes into a theater production. At first they may balk at your attempts, even turn up their noses; later, most of them will graciously thank you for these opportunities.

2. Assign them projects for writing and organizing their own music, film, or video presentations. Trust me: After teenagers have tasted the class of *special* media, the junk media will reveal itself for the rubbish it really is. And this is doubly true if they participate in a process where they help to create some worthwhile media projects themselves.

3. Risky, Risky, Risky! Read rap lyrics aloud to them, *as though you were simply reading another essay*. You may choose to do this with lyrics from Eminem (as I have—uncensored)! Often students have told me they were shocked to hear what they actually *heard*. Some kids confided that they had been attracted to the beats of the songs and ignored the words, thereby discounting the distasteful messages about women these "artists" were presenting. When they actually paid attention to the lyrics, boys and girls were shocked in about equal numbers.

Teenagers

Frankly, very little of this is your fault; junk is what you're being fed. If somebody came to my home every day and offered me Big Macs and fries—with a chocolate shake from In-and-Out Burger—I would devour all of it in about 2.4 seconds. *You* don't know that what you love is junk, or you maintain the unrealistic notion that one man's junk is another man's art—which is very sweet, but short-sighted. You will, as generations before you, pursue the music, movies, and television you adore, no matter what the terminally old and unbearably crabby happen to warn you about. My three suggestions are not mandates; however, since I believe strongly in what I'm saying, and I'm worried about your mental and emotional health, give them a try—*pweeese!*

1. March to the beat of a different drummer. Just because everybody else raves about the cool songs from Rape'em-Stab'em-Kill'em, you don't

have to. Feel free to decline their invitations to partake in this jungle of misogyny. You have a mind of your own. Use it.

2. For one month, take your parents' and teachers' advice about media. Don't fight with them, don't rebel, and, most of all, don't pretend to do one thing (take their advice) and then do another thing (lie and say that you took their advice). After the month is over—but not until then—go back to your old ways. Two glorious effects here: first, your old media tastes will seem *junky*; and second, you will thirst for—even crave—more of your parents' and teachers' recommendations.

3. Your tastes are normal. Don't worry about it; you're a teenager! Always control your *behaviors*, treat people well, and stay out of trouble. No matter how much junk you eat, you have a mind and a soul and a heart, and what you *do* with those—not your tastes in music—ultimately makes you who you are. Yes, the media have a potent effect on you, and yes, the world is different today—far more demanding, far more needy—partly because of the intoxicating effects of media, but in America you are the planners of your destiny and the masters of your soul. And the really cool thing is that much less soul pollution makes our lives a great deal more bearable, even to the point of being (gulp!) *pleasant*.

If you still consider yourself a doubter, a naysayer, I present to you the words from a note a female teacher and very close friend of mine found in one of her students' writing portfolios: Two of her male students had been passing a note back and forth during her class, and one of them had inadvertently forgotten to remove the note from his writing portfolio before he turned it in to her for grading. I had taught one of these boys the previous year and knew that he listened to the genre of rap music I have condemned in this book. I had already spoken with Kelly about the rubbish that constantly streamed into his consciousness through his iPod and car stereo system.

Obviously, my words had fallen on deaf ears.

Please believe that the following note is a by-product of some of today's so-called musicians: the way they talk, their artificial swagger, their blatant disregard for authority, and their loathing of women.

Evidently, these boys' "prose" made references to one of their so-called girlfriends. Stop reading here if you're even slightly prudish. I'm a grown man—well, agewise—and even I found this very tough to take:

Yo! What the bitch?
Got balls? Got dick?
I got balls. Did you ask her?

She gonna suck tonight?
Yo!
Don't be 'fraid. You gonna fuck her good.
Yeah.
Gotta jam it.
Yeah. But stop. Yo make me crazy.
Fuck you.
Yeah.
Yo!
Fuck off.

This young teacher is a kind, gentle, dignified, intelligent, generous, classy, beautiful woman who brims with integrity. And so this is what she pulled from her student's notebook at two o'clock in the morning, as she slaved tirelessly to help him by carefully editing his writing. This was his way of saying, *Thank you, Mrs. Jones . . . for all your hard work, help, and kindness.*

Yo! Bitch!

14

They Bombed Hiroshima, Didn't They?

IS THAT GOOD...OR IS THAT BAD?

He strolled into the room and quietly laid his books on a desk. Class would begin in about three minutes; soon the teacher would be droning on about something utterly irrelevant to his life. Entirely removed from his surroundings, the small plastic gadgets in his ears piped in the words that resounded repeatedly in his head, chorusing the ideas that he has heard about sex and violence and crime—and women:

> Give me some time you motherfucker / But you ain't got the goods and I ain't got the courage / to blow you away / I ain't got the courage to blow you away / You lied like every other pig in town / You spent too much time with that bitch you own / And you never got the sign / You never got the line / Your fuckin' never got off her dime![1]

He could play that rap refrain in his brain without the assistance of an iPod, one of the most popular play toys known to post-9/11 teenagers. But the iPod somehow gave him power. The iPod increased his *status*. He had become the latest of the Boomers' grandchildren to use a technology the Boomers had only dreamed of: music *you* choose, music *you* take with you, music you listen to at your whim!

American high schools and middle schools, however, have not joined the hippest of all music generations in promoting the iPod craze; very few school officials condone them, allow them, or use them. The acceptance of iPods in American secondary schools has grown tantamount to the acceptance of the small transistor radios of the 1960s, when kids snuck them into schools in order to hear the World Series (played during the daytime back then).

As a teacher, I *loathe* the use of iPods at school for three main reasons:

1. *They disrupt the kids' concentration.* Students should be thinking about what's happening at school—ideas about algebra, government, and Whitman—not Snoop Dogg's latest bout in jail or Eminem's most recent confrontation with guns and cops. At the very least, they should be looking at the school's "Vision Statement"—no one can figure out its significance—that is plastered on the walls of every classroom.

2. *They lose them.* Bureaucratic nightmares over lost iPods tend to thwart the benefits of being ever-connected to the woes of young convicts who lament about their bitches standing them up and their homies talking shit to them.

3. *They scare me.* Not literally *frighten,* but just knowing—or having a good idea—what is being heard in those earphones at any precise moment is enough to rattle my nerves. I might try denying my most subjective assumptions and pretend as though my students were listening to the Righteous Brothers, but I have a feeling I won't be fooling myself for long.

Okay. I'm probably battering around too severely the presence of portable music devices. After all, we've all used them at one time or another; in fact, when I go to the gym, I wear a headset while working out. True, I listen to AM radio talk shows that would bore the ever-lovin' tears out of most teens; and, true, a huge antenna juts in the air off the front of the headset making me look like a Martian—but I do wear a headset. I've told my students that while they're in my classroom, they're not allowed to even *show* me an iPod (or other such contraption) before, after, or during class, unless it has one of those pointy antennas.

Naturally, they laugh. But I'm serious.

The newest technology has been both a boon and a bust for modern educators. Seeming to compromise the effectiveness of educators, some of the most modern advances have presented thorny challenges. Technology has always presented an enigma, a whole series of contradictions, paradoxes, and hypocrisies: for example, one of the most amazing advances of modern man has been the invention of the automobile. Who can imagine today's world without cars? Besides pleasure transportation, the entire economy now depends on materials being transported by vehicles on wheels; yet, a couple *million* Americans have been killed in automobile crashes since the early 1900s. In the last decade, 10,000 more teens died in the United States in car crashes than members of the military who died during the entire 10 years of the Vietnam War.[2]

The same concept rings true for nuclear weapons. While you hear so many intelligent, knowledgeable people condemn the technology of the arms race, this fact remains: the United States *exists today because of its possession of nuclear weapons!* The sheer number of Cold War enemies who would have overrun this country looms as a terrifying concept, but without the deterrent of the hydrogen bomb and the balance of power, the United States probably would not exist today. More than 2 million more Japanese civilians and soldiers—not to mention a million more American military personnel—would have perished during the latter part of World War II without President Truman's determination to drop the atomic bomb on Hiroshima, on August 6, 1945. We all may be alive today by the grace of the atomic bomb.

Technology, when used well, benefits humanity. Technology, when used unwisely, destroys a little more of humanity every time it is used. Without enough care and concern, technology in the wrong hands has the ugly potential for obliterating civilization.

On a micro level, consider modern teenagers: I've thought really hard about this, and I can't remember too many advances in pop culture technology—except for television, of course—that had affected teenagers prior to the advent of VHS and CD players. The needle on the record player served my generation just fine, but in the late seventies the old needle-driven Victrola began to wane with the arrival of the new eight-track tape systems. From this time forward, technology—especially related to the media and communication—has sped at such a breathtaking pace, many other old codgers haven't caught up either.

MUSIC TECHNOLOGY: THE POUNDIN' OF THE DRUMS

Recently, I spotted two boys sitting in a local buffet restaurant with a woman who appeared to be their grandmother. As the boys ate, they listened to small earphones that were connected to iPods. My first reaction was one of minor vexation; their blatant rudeness surprised me. Two teenagers drifted alone in their private music worlds (scary or what!), while their grandmother, who sat with them and had probably paid for their dinners, had been temporarily excluded from their lives.

I walked over to them and introduced myself: I told them I was in the process of writing a book about teenagers. Mind you, it took almost six hours to gather their attention (okay, a *slight* exaggeration), but eventually my obnoxious persistence convinced them to turn their sets off and remove their earphones.

After the formalities, I asked the teens, "So, what are you guys listening to?"

One said DRS and the other muttered something unintelligible.

"How much do you listen to your iPods?" I asked a totally useless question.

Their responses were vague, so I turned to Grandma; the boys were understandably suspicious of an old geezer who had wandered over to their table and asked them weird questions about their iPod habits.

"Does it bother you?" I probed Grandma.

Grandma knew immediately where I was headed. "Yes. If they want to eat dinner with me, they have to be civil. You should be very nice to your food provider, you know!"

She laughed.

I wondered why she tolerated their abuse; I said, "If I did that with my wife—if I put a headset on while we ate at a restaurant—she would lean over and rip it off my face!"

I immediately recognized the inappropriateness of my boorish comment and wanted to change the subject. My lambasting Grandma for not taking charge would not endear me to anyone at the table, so I needed to drop it—fast.

But before I could decide where to take this, one of the boys—the older one—chimed, "If she told us to take 'em off, we would—I would."

I looked to the younger kid for confirmation; he let his head droop.

"Seriously," the older boy persisted, "I usually do what my mother tells me; so does he."

He had alluded to his younger brother, but my mind momentarily dwelled on the reference to the woman at the table as his *mother*; actually, this provided temporary satisfaction. Several times strangers have referred to me in the presence of my children as *grandpa*. If nothing else, it was good to see another ancient-looking parent out there: comrades in arms.

I looked at the younger boy. "Don't you think it would be nice to have a conversation with your mother at dinner?"

He shrugged. Not a big talker, this guy.

I continued, "Why do you to listen to music at dinner—while other people are eating with you?"

The older boy shrugged, pointing to his mother, "She doesn't mind; she likes to sit there and *not* talk to us."

The younger boy added a grunt.

I decided this to be going nowhere, except maybe to the point of alienating my three subjects, so I fired a point-blank question at Mother:

"How can you stand it?"

I hoped she wouldn't throw her bowl of banana cream pudding in my face; she replied, "I'm used to it."

"You like it?"

She momentarily glared at me and then turned her ferocious stare on her sons. "No, I don't like it. But they gotta eat," she added matter-of-factly.

And I wanted to say, "Well, yes, they do; but they don't have to eat at a place like this, where they have every greasy, grimy, delicious food known to modern mankind—especially adapted to the voracious taste palates of American teenagers.

Ever heard of bread and water? That'll convince them to take off their headsets during dinner!"

But instead I sat there with a forced, gaping smile and said absolutely nothing. Finally, I lied, "Whoops! Those are my kids calling me to leave!"

And I excused myself, waddling back to my family, under the scope of my wife's glare, as if to ask me, "Is writing this book really worth making a blithering idiot out of yourself all the time?"

Tough call. I really had to think about that some more.

My students laugh at me when I tell them my views on music technology. Back in the seventies, when stereo first became a big deal, I had said, "Hmm...I'm not sure if I like that sound."

"Why?" The seventies kids had asked incredulously.

"Well, there's something to be said for music that filters through only one speaker. The sound is more solid, fuller; in fact, for my old doo-wop records, I *like* the scratchy sound the record player produces. Without the scratchy sound, it just wouldn't be the same."

Which, of course, *was* the point for these kids. They didn't *want* it to be the same! The *same* was *out*. Stereophonic music bellowed all over the school. In those days, if you weren't "stereo," you were a total geek; homosexuals in the Marine Corps received nicer treatment.

As the modern machines sounded truly better, my arguments for the old mono sounds echoed hollow. I could no longer justify not using at least an eight-track tape player; I even bought a car, a brand new Mercury Cougar, with an eight-track! How I beamed with self-assigned coolness every time I inserted one of those oversized tapes into the huge insert slot near the bottom of the tape deck! My semimastery of modern music technology gave me my hippest moments as a high school teacher; after all, I was using *their* machines to play *my* music! And what could be hipper than that? Some of my students—who then were not much younger than I—even liked the same musicians: Gordon Lightfoot, Dan Fogelberg, and Cat Stevens. We not only shared in the technology for *playing* the music, we had the same *tastes* in music, as well! What a glorious time!

Unfortunately, I couldn't keep up: not with music, not with technology, and not with teenagers' voracious appetites for new things. They rapidly progressed from the tape deck to the CD player's multisystem sounds world, while I still tinkered with my record player, hoping I could catch Radio Shack at just the right time for a new needle; unfortunately, Radio Shack stopped storing those needles, and I once again was left behind in the technology boom.

Maybe that's been the source of my hostility toward the iPod. I don't know how to *put* the music on the dang thing to begin with, let alone play it when I go to the gym! While I'm with my wife and kids, listening to an iPod would be a definite no-no. You can't teach an old dog new tricks, and, incontestably, I *am* an old dog.

These are definitely new tricks.

CELL PHONE TECHNOLOGY: "IT'S, ME, STUPID, CALLING!"

For teenagers, no other piece of modern technology has demonstrated itself to be as utterly useless and counterproductive as the cell phone. Sure there are some benefits: In the event of a major earthquake or a terrorist attack, you're going to have to call whomever to talk about whatever. And if you're stranded somewhere on the freeway in the middle of the night, having that little contraption to summon a tow truck just may save your life.

Somehow I wish cell phones could be fitted to work *only* for these kinds of emergencies. In reality, do cell phones cause more harm than good? Several disadvantages to cell phones in the hands of teenagers cry out for your examination. I admit that some of my objections seem to be mere annoyances, but I beg you to compare the *accumulation* of these problems with the aggregate advantages to the technology.

Teenagers Drive While on Their Cell Phones

I once believed that the scariest sight I had seen in my entire life happened in a movie, when Godzilla rose from Tokyo Bay, poised to make his last—and probably fatal—strike on the city he had previously crippled. Now, I have a new "scariest sight": a 16-year-old girl, cell phone in hand, sitting behind the steering wheel of an automobile! Last year one of my female students returned to class after a bout in the hospital; she told me about flying 90 miles per hour down the freeway at one o'clock in the morning, while talking to her boyfriend on her cell phone. Not surprisingly, she crashed, causing great consternation to her boyfriend, who had heard the whole thing on *his* cell phone. She related to me the "horrors" of that moment with the nonchalance of talking about dropping a pan of chocolate chip cookies on the kitchen floor.

The frightening truth: Teens are four times more likely to be distracted while driving...and 16-year-olds have a crash rate almost 10 times higher than 30-year-olds.[3] Teens, cell phones, and driving don't mix.

Kids Use Their Phones to Cheat

Rather easily, actually. Text messages are the order of the day. Need an answer to Number Five on the test? Type the question to Sally, who is in her history class; she'll speed back an answer. Admittedly, most teachers don't—or can't—catch the cheaters. I have no idea about the number of students who have cheated by cell phone in my classes, and, to date, I have not *caught* even one of them. A shifty restlessness sifts through the air on test days, however.

Phones Go off in Classrooms

Have you ever sat near someone whose cell phone went off in a movie theater? Most people find this obnoxious. And at school it's worse than obnoxious. Teachers have to police this to the nth degree, which adds more burdens to already overburdened teachers. Recently, the phone sounded under the desk of one of my best students. My policy—when this happens—is to take my students' phones away from them; they can pick them up from the security office at the end of the year. This time, however, I said to the kid, "Bill, I won't take away your phone if you tell me one thing."

He looked at me as though he had been handed a last-minute reprieve from the gas chamber. "Sure. What?"

"Just tell me who's stupid enough to call you while you're in class."

"*What?*"

"Yeah."

"Why are they *stupid?*" he asked, annoyed.

"Because they know you're in class, and they called you anyway." I said softly.

"Maybe they *don't* know," he responded defiantly.

Sighing, I held out my hand. "Just give me the phone, Bill."

"Okay! Okay!" he snapped, quickly checking his phone to find the information I had just requested.

"Who was it?"

Sheepishly, he answered, "It was my mother."

The class roared with laughter.

"Your mother doesn't know you're in school?" I smiled.

"She knows, but I forgot to turn my phone off. She leaves me at least one message a day on the voice mail."

"Awwwwwwww...!" said the class.

"That's nice," I added.

"She says, 'I love you, Bill,' and stuff like that."

Again: "Awwwwwwww...!"

I grinned and turned away, announcing, "Normally, I would take his phone and give it to security, but Bill's honesty is way too cute for punitive measures."

A boy, who could not have known what *punitive* meant, piped up, "Does this mean that I can turn my phone on and you'll give me a freebie when it goes off?"

I quipped back, "Nope. Doesn't mean that at all, Josh. For you, it means a short walk to the office on the last day of school to get your phone back."

My inequitable distribution of justice both amused and angered my students. But I didn't care. Point made. Keep them off. They're annoying. Sometimes nice kids like Bill get special dispensations, but for most of my students the letter of the law prevails.

Cell Phones Distract

A boy in my Sunday school class, during my stirring lecture about God and the Holocaust, had been fixating on his cell phone; finally, I had to interrupt him: "Gary, *what are you looking at?*"

He snapped his head up. "Huh?"

"What are you…?"

"Nothin.' The time. I'm just watchin' the time."

"Must be fascinating."

"Huh?"

"Me, Gary. My wisdom about God and the Holocaust. Obviously, you're riveted."

I'd embarrassed him enough. But sometimes I wonder what happened to just glancing at a watch for the time, or studying the second hand on the clock on the wall, as it painstakingly moves around the dial. Ah, for the love of the good ol' days!

One girl in my fifth-period class filled me in: "Mr. G., kids have a way of hiding their phones in class, playing games on them, and text messaging. One guy in here yesterday during our discussion of *The Catcher in the Rye* told me that he played out nine rounds of Wild Woody."

Now one might argue that a veteran teacher should be able to pick out a boy playing Wild Woody—whatever that is—and nip any potential problems in the bud. But the reverse is true. The younger, technologically savvy teachers are much better suited to busting the cell phone criminals in their classrooms; they are more tuned in to their devious little maneuvers. I, however, hide woefully in the illusion that my classes are so interesting, so inspirational, these kids would never stoop to playing games, going on the Internet, or text messaging during *my* classes.

I know; I'm in denial. And I've never been to Egypt! (Get it?)

Teens Commit Cellular Subterfuge

Cell phones have cameras! They're tiny, but they work. They also have audio and video recording devices. This might vary from state to state, but in California it's unlawful for a student to record—video or audio—in a public school without an instructor's permission. Lawsuits have been filed over this. In a local district many years ago, one student with a video camera caught another in the corner of the woodshop tokin' on a joint (smoking marijuana); the guy's parents sued the amateur photographer—and won!

As YouTube has gotten so popular, unsuspecting teachers have become particularly susceptible to unwelcome celebrity status on the Internet. A few clicks on YouTube and you see teachers ranting and raving, sleeping in their classrooms, or flirting with students. Before you think this is a good thing because it provides a check on unprofessional teacher conduct, consider how modern technology has given us license to edit, splice, and otherwise manipulate these audio and video-tapes so they may be heard or shown out of context. Innocent people are drawn into scandal, and lives go up in smoke. None of this would be prevalent without the advent of a tiny device, one that can be held in the palm of a small hand, concealed from the view of the intended victims of video or photographic gossip.

Last year I confiscated a cell phone from a student who let it ring twice during a single week in my classroom; unfortunately, after I stuck the phone into my coat pocket, I forgot about it and carried it home. Immediately upon returning to school the next morning, I took the phone to the security office, but no one was there; I then inserted the phone back into my pocket and brought it to class with me. At the end of first period, I received a call from one of the assistant principal's secretaries; the conversation went something like this:

Secretary: Mr. Gevirtzman, a Mrs. Smith called yesterday afternoon and asked about her son's cell phone.

Me: Oh, yeah.

Secretary: She wanted to come here and pick it up.

Me: I thought the policy was to have the parent pick up the phone at the end of the school year. It's only February.

Secretary: The policy changed.

Me: Really? Were we informed? The teachers?

Secretary: I don't know. Anyway, Mr. Gevirtzman, Mrs. Smith was irate; she wants the phone.

Me: What? She had no other phones in her house?

Secretary: Do you have her son's phone?

Me: Yes, I do. I tried to turn it in to the security office this morning; nobody was there.

Secretary: Will you bring it here now—to our office?

Me:	I have a class.
Secretary:	We'll send security to get it. As I said, Mrs. Smith is—
Me:	May I speak with Mrs. Smith?
Secretary:	I guess. Do you wish to make an appointment with her?
Me:	Please. Can you set something up for tomorrow morning at 9:00?
Secretary:	What if she can't make it then?
Me:	Well, we won't give her the phone.
Secretary:	What?
Me:	Don't give her the cell phone, unless she meets with me first. It would be the right thing to do.

I knew that she wanted to remind me that the *right* thing would have been not to take her son's cell phone home with me in the first place; all of this would have been avoided. But that was water over the dam—or whatever. I now desperately wanted to meet with a parent who would get angry with a teacher for taking a disruptive cell phone away from her precious little child. Already seeing a book in my future, I knew she would be quotable.

I was right.

Although the administrative staff had wimped out and returned her son's cell phone the afternoon before our meeting, Mrs. Smith met with me as scheduled.

Her first comment after the preliminary niceties took me off guard: "Did you use the phone to make any calls?"

"No," I stammered, "I didn't think it was the proper thing to do in this case."

Which, of course, was an awful answer, since it suggested that in *another* case, taking a student's cell phone home and making phone calls would have been the proper thing to do. Knowing that my response stank, I added, "Except for the three calls that I made to London, and—oh, yeah—the one to Paris."

My smile faded, when she changed topics, completely ignoring my feeble— *pathetic*, actually—attempt at humor. "You had no right to take the phone home. It's like stealing his property."

"Yeah, well, more like borrowing it without his permission and then not using it," I retorted—sinking, sinking. "Mrs. Smith, I do apologize for accidentally taking the phone home. But as of now, your son hasn't apologized to me for letting it go off in class."

"Big deal," she snickered.

And then I let her words sink in, repeating them several times in my mind: *big deal*. To her, it was no big deal; phones probably go off around her all the time.

But her inability to distinguish between phones ringing in the mall and those ringing during a teacher's lecture in a high school classroom baffled me.

Big deal?

And for one of only three times in my entire teaching career, I lost my temper with a parent.

"It *is* a big deal!" I snapped. "Ever since we began allowing those friggin' (I'm not sure; I may have used worse than *friggin'*) devices on campus, there's been nothing but headaches! He knew the rule! He knew the consequences!"

"Was one of the consequences that you would steal his phone?"

"I didn't steal his goddam phone!" I yelled at her.

Very unprofessional.

I roared nonstop. "I stuck it in my pocket and accidentally left with it. I never used it and came right back to school and went to the office and it was closed but I finally got it there and now you have it!"

A red-in-the-face Mr. G. frightens people.

What infuriates me: without official, institutionalized permission to bring cell phones to school, there never would have been that unpleasant confrontation; there never would have been that explosion of classless demeanor, leading me to remorse and reflection.

Yeah, I'm an idiot for leaving the premises with a student's cell phone. But his mother is wrong for allowing a phone to interrupt my class. And the school is cowardly for instituting a policy that appears to be toothless around assertive parents.

THE INTERNET: MYSPACE ISN'T JUST "MY SPACE"

The potential devastation revolving around children and the Internet has already been well documented. Everybody knows of the hazards involved in underage kids visiting sites like MySpace and FaceBook.

A few years ago, a quiet girl sat in my honors English class. Cal had dark Asian features, with a too-infrequent radiant smile. Cal usually waited to be called upon, saying very little in class; she came to school every day and always completed her homework assignments.

And then she disappeared.

Cal's absence came during our annual spelling bee; she spelled words better than most of her classmates, and her participation in the bee had been greatly anticipated. The competition went on as scheduled, and then another student casually told me that Cal had fled to the Philippines with her 34-year-old boyfriend, a man she had met on the Internet.

"Did she know that he was 34?" I asked the student wide-eyed.

"She knew he was older," my student replied.

"Older," I scoffed, "is about 17 or 18. Not *34!*"

Cal could never have met a pedophile and run off to Southeast Asia, if not for unsupervised use of the Internet.

I'm reminded of the doctor who asked his patient, "When does it hurt?"

"It hurts when I touch my shinbone with my finger," the patient replied, showing the doctor that applying a finger of pressure on his shinbone sent streaks of pain up and down his entire leg.

"I know how to solve the problem," the doctor winked.

"How?"

"Just stop touching your shinbone with your finger," the doctor smiled, imitating the finger probe that instigated the intense discomfort.

Then he left to his harried schedule.

The serious nature of child abductions and kidnappings cannot be underrated; yet, we *permit* our children to engage in behaviors and activities that tempt them into the darkest corners of their souls—caverns they would not have entered if not for a new technology that allows them to go there.

Just stop touching your shinbone with your finger.

Personally, I don't get the whole Internet thing.

Sixteen-year-old girls typing away in chat rooms, posting on message boards, or lifting their shirts on MySpace are tragedies waiting to happen. When I discuss with my students these high-risk behaviors, their answers echo: "It won't happen to me. I'm careful."

Cal later returned to the United States and went to a continuation school to make up her lost credits. As far as what happened to her in the Philippines, no one is talking about it.

Most schools now require parental permission for children to go on the Internet. At our school, the kids have a special sticker pasted to their ID cards, allowing them to surf the Web; in addition to this precaution, our district has established a system that obstructs more Web sites than those it allows the kids to view. Even teachers—and it's sometimes frustrating—must face the mortification of typing a forbidden word on a Google search engine, only to be informed that the site has been blocked.

Educators also worry about a new form of cheating, via the Internet. But just as the Internet accommodates teens who have the desire to cheat while writing papers or doing research, the Net also offers several vehicles for *catching* cheaters.

Last year, I assigned a short research paper. Students had to take a position on a topic and then come up with several sources to support that position. While I graded student work, my antennae were up, as I scoured the papers for plagiarists. One sure sign of plagiarism is a paper that lacks the familiar voice of a particular student: After several months, we teachers get to know our students well, familiarizing ourselves with their styles of writing and basic skills levels. One paper I read encompassed some rather sophisticated ideas for reforming the welfare system, its cogent analysis quite persuasive, incorporating an enormous amount of research from expert sources. The girl who wrote the paper had pulled a paltry C grade in my class for the three previous grading periods, and this re-search document was clearly out of her league. Before the advent of the Internet, however, there had been little recourse; I would have mumbled something to the student about how suspicious I was, only making the kid dislike me even more. Now, however, I used a rather primitive Internet method for finding out what I needed to know. I typed the first line of the paper into a search engine ("The alleged abuses of the state welfare system are embodied in the fallacies inherent in the program Aid to Families with Dependent Children..."): Bingo! Not only did that *exact line* come up, so did a whole paper, almost identical to that turned in by my student!

My subsequent encounter with the student further exposed her character: After I had requested that she speak with me, Sasha meandered over to my desk. I held the suspect paper in front of me with one hand, waving it, as I spoke. "Good paper, Sasha."

Busted!

Her upper lip quivered. "What's the matter with it?"

"Well," I continued with my lowbrow sarcasm, "there's nothing wrong with the paper per se; as I said, *good paper.* Too bad you didn't write it."

"I wrote it!" she blurted defensively.

"Sasha, I didn't mean, like, by *typing* it on your computer. Or did you even do *that* much?"

Her shoulders sagged. "Okay, I did have some help."

"What kind of help?"

"My brother helped me a little."

"By letting you use his paper and call it your own?"

"No!"

"Then—what?"

Sasha would have rather been anywhere in the universe than here. She said, "I copied some of it, and he helped me write some more of it."

"Where did your brother get the paper from?" I asked, setting up for the kill.

She frowned, seemingly dismayed at the direction I was now taking. "He wrote it; at least, I think he wrote it."

"Well, Sasha, what would you say if I told you I typed the very first line of your paper into Google, and, lo! There was your entire paper—verbatim! What would you say about that?"

I almost felt sorry for her and was about to offer some leniency.

Until she *had* to say, "Big deal, Mr. G.! Everybody does it now! Everybody copies stuff. You can even buy whatever you want right off of those Web sites that sell 'em cheap. Well, not cheap, because sometimes it costs..."

But I let her words fade into the recesses of my brain, as I mulled over two important points of refutation to her defense: first, not *everybody* does it. Most of my students—maybe all the rest of them—struggled to plow through this assignment; and, second, even if she were right—and *everybody* does it—it's *still* a big deal. Cheating is always a big deal, because when you cheat to *win,* someone else *loses* unjustly. That someone else is not always a teacher or a person who can afford to take the ill blow of the cheater. A teenager cheats for a better grade; another teenager does not get into college or rank as high in the valedictorian competition as the kid who cheated. And who would like to graduate from a high school that has a known reputation for having more cheaters than any other school in the state—or has enough cheaters to soil the school's reputation in the college admissions process?

Fortunately, since the cheating incident happened in my class, other vehicles on the Internet have become available to teachers to help them in nailing cheaters. Some teachers require students to write all their papers on the computer and then send them online verification programs, checking that their work doesn't exist anywhere else in cyberspace. Other official Internet programs can now validate research sources, the authenticity of other writers' contributions to the students' papers, and the accuracy of the paper's information.

I still adhere to the old-fashioned method of typing a line or two into the search engine and waiting to see what comes up. In a rather macabre, sadistic way, it's fun to catch somebody so lazy that even *my* antiquated methods can nail her.

The technology of the Internet is useful. But it's also deadly.

It's not that the technology itself is inherently evil; the *use* of technology can lay the foundation for good or evil. It's like money: money itself is neither good nor bad. The manner in which money is *used* can be good or bad. When I hear the idiom, "Money is the root of all evil," I cringe; it's absolutely not true. And the same goes for technology. By itself the atomic bomb is inert; it just sits there. If a terrorist gets hold of a bomb and annihilates Chicago, it's evil. When President Truman ordered a bomb to blow up Hiroshima, it *wasn't* evil; it saved hundreds of thousands—maybe *millions*—of lives.

MR. G.'S HOME-GROWN ADVICE

To prevent the horrors of teenagers abusing new technology, I have three pieces of significant advice for each of the three groups: parents, teachers, and teenagers.

Parents

Once again, you have the ultimate responsibility.

1. Teach your kids appropriate uses for the computer. Set restrictions and boundaries and *enforce* them. Use the programs that block children— even teenagers—from places they are most likely to find trouble (like those porno pages you and your spouse visit on Saturday nights).

2. Establish suitable guidelines for using cell phones, iPods, and the like: for example, no iPods may be worn when your kids are around actual human beings. No cell phones may be used, except for real emergencies or to *receive* calls—and only when they're from *you*.

3. If your kids have their own computers, *locate them right next to yours*. If this needs any explanation, you need to reread the section about the Internet in this chapter.

Teachers

For us, technology challenges have become more daunting than ever. But keep in mind that teenagers value structure; and when expectations are clear to them, they usually rise to the occasion.

1. Be tough: No iPods in your classroom—period. Those that are visible— on or off, before class or after class—will be confiscated. Cell phones are to remain invisible; those that go off during class will be confiscated. And then enforce those two rules! At first, you will feel like an ogre, but eventually, it'll be fun. The best thing: you won't see any more iPods or cell phones in your classrooms.

2. Teach your students the benefits *and* harms of modern technology. It's called *costs versus gains* analysis. Your most astute students will understand you.

3. Monitor the computers in your classroom. Make sure parental permission has been given for use of the Internet. Teach proper use of the Internet for research and for some really cool sites—like those that broadcast Major League Baseball games from 40 years ago!

Teenagers

It's your call:

1. Be one of the few kids who doesn't leave the house with an iPod, Black-Berry, or miniature video game device. Be one of the few kids who

doesn't carry a cell phone around everywhere—or has it turned off, but ready for sudden crises. A female student told me that on a date with her former boyfriend, he answered three calls from friends on his cell phone! After that, she dumped him. Some students in my classes related scenarios in which guys called friends—or took calls from friends—on their cell phones for the purpose of reporting their *progress* while on a first date with a girl! I shook my head and told the classes, "Pretty jerky. And if she put up with it, she's pathetic." My students agreed. If you have an iPod, don't wear it when you're with friends. Don't let technology reach its potential for breaking down the codes of manners and common courtesies that still protect society. Teenagers should not have to live by a different set of rules from the rest of us: Rude is still rude.

2. Limit your hours. Decide how much of your time is *really* worth talking on the phone, playing video games, messing around on the Internet, watching TV, and listening to music. Just how valuable is your time? For that matter what is your *life* worth? Make a reasonable schedule for yourself, cutting down on your technological brain barbecue. Limit yourself to a healthy number of hours per week—and then *abide by that*.

3. Surf the Web oh-so-wisely. Do you have to be reminded of the ghastly crimes that have been perpetrated on some young people who had messed around on the Internet? Do you have to be told that the 15-year-old cheerleader who agreed to rendezvous in the mall parking lot could be a 44-year-old balding pedophile with mats of hair covering his back? Of course, you already knew those things! Protect yourself accordingly. Also, giving away personal information in chat rooms or on posting boards—or taking off your shirt or pants in front of a video camera for MySpace—doesn't exactly present you to the world in the most sophisticated, dignified manner. You are *asking* to attract a person who yearns to nab someone in real life even more undignified and unsophisticated than he is.

Teenagers have always been bombarded with problems associated with change and progress. Yes, these troubles have intensified, but teens today really do have the power and wherewithal to cope. Lots of healthy, helpful ideas about technology have recently surfaced. Equipped with these ideas, kids and their parents can survive the modern era together, *using these recent advances to their benefit*: the advantages of technology in the micro world—microcosmically analogous to the benefits of unleashing an atomic bomb on Hiroshima.

15

Good and Plenty

MISS BIKINI BABE'S INADVERTENT LESSON

It must be nice to teach the *good* kids.

Throughout the years I've taught high school, the following oft-heard comment about my own teaching situation has miffed me more than any other: "What's it like to have the good kids all day long?"

Here's why this seemingly innocuous remark has bothered me so much: Just because a student was taking all advanced placement and honors courses, it didn't necessarily equate to her being a "good" kid. I have discovered that some of the creepiest kids I've taught over the years have been in some of my honors courses; conversely, some of the sweetest have been among the dumbest kids in the whole school. Simply, there are no interrelationships between intelligence, high grades, and goodness. There is, of course, a statistical correlation between high grades and successes later in life, but those successes do not guarantee *goodness* either.

Gerald and Jack were twins. They worked hard in school, tutored elementary school children in their afternoons, and helped their mother take care of her dying father, which meant leaving their beds in shifts throughout the night to make sure that their grandfather was comfortable. Gerald and Jack had been diagnosed with retardation disorders that certainly qualified as official learning disabilities. They barely made it through high school (this was before the designation *special education*) and graduated with grades that made their going to college about as probable as their diminutive stature made probable their playing basketball in the NBA; however, I would have trusted Gerald and Jack with my life. Nobody was kinder, sweeter, and more altruistic than Gerald and Jack.

Saul often arrived late to my zero period class. His eyes were dulled from sleep deprivation, and he could barely hold his head up. I never knew the reason for Saul's lack of sleep (and from the smell of things, lack of proper body hygiene, too), but at the time, I didn't care. I suspected late-night—sometimes all night—video game playing. But *then* the bottom line for me was that Saul had pulled an A in my class, one of only two students who had attained such a feat. Saul came from an Asian American family that mandated academic success, and he lived up to their demands. He eventually graduated, but I'd forgotten about him, until I heard from a school counselor that Saul languished in prison.

Saul had not been playing video games all night; he was actively involved in an Asian gang that, like other gangs, had as its core purpose hurting people. Saul inherited that dubious distinction, too. And despite his native intelligence and motivation for his studies, Saul was also a gangbanging criminal.

One of our most celebrated, deified American authors was Ezra Pound. Pound was tried for treason after trying to sell out America with his cohort, Benito Mussolini (who was not trying to sell out America; he merely wanted to destroy it along with *his* buddy Adolph Hitler). Pound eventually wound up in a hospital for the criminally insane; however, he was freed after some of his friends in the literary world (such as Robert Frost) pled a case on Pound's behalf: Pound, after all, could not be evil. He was an artist! A writer! These *benevolent* authors won their argument in front of a judge who, likewise, believed being a talented writer mitigated Pound's tendency to be a creep.

Bad kids can be smart; good kids can be dumb. They are not mutually exclusive, but it's the case more often than most people think.

One evening in August 1988, I had the luxury of being in what was then my favorite spot in the entire universe: basking in the Jacuzzi at the (now demolished) Stardust Hotel in Las Vegas, Nevada. At the time, I was not married; I wasn't even dating anyone in particular, playing the role of a lone, single dude—a stud—on the prey, on the loose, scammin' the chicks in the Sin Capital of the World!

Just when I was thinking, now, what could be better than this?—it got even better: the goddess of my life (well, at least until I met my wife and realized *she* is the real goddess of my life), clad in what might have been a tan bikini (I'm still fuzzy about the details, of course), stepped into the Jacuzzi and parked her 20-something body directly across from my 30-something body (and admittedly, my 30-something body did not compare to her 20-something body when it came to its, well, allure). Despite this, she became flirtatious, friendlier than I had the right to hope.

My memory comes up short in its recollection of the beginning of this conversation. What I do remember about the rest of our talk, however, is still quite fresh; I have been accused of having a selective memory, and this may be one terrific example of its selectivity.

Finally, on one of these solo Vegas trips, I would focus on something more important than "Should I double down on a nine against a dealer's seven?"

The potential for winning the lottery in the—albeit probably brief—romance department suddenly struck me as being quite substantial.

For a guy this is a *very* big deal.

"And, so," she asked casually, bracing her back against the wall of the Jacuzzi, exposing a sizeable portion of her (gulp!) breasts, "what do you do?"

Panic enveloped me. "Huh?" I stammered.

"What kind of work are you in?" she smiled demurely.

Now I knew I was toast. Women like this did not date high school English teachers, especially ones who also coached the nerdy debate team. Women like this dated Guido, the silver-haired, slick-lookin' guy who played three circles simultaneously at the blackjack table, stacking $15,000 in chips in each of those circles. Girls like this patted Guido on the arm every time he shoved another mountain of those chips into the circle to replace the one that had just been sucked up by an apathetic dealer.

But here I was: *stuck.* "I'm, uh, a, uh, tea...cher."

My usually booming voice suddenly became inaudible; the word *teacher* came out in five syllables.

Naturally, she had me repeat it! "*What?*" she leaned toward me, clearly already having lost some interest.

I quickly sucked in my breath and hoped my sudden burst of energy and feigned pride would fool her. "A teacher!" I said, forcing a smile. "I teach high school English!"

What does Miss Bikini Babe say *now?*

I waited; believe me, I was tempted to fill the void in our discourse with "Only kidding! Come on! Do I look like a—a—teacher?"

But I didn't get the chance.

She asked pleasantly, as though she were still interested, "Oh. You teach English? You look like a gym teacher."

To which I sank below the surface of the water, disappearing for about 10 seconds, hoping to drown before her very eyes.

When I realized she still wanted to speak with me, I half-joked, "People have said all kinds of terrible things to me in my life. But a *gym teacher!* Humph!"

And then she waxed serious. "How do you do it?" she asked, her voice trailing off into a tenor of sympathy that I didn't like. I had to be her hero, not her victim, the man that she wanted to cuddle—not fix.

Well, on second thought . . .

"How do I do—*what?*"

"How do you put up with those fucking losers all day?"

Whoa! I assumed she referred to the teenagers—not the adult teaching staff that I worked with, but her sudden change in tone rubbed me the wrong way;

plus, her condescending profanity seemed to come from nowhere, stunning my equilibrium.

If I could have stopped *looking* at her, I might have been able to muster enough courage to stand up to her; after all, these were *my* teenagers that she called, uh, "fucking losers"! And no one—but *no* one—refers to my losers as *fucking* losers!

What's more, they were *not* losers; at least, the vast majority of them were not losers. Most of them—even the ones I wound up failing at the end of the term—were decent kids: sometimes charming, often amusing, and always needy. All kids are needy. And those who *were* losers turned out that way usually because of *adults*.

I am so embarrassed to admit this next part; in fact, as I write this, I'm thinking of omitting it entirely during the editing process. However, male that I was—and still am to a certain extent (that extent determined more by my advancing age than anything else)—I still desired to make her acquaintance something a little more, er, significant during my brief vacation in Las Vegas. Any glimmer of hope to meet this modest goal would be established in the next few moments.

I could not completely ignore her comment about my "fucking losers," so I tried to temper her remark, while putting her in her place. My verbal come-back shined with brilliance: "I, uh, well, I just gotta put up with 'em, I guess," I muttered.

"Oh."

"So, you—would you like to have a drink later? In the bar? Or, I guess . . . Yeah. I guess it would have to be in the bar."

My wimpy come-on did not exactly remind her of James Bond.

She turned a little red. Was she angry, or embarrassed for me? You know: the guy who must find ways to put up with "fucking losers" every day. "Actually," she answered slowly, groping for words, "I have to—I'm leaving town tonight; I'm going to the airport. I'm flying back to Chicago."

"Tonight?"

"Yes," she forced a grin. "But it was nice meeting you."

I never hated my profession as much as I did the moment I saw her wet hand extend in my direction for the formal good-bye handshake. Everything about my job, not to mention the kids, reeked of second-class citizenry—at least second-class *guy-ary*. Being a teacher of mutants did not qualify me for her social circles, especially those during our mutual vacations in Nevada.

But here's the upshot: This whole episode made me wonder why I had been so bothered by her rude verbal attacks on my teenage students and—by extension—my profession. I mean, if only she could see these kids in my classroom: their raised brows at some of my most provocative assertions, their hearty laughter at some of my most awful puns. If only she could witness these kids at speech tournaments: their nervous, sweaty hands in their laps, as they sit in the auditorium waiting for the awards assembly to begin, many of them sick with worry about what to tell their parents if they don't come home with the first place trophy. If only she could watch these kids on the ball diamond, as they celebrate the winning run in their last at-bat, wildly bear-hugging each other's bodies to the ground. Even after a loss, emotions fill the field, usually with a palpable determination to fight off the demons of losing, in order to welcome the angels of winning (the next game).

And these kids are—in her shallow, ignorant, misinformed little mind—*fucking losers?*

THE GOOD, THE BAD, AND THE JOYCES

Teenagers may be divided into three categories (actually, 3,000 categories, but for this chapter, we'll make it three):

1. *The Misfits:* We don't want to confuse these kids with those who have been afflicted with the anti-Midas complex. The anti-Midas kids come with sound motives, good hearts, and decent attitudes; the Misfits are those who may lack all three of these character ingredients. They chronically immerse themselves in activities that are illegal, immoral, unhealthy, and unsafe. They never listen to reason, and their decisions are always incredibly selfish—practically sociopathic. They publicize themselves as being hell-bent on destruction, seemingly oblivious to right and wrong and indifferent to those who would try to help. This group dramatizes the notion of teenager rebellion at a toxic level. These kids are headed—or have already been—to prison, either physical incarceration or internment in their own souls.

2. *The Goodie Two Shoes:* Yes, they are a small group, but they stand out for that reason. Most of the other kids have ambivalent feelings about them: on the one hand, Goodie Two Shoes teens stand out because they seem to be so, well, *good;* on the other hand, a perennially good teenager is downright weird. Teenagers who strive to do the right thing all the time—and often succeed—fail to fit form. They speak well of their parents; they obey all the rules set down by their teachers—*all of them.* They never speak unkindly of anyone else—at least no ordinary person. They do, however, have ill will for those who are evil—part of a Goodie Two Shoes's charm. These teens send cards to people they hardly know for their birthdays. They call friends and acquaintances who are sick, just to cheer them up. They donate to charities and do walks for disease

prevention programs. They hardly ever raise their voices in anger and willingly mediate others' disputes. They don't laugh or direct insults at people who are less fortunate, and they sometimes chide others for doing so. They refuse to nag over the small stuff, but they implore for changes of behavior over the big stuff.

These kids are *perfect*.

And it's true. As close to perfection as one can get, these teenagers break the mold of the complexity that dwells throughout their alien kingdom. Hardly any *adults* come close to their levels of goodness, so sometimes it's the *children* who take on major responsibilities—whether they want to or not—as mentors and role models, often leaving their elders in bemusement.

3. *Everybody Else:* Venturing an estimate: around 90 percent or more of teens fall into this category. Who are these teenagers? They *sometimes* perform activities that are illegal, immoral, unhealthy, or unsafe. They *sometimes* refuse to listen to reason, and their decisions are often incredibly selfish. They *sometimes* seem hell-bent on destruction, seemingly oblivious to right and wrong and indifferent to those who would try to help them with their problems; however, more often than not, they come around, steadfast to the good advice—rather than the bad advice—they have been given all their lives. This group epitomizes teenager rebellion in its most benign forms, rarely to its most noxious intensity. These kids eventually grow into mature, responsible adults and often model citizens. Some of these teens—later as adults—advance to the upper echelons of American society, having left their most erratic years behind them. If ever the term *typical teenager* was appropriate, it would be the correct euphemism to describe these adolescents.

Despite the organizational tidiness in the purity of these three categories, many teenagers wallow in confusion over what they see as a lack of incentives to have good values: Paul's personality seemed to change overnight: Nothing like the wrath of a woman scorned—or something like that. But in this case, it was Paul who had been scorned too many times.

I don't get it. I'm a nice guy, so I like to let people know that. It seems like the better I treat a girl, the more she gets turned off to me....I bring my dates flowers. I always get them home on time. I never take advantage of them, even if they're willing....I don't call them names like lots of guys do....And I never kiss and tell. So, why can't I get girls to like me?

There must be something about me that turns off the girls. I talked to a girl I sorta liked for a while but didn't like me back—Carol—and you know what she told me? She said, "Paul, you're a really nice guy and all; maybe you're *too* nice." And I'm, like, *too nice*. . . . What does that mean? How can a person be *too nice*? Does it mean I let girls walk all over me and take advantage of me? Because I don't. I just treat girls the way girls should be treated, like my dad tells me girls should be—and want to be—treated: the way that my dad treats my mom. My dad loves my mom, and it really shows. He's polite to her and says "please" and "thank you" and stuff like that. He doesn't ever call her names or hit her or anything.

So, I'm constantly wondering what it means to be *too nice,* and I'm thinking maybe I should change all that. Because the way I'm treating girls now isn't doing me any good. So maybe what I gotta do is be a lot more assertive with girls. Hey, don't worry. I'm not at the point where I think it's all right to hit girls or anything. Not yet.

Eighteen years ago a young lady in one of my honors American Literature classes wore a special gleam in her eyes. Joyce always smiled, seemingly able to handle gracefully even the toughest duress. At the end of her junior year, she said the following to me:

"I'd like your permission to be your TA (teaching assistant) next year."

"Sure," I answered quickly, "that would be nice. You'll have a position in one of my 11th-grade honors classes."

Content with that philosophy, she smiled broadly. "I think I can handle that."

The next year Joyce became my TA in my honors American Literature class. She was always punctual, never absent, and rarely in a sour mood. Now in a position of greater authority, she embraced all of the virtues I have taught my students. Her altruistic behavior shone above all. When I had the sniffles, she offered me a tissue. When I coughed, she gave me a cough drop. If my voice rasped, she handed me a throat lozenge. Remarkably, she never asked for anything from me in return; Joyce performed her duties as my TA with the grace and generosity of a saint.

So I waited for the other shoe to fall.

But it never did. When Joyce graduated high school, I gave her some small gifts, and with tears in my eyes, said good-bye. At that moment she revealed to me, "The reason I wanted to TA for you is that I knew I couldn't take your class again; so being a TA for honors English was like watching one of my favorite movies for a second time. Thank you so much, Mr. G."

Joyce and I still maintain close contact with each other. She is now a high school English teacher herself. She is also a mother. All of her children are lucky to have her: teacher or mother. A genuinely good person, Joyce makes the world better every day of her existence.

There aren't too many teenagers like Joyce—heck, there aren't too many *human beings* like Joyce. When the Jacuzzi Bikini Babe had condemned *my* teenagers with such raunchy suddenness, I reeled with resentment. For one thing, I didn't like the abrupt change in the whirlpool's atmosphere; for another thing, she was dead wrong. Most teenagers, while not bordering on sainthood like Joyce, occasionally reveal their overall decency. But it's not until young adulthood that they contract graciousness and civility. Once we were *all* teenagers; it's kind of frightening to contemplate how adults viewed *us* during those confusing, unsettled years—isn't it?

Not quite one of the Joyces, yet—but working on it very hard—is Jimmy. Jimmy's dad epitomizes a certain type of American father that might be lampooned in a film satire about the plight of the modern American teenager, except no one would believe a man like this exists in the real world.

Jimmy spoke with me during a recent evacuation at our school. Workers had ruptured a natural gas line, prompting more than 2,000 of us to file into the football stadium. During those two hours, most teens frittered their time away; Jimmy, meanwhile, spilled his guts to me about his father, his upbringing, and his girlfriend.

He told me that his mother died when he was 10. She'd been addicted to drugs, and to support her habit, she frequently brought men home. Jimmy tearfully reflected, "I watched this happen night after night—a stream of men coming into my house—and I would cry myself to sleep. Most girls want to be a Daddy's Girl while they're growing up. But me, I wanted so much to be a Mamma's Boy. I wanted my mother to *pay attention to me*—just know that I existed. But she didn't—and I was so jealous!"

The one man she married—Jimmy's dad—eventually wound up having four children with four different women, but he married only two of them. He'd been a drill sergeant in the Marine Corps and took some of those tough guy strategies into his home.

With his head bowed, Jimmy told me, "My dad wonders why I haven't had sex yet. He screams, 'What's the matter with you! You some kinda faggot!' What am I supposed to say to that? I've got a girlfriend, and we were going to wait to have sex. But now she's suddenly decided that we should do it. The thing is, Mr. G., I'm not ready for sex! I never wanted to marry a woman who'd been used a bunch of times, so I don't want to contribute to that problem in society. And I'm a Christian; it's pretty clear what my religion says about sex before marriage. But my father, he...he lived a life that he now wants *me* to live—if I did some of the raunchy, thoughtless things that he's done, it'll somehow validate his past."

Jimmy's father isn't religious, and Jimmy may be right about his validation theory; nonetheless, Jimmy felt that his father measured his son's manliness by the frequency of his sexual conquests.

And by something else: Jimmy continued, "My father is demanding that I join the Marines after graduation; I want to go to a community college and get involved with law enforcement—maybe work with the juvenile parole board. But my father says that college is for faggots."

Currently (2008), Jimmy is a senior and works as a teaching assistant in one of my 11th-grade English classes. He's bright, bold, and—most important—he laughs at all my jokes. He explains his commitment to goodness this way: "A couple of years ago I was watching the news and heard about a little girl who'd been murdered by her mother's boyfriend. This really got to me, so I began to cry and threw a shoe at the mirror. Right then, my father walked into the room and beat me with his fists. He claimed that it was about the mirror, but I was crying for a little girl who lost her life to a monster *her own mother had brought into her house*—and didn't protect her from! My father has me in therapy for anger management, but I've never hurt *anybody*. My anger and pain are for the pain of others, Mr. G. My grandma [on my mother's side] taught me that love and kisses go a lot further than beatings and name-calling. But I'm for the death penalty for murderers, because it's pure justice in a world that lacks any kind of justice. I'm going to make the world a better place. I am. I really am."

Jimmy comes from the mold of a Joyce.

One last word to the wise: Sometimes it's the good kids who hurt the most, and we don't have even the slightest idea they are in such emotional pain; after all, the exterior of a human being is designed to hide the interior. One of the most popular pieces of literature that I have taught on this subject is a 19th-century poem by Edwin Arlington Robinson called "Richard Cory." My students go wild over this poem because they can relate to it. Their profound empathy for a man everyone admired—but who wound up killing himself—has always intrigued me.

Just how many Richard Corys *are* there?

So on we worked
And waited for the light
And went without the meat
And cursed the bread
And Richard Cory
One calm summer night
Went home
And put a bullet
Through his head.[1]

MR. G.'S HOME-GROWN ADVICE

For what should I offer advice here?

How to be good?

And what does that mean? Teenagers *are* good; if they weren't good, I wouldn't have been a high school teacher. If I didn't like hanging out with them, I wouldn't have coached baseball, directed theater, and sponsored the debate team. People generally don't volunteer to do more of the things they despise.

When my own two children become teenagers, I had better like *my* teenagers a whole lot more than I see most people liking their own teenage kids. Ranting, raving, condemning, and criticizing teens is not my style. True, I enjoy making fun of them, laughing at them, and goofing around with them, but I also *like* them. My positive feelings for teenagers—especially the "good kids"—govern my decision making concerning them.

So here's what it takes to be *good*.

1. Don't do bad stuff; stay out of trouble. Self-control is the key. In today's society, people think if you aren't bad, you're good. So *stop being bad!* Street racing, driving drunk, skipping school, and plastering graffiti throughout the neighborhood are all terrible choices.

2. Treat others thus: "After I am dead, how do I wish to be remembered?" For many, contemplating this is truly frightening—but motivating.

3. Be fair; this means, in all aspects of your life, strive for justice. Root for bad things to happen to bad people, and for good things to happen to good people. And help to make it happen.

4. You don't have to express an opinion about *everything*. Unless you're sure you're right—and unless *something good* can come from your opinion—keep it to yourself.

5. Work on your prejudices; don't allow them to become behaviors. If you hate all those (name the group), keep it to yourself and *don't act upon it.*

6. Respect members of the opposite sex. Boys: Put girls on a pedestal; men protect women, not use them. Girls: Don't tempt boys; women tame men, not tease them.

7. Know that something or someone is bigger than you are, more important than you are. For many, God fills this role. Even if you don't subscribe to God, look to a higher authority than you for comfort, advice, and—rules.

8. Don't love everybody and don't respect everybody. Decide who has earned your love and respect. Not all people *deserve* love and respect. Charles

Manson didn't; neither did the guy who walked into Virginia Tech and slaughtered 32 innocent students and teachers. *Judge!* If you love everyone—*even evil people*—your love will mean a heck of a lot less to those you *truly* value.

9. Have manners. Nothing shouts "polite person" like "please, thank you, and excuse me." And if you're not sure, learn all the other proper words, phrases, gestures, and body language that promote courtesy.

10. Don't pass gas in public. Even some of the silent ones are deadly.

It always cracks me up when someone says something like "Even though I tortured the dog, crashed the car, cheated on my wife, stole the money, raped the woman, attended a Los Angeles Clippers basketball game, I'm still a really good person." Really? What, then, *disqualifies* someone from being a good person? Even Hitler fed his dog; too bad he also had a few "minor" faults. Teenagers should think of themselves as adults who are wearing the training wheels of life. Occasionally, you will make a bad decision—but unless it's a terrible, terrible decision, you will recover. You can ask other people for forgiveness and make restitution for what you have done wrong; everyone does wrong sometimes. But in the total scheme of things, some people are just *better* than others because they *behave* better. They carry themselves with more grace, they bestow themselves with more dignity, and they portray themselves with more pride. Striving to do better does not mean you're a perfectionist; no one is perfect. But it shouldn't keep you from trying to be more like the Joyces.

Finally, a few words from a good boy; he's 17, and his name is Jack:

I'm not special or, like, a big shot or anything. . . . I guess my secret is that I keep my mouth shut a lot, even though I speak up when I have to. . . . I go to church, love my parents, and take the trash cans outside on Mondays. . . . I'm a practicing Christian, but I'm tolerant of other points of view. I hate rude, obnoxious people, and I stand up to them when it's necessary. I try to do what's right all the time, even though lots of times I fail. I guess the key for me has been the love and protection of my parents. They give their whole lives to me and are always there when I need them. . . . They teach me how to be good; they model it all the time. My parents: I wouldn't be the person I am now, if not for them.

16

You *Vil* Go to Ha'vid!

YES, STEREOTYPING UP THE—WHATEVER!

At the first sight of a baby emerging from her mother's womb, several frantic events occur: The mother strains to bend forward, catching a glimpse of her tiny miracle; the father's hands shake like those of a nervous piano player, as he awkwardly cuts the umbilical cord, an act he has played out in his mind at least 5,000 times. Doctors and nurses scurry to and fro with all kinds of pans, scoops, and other scary-looking devices. And at the touted moment of birth, the doctor slaps the baby on her rear, causing her to cry, reassuring everybody that all is right with the newborn, that all is right with the world.

Now picture this scene: A Jewish child is lifted from her mother's womb. Her mother leans forward, hoping to catch a glimpse of her new daughter, but her father does *not* strain to sever the cord of life that joins mother and child. Nurses and doctors carry pans, scoops, and other devices, but all eyes are on the father. As the doctor slaps the newbie on her behind, the father shouts—sounding like Tevia from *Fiddler on the Roof*—"You *vil* go to Ha'vid!" A nurse immediately thrusts the latest *Sesame Street ABC Book* in the direction of the mother, so her new daughter can begin studying for her SATs, while she is being cleaned and tested postdelivery.

Typical (with only *some* hyperbolic stereotype) for the delivery room at the birth of a Jewish baby.

Or Asian.

Asian parents are similarly obsessed when it comes to the formal education of their children.

The United States of America faces a crisis in education today. Much of the problem has to do with the all-or-nothing approach by cultures, families, and religions that feeds into the whole education process. The sensible middle ground has been lost, decimated by parents who will stop at nothing to make sure their child is admitted into a superior...*kindergarten?* And by parents who have absolutely no clue about what their children are studying, what kinds of grades they are earning, or even if their children have been *attending* school! The stereotypes: In some cultures, education is of foremost importance. Kids who don't finish high school disgrace the family; children who don't go to college are thrown out of the house. In some other cultures, making minimal amounts of money in order to help pay the family's bills serves as a motive *not* to attend school. Some children don't attend classes because they are required by family to babysit younger siblings; other times, frankly, parents don't really care if their kids go to school or not.

Quon joined competitive debate in high school for one reason: release from colossal amounts of daily tension. Quon's parents pressured him to have not just excellent grades, but the *best* grades of anyone in his high school graduating class! In the late seventies, getting into a good college was infinitely easier than it is today; however, that did not stop Quon's parents from applying unnecessary pressure on Quon.

"My mother went to the kindergarten teacher the very first day of class and asked her if she planned on teaching us our multiplication tables," Quon reflected much later. "When she said no, my mother immediately pulled me out of school and put me in a Catholic school. And she was *mad*. Which was really weird, because the Catholic school didn't teach any math skills other than counting to a hundred. And it wouldn't have mattered anyway, because I already knew my multiplication tables. My parents taught them to me the summer before I got to kindergarten."

Quon told me his depression started in the fourth grade, when he failed to win a spelling bee! His mother had called the principal before the contest and asked if she could have a list of potential spelling words; of course, the fourth-grade teachers adamantly refused to cough up a list. "My mother thought my edge had been compromised," Quon remembered. "She figured the way for me to succeed was to have an edge: that meant working harder than anyone else or taking the initiative to ask the teachers for special favors. She was really ticked off when I lost, but it lifted a heavy weight off me. Since I didn't have the list, we could blame the teachers and principal for my losing the spelling bee. My mother was madder at them than she was at me."

How much did Quon's Chinese ancestry figure into the academic pressures that he felt?

"Almost entirely," he answered quickly. "You look at Asian families in America and all you see is motoring for financial success. You're going to college; that's a given. But the real question is, what will it take for you to get there."

A national poll asked parents this question: "Would you approve of your child's cheating—without getting caught—if it meant getting into the college of her dreams?"

No, I would not approve (38%)

Yes, I would approve (40%)

Don't know (22%)[1]

One way of looking at these numbers is to shrug and say, "Well, only about a third would approve. That's not too bad, given the academic climate in America and the state of morality today." Another way to look at these numbers is to shriek, "Oh, my! Almost two-thirds of the parents (62%) would not disapprove of their child's blatant academic corruption in order to get ahead!"

One of my so-called driven students condoned the concept of cheating for the purpose of getting into a college of his dreams. He flippantly commented, "Kids get into college for all kinds of quirky reasons—and they get rejected for weird reasons. In this case who gets hurt?"

His shortsighted analysis failed to recognize that someone *does* get hurt: Someone will *not* get into college who should have, because of the cheater. The cheater gets in; the student who played by the rules does not.

Quon's father showed up unexpectedly one Saturday afternoon in the middle of a speech tournament on another high school campus (not far from our own). I had never met his father before; his mother, however, had become the laughing-stock of our school—and the subject of daily gossip around our speech squad. She sometimes came to school during lunches with Quon's specially prepared meals (really weird stuff, like peanut butter sandwiches with celery sticks tucked inside the decrusted bread slices). Later Quon admitted how embarrassed he'd been when friends and other classmates chided him, not only for the odd array of lunches that his mother brought him, but for the ridiculously frequent appearances of his mother on our campus: to visit Quon, to challenge a teacher, to complain to the principal.

So it was that Saturday afternoon that we all welcomed Quon's father to the host campus of the local speech tournament—especially since we'd been so used to seeing Quon's mother—and we were additionally pleased to notice he'd brought with him boxes of pizzas, as many as his arms could carry. What luck that Quon's father had decided to join us! What a gracious gesture: bringing pizzas for the entire speech team! Eating pizzas would be a pleasant way of waiting for elimination rounds announcements.

Quon, too, sat nervously, eager to discover if he would be included in the quarterfinal debate pairings. Only the eight debaters with the best records (out of

50 debaters) after six debates would advance to the next level; shattered nerves usually flooded the atmosphere.

I asked Quon's father if he wanted to judge a debate round or two. Parents often contributed their time to judging, giving them a bird's-eye view of competitive speech.

No, Quon's father did not wish to judge.

Would he like to watch a round without the responsibility of casting a judge's ballot?

Nope. He didn't wish to do that either.

If Quon made the first elimination round, did he intend to watch Quon compete?

A panicky shaking of Quon's head behind his father relayed what Quon thought about such an idea. But not to worry: Quon's father had no intention of watching him debate in the quarterfinals.

Had Quon's dad simply shown up with lots of pizzas and decided to sit there with a lost, goofy grin on his face?

Time would tell the story.

Quon did not make the elimination rounds that day; he had compiled a record of three wins and three losses in Lincoln-Douglas debate, not good enough to continue in the tournament. A couple of his teammates, however, made the cut, so Quon did what all my students were used to doing when they attended speech tournaments: He became a spectator for the other speakers—a rooter—affording him an opportunity to take notes, helping him to improve his debating skills. And our advancing speakers always appreciated the support of others.

In a quirky turn of events, both of our debaters closed out the tournament; that is, after all the dust had settled, they were the only two debaters remaining. They would not have to debate each other. It was always a glorious triumph when a "close-out" occurred; and Quon, like the others, basked in the sunlight of victory with his winning teammates.

Unfortunately, Quon's father had viewed the day's events otherwise; in fact, when Quon wandered into my classroom before school on Monday morning—presumably to pick up his personal results and feedback (the judges' rankings and critiques)—he looked like someone had squeezed him through one of those old-fashioned washing machine ringers.

"I have to quit the team, coach," Quon garbled, his face displaying obvious anguish.

Had I heard him right? "What?" I asked.

"Don't—don't make me say it again. Please. And don't make me explain it."

His face said otherwise, but the situation demanded some levity. "A three-three record for the tournament isn't so bad; I wouldn't take it that hard, Quon. Now, if you had lost *one* more debate, I'd say, yeah, quit the squad."

Quon wasn't in the mood for my flippancies; the only thing he wanted to do was tell me what happened between him and his father Saturday night after they left the speech tournament. Evidently, the minute they got inside their car, Quon's father began slapping him about the face and side of the head, his anger seemingly pouring out of nowhere. What had been up until that moment an affable, generous man with pizzas and smiles had become a raging lunatic.

At that time, what Quon told me defied credibility. Since I have become more familiar with different cultural attitudes about education, I now understand the truth of what Quon confessed to me in 1988. Quon's father berated—lashed out at—Quon for *wasting his time*. According to this dad, after Quon had been eliminated from the competition at the speech tournament, Quon had done absolutely nothing to better himself: He did not practice his speeches anymore; he did not bring something to read or study; he did not do his homework for his AP classes. *Quon had gone to support his teammates!* Wasted time! No productivity! No apology for it—or if we really want to dig—no remorse for *losing,* especially since his father had sprung for pizzas and come to the tournament for the sole purpose of hearing Quon's name announced for the elimination rounds. No name. No elimination rounds. No trophy.

> So, this is what you do all weekend, Quon? This! When you could be studying! You could be working hard to get ahead in life. You could be beating all the others in their studies, because you take the time and you make the effort to study! You sit and you watch debates about air pollution and saving the rain forests! You? What good is that? How will it help you later in your life, Quon? And why didn't you bring your books so you could work while you were waiting for the next debates to be announced? Why did you just sit there, jabbering with your friends and teasing the girls? Why? You will not do any more of this debating. After I tell your mother what it is that you do with all your precious time on your weekends, she might not ever let you out of the house again!

For some in the Asian culture, the pressure for success rides the crest of daily routine. My wife comes from a family of Japanese heritage, but they are very Americanized. My wife graduated from an expensive private college and became an English teacher. Her sister—after 40 billion years or so—finally graduated from the state college system. Her brother *almost* earned a prestigious degree from the state university system; he came up a class or two short. This does not typify a family of Japanese culture. Maybe it's because they have been in the United States forever; perhaps, some healthy American habits have rubbed off on them. Not by any stretch of the imagination can they be classified as failures; on the other hand, none of them committed suicide because they didn't sit at the top of their classes with degrees in chemistry or biophysics.

My wife graduated college with a friend of Chinese background. From the earliest she could remember, Emma had been told by her parents that she *would* become a doctor. Emma and my wife were close, but they didn't have the same mindset about their educations. My wife married me and began her teaching career, later taking time off to become a mother; Emma immersed herself in medical school, often lamenting the rigors of New York University.

Today Emma toils as an orthopedic surgeon somewhere in Pennsylvania. My wife lost contact with her shortly after our wedding, but her struggles to become an orthopedic surgeon paid off; she reached her goal. Emma succeeded—and with parents who had very strongly suggested her destiny.

Every once in a while my wife thinks of Emma and wonders if she's happy: embroiled in the turmoil of a hospital, on call 24 hours a day, dubious about her own ability to have a family, and emotionally drained by the demands made by desperate patients.

But Emma's mother had expected her to become a surgeon.

And Emma didn't disappoint her.

PRYING PARENTS: PUSH AND PUMMEL

I had taught the honors classes for more than 20 years and had multidimensional experiences that not too many other teachers have experienced with high-achieving teenagers.

Oscar found himself at the tail end of an unusually stressful 11th-grade year: Conflict in his family life had become unbearable. He stood tall and sturdy; at age 16, his strong body belied his minimal strength of wisdom about life. Having agreed to help me transport some furniture during one of my frequent bachelor moves, Oscar drove his enormous pickup truck to my apartment building. Today his face bore 30 years, almost twice his actual age.

Always eager to help, his first comment—actually a question—when I greeted him, surprised me: "How long do you think this is gonna take, Mr. G.?"

Apprehension roamed all over his face. "I'm not sure," I shrugged. "If you think it's taking too long, you can go home any time you want."

"It's not that, Mr. G. I've got chemistry lab to finish up, and my dad's been on my case all weekend."

And then he told me something revolving around chemistry, like having to find the microbes in the alloy that stimulates the molecular balance in osmosis of the right ventricle....

Whatever.

No matter: Oscar was now mired in a swamp of demands and commands made by his parents, teachers, and, unfortunately, me. Had I known his plight, I never would have rushed to judgment about the inconsistencies in his original oratory that he prepared for Saturday's tournament. I never would have chided him for missing one of the daily literature assignments in his honors English class. I never would have bothered him about using his truck for my moving expedition. Guilt besieged me; I hadn't put two and two together. Oscar always carried himself with such dignity and diplomacy; he never complained to anyone about his home life or his health. His politeness was an anomaly around other teenagers—who hardly knew that words like *please* and *thank you* existed. What's sometimes scary is that the kids who attract the least attention are the ones who venture on to bigger problems. No one notices them, as they plunge through young adulthood, radiating a carefree image of having everything under control.

"Everything's just piling up, Mr. G.," Oscar said, sitting at the steering wheel of his oversized truck. "My mother wants me to help take care of my little sisters when she has errands to run—which I suppose would be okay, but she stays out for, like, two or three hours, and I never have that much time to spare....My dad, who just left my mom and probably should just keep his mouth shut, won't let me get a job, because he says that my job is school—which is true—and then he tells me that if I need money to just come to him—which I do, but then he never has any—which he actually doesn't, because his doors installation business isn't that steady. Besides all of that, my parents—especially my dad—are always putting all this pressure on me to pull off great grades—which I do—but I really struggle in chemistry and physics. And then I have my other school clubs that you never really want to hear about, because you seem to think that speech is the only game in town—which, it is my priority, because it's got the best people in it and the best-lookin', all-around, got-it-goin'-for-them chicks in the school. I always have speeches to work on, which is okay, because I like doing that—but then you have me write all these other essays and papers in your English class, even though you probably don't have to do that. That position paper we gotta turn in next week is a killer. I guess I really shouldn't be complaining to you right now about this, but...Mr. G., I'm goin' *crazy!*"

Oscar was close to losing it, his face wrinkling into an expression of agony, his eyes glistening with moisture.

I sighed and put the tips of my fingers softly on the edge of his shoulders. "These are the things you needed to come to me about, Oscar; I can't read anybody's mind, especially yours."

"Not asking you to read my mind, coach."

"Anything—I mean anything—Oscar, that is assigned by me in class is negotiable. You just have to let me know."

He shook his head, an incongruent gesture, considering his response. "I know. I guess I was a little late. And you're not the only teacher I have, Mr. G. Mr. Lanker is cranking up the AP History stuff, especially now that we're back from spring break. All this shit—sorry—that I told you about in chemistry, it's driving everybody *insane!*"

I leveled with him. "Tell me what you want me to do—how I can help you. If you want me to, I'll talk to Lanker and the chemistry guy."

Again he shook his head. "No, don't do that; they get pissed off at you as it is."

"They do?" I asked incredulously. "Why?"

"Because they see all these students spending so much time and giving so much effort for speech stuff. They're jealous. And they think you take us away from school too much for speech tournaments."

I wanted to bop the chemistry teacher over the head with a large test tube. As for Mr. Lanker, I liked him a lot, because he was a good, honest guy. But I also thought he gave too much work to his students—when they could have been honing their debating skills! I had control over, well, only me. Big speech tournaments lurked in the distance, so I knew I had to give this kid a break.

"What if I let you off the hook with the position paper project," I suggested. Before he could shake his head and give me that "can't take any special favors" malarkey—which was pure Oscar—I added, "It's not as though you won't be turning anything in. Take your debate case, your first affirmative speech [the one that begins the debate], polish the mechanics [grammar and punctuation], and make it your position paper. It isn't as though you haven't already done a whole bunch of research on the pitfalls of the criminal justice system; just use it in a way that will help you with my class."

He didn't respond to what I believed a gracious gesture; I took that for a yes. Oscar had strong principles, and he usually stood by them. Now on the brink of self-destruction, he would grasp onto any help he could get, while teetering on an ethical dividing line.

And this is how I can help the students whose parents drive them to the verge of craziness. I can't let these kids cheat; I can't sanction blatant favoritism at the expense of other students' welfare; I can't condone policies that would cause students to suffer academically in my classes; however, I *can* offer creative methods of meeting academic standards, as I go to war to protect students from unfair burdens placed upon them by other teachers or administrators. I like doing that. The motivated teens, the ones who create goals for themselves and remain focused on those goals, deserve much better treatment than we seem to have given them.

GIVING THE SHAFT TO OUR BEST AND BRIGHTEST

The truth be known: Most high schools in America—maybe all public education—give too much attention and steer too many resources toward the students who languish at the *bottom* of the academic ladder. We want these kids to stay in school, earn a diploma, and stay out of trouble. We worry ad nauseam about their self-esteem, self-respect, and self-image. But what about the students who come to school every day *prepared* to learn? What about the students who find themselves on an upwardly mobile fast track? The sad truth is, compared to the investments we make in the so-called at-risk crowd, we do virtually *nothing* for the achieving crowd. It's no wonder I have heard the best and the brightest at my high school make comments like these:

I hate this school; they treat us like babies.

If we were trusted, we would be more mature.

If you cause trouble, they pay out money for cops and counselors. They spend tons of money trying to keep you in school and off the streets, and then they pay for extra help like tutoring. But if you're on the speech team, you have to sell Christmas wrapping paper to pay for tournament entry fees!

The bad kids always ruin it for everybody. The other day somebody stopped the toilets with a bunch of toilet paper; they wound up closing most of the bathrooms for the rest of the week.

We don't even have an academic decathlon team at this school. They pay a bunch of teachers for babysitting the kids assigned to Saturday schools, but they don't pay anybody to coach an academic decathlon team!

The college-bound students are cheated. Most of the brainy students perceive that the system works against them; they receive scant attention, an indifference that magnifies their resentments toward the entire education establishment. Parents should be the first to go to bat for their kids in these situations, but it's the parents who are often the source of bigger problems. When individual circumstances are carefully deconstructed, they look something like this:

1. Students are left alone to suffer their academic stresses. For them, no one understands; no one relates. *Parents exacerbate their woes.*

2. Pressures to succeed, to receive the best grades, can become unbearable. Some students turn to drugs and alcohol. There have been documented cases of suicide.

3. Students spend outrageous amounts of time and money taking extra classes (that they had no time for in the first place) to prepare for college entrance exams like the SAT. Their resentment levels dwarf any feelings of satisfaction.

4. Many of these students curtail or cut out completely their extracurricular activities or sports participation. Hemmed in by their AP and honors class loads, they realize their nonacademic life choices are virtually nonexistent.

5. Boys give up their hopes for going to college; sometimes they dump their dreams so drastically, they barely earn a high school diploma.

6. Families have internal disagreements about the amount of pressure to put on children for academic success; thus, permanent family feuds have evolved into alienation from parents—or divorce.

7. Parents have sued other parents and school districts for issues related to valedictorian or other class-standing honors. In New Jersey a girl sued her school district for the right to be lone class valedictorian. She also filed for punitive damages in excess of $2.5 million![2]

8. Especially at the lower grade levels, reported cases of physical child abuse have been well publicized. Some of my students have told me that they had been beaten, locked in closets, ignored, starved, and other horrors—because of their inability or unwillingness to achieve at the highest academic levels, even in *kindergarten*.[3]

9. These pressures precipitate higher rates of promiscuity among girls. Any extraordinary stresses have this effect, but academic stresses overwhelm teens, causing them to make even more emotional—and worse—decisions, such as hopping in the sack with boys who pay attention to their cries for help.

10. Cutthroat competition for colleges breeds cheating, bribery, and unabashed nepotism.

Teenagers have become pawns, and their parents willingly play the game. Wild, wide-eyed parents who badger, barter, and bargain with school officials are worse than parents who stay away from schools altogether. Yes, parents who remain distant from their children's lives at school may be doing colossal harm to their children. But parents who stick their noses in all the wrong places and then proceed to stink up the joint with their hideous manners, unrealistic expectations, and dogmatic decrees may be doing irreparable harm to other peoples' kids, too.

THE GALL GETS BADDER

Quon's mother wielded a reputation around the school that brought most teachers and administrators to their knees. For three years she had remained a slight nuisance, a bit of an irritant to me. But all that changed during Quon's senior year. It happened on a student-free day between the first and second semester. Our district kindly provides time for its employees—teachers mainly—to prepare for the second semester by telling our students not to come to school for a day. So I cheerfully made my way through the corridor of the main office, the bulk of my work behind me, looking forward to going home.

When I unceremoniously bumped into Quon's mother.

Quon's mother resisted the stereotype of the middle-aged Chinese woman who would mercilessly hound *anyone* in order to push her own child upward. She stood only about five feet tall; her unusually thin body was clad in a dark business suit, giving her professional flair. Despite this, she looked no older than our students.

After we exchanged pleasantries, she narrowed her eyes at me. "So, how is Quon doing this time?" she asked tenuously.

In a hurry, I shrugged, fighting my will to leave her standing there. "Quon always does good work."

"Not in speech class," she shot back.

Technically, she was right; even though Quon stood out as one of our hardest workers in speech and debate—with some of the most successful tournament results—he found it difficult to arrive on time to speech class; it began at 6:50 A.M., and the early hour had become a problem for several of the speakers. I, therefore, had to construct a tardy and absence policy that spoke to the problem: After so many tardies and/or absences in zero period, a student's grade would go progressively down.

Quon received a lowly D at the end of the first semester. His friend Dan, also a great, hardworking chap, wound up with even worse consequences for his lackadaisical attitude: He received an F. While I loathed the rigidity of this policy, the tardy problem disappeared overnight. We had already gone through another full semester without Quon receiving any tardies or absences in zero period; Dan still struggled, but even he had considerably improved in his punctuality.

So I responded to Quon's mother's question cheerfully. "He's doing great in speech, too! He's received an A in both classes he takes from me!"

Her face didn't change; it remained stoic. "But he received a D from you last semester."

"Yes, well, we talked about that problem months ago; it's solved now."

Her eyes blazed. "No, it is *not* solved, Mr. Gevirtzman. That D may keep my son from the University of Chicago."

Teacher reality check time: *Why did I become a teacher! Why!*

A parent came to me and challenged a grade; she pointed to personal concerns that were, frankly, irrelevant to that grade—not by any means the first time I'd encountered a nutty parent. But this felt different. To hear that my D grade for a great kid like Quon—because he couldn't get to class on time in the wee hours— would thwart his college intentions, tugged at my conscience. Her words had not rung hollow. And I *swear*, I would have paused for a moment, nodded, and told her something like, "Yeah, you're right. Quon paid a very high price for being late. I know he was exhausted last semester. Maybe I was too hard on him."

I would have raised his grade to what he probably deserved without my cocka-mamie absence/tardy rule: an A. *I would have done that!* In fact, I had formulated those very words, and they were about to exit my mouth *when . . .*

Quon's mother screamed at me, "You *must* go into that office and change his grade to an A! You must do it right now!"

She was panting.

I stared at that small body attached to such an enormous presence, but I could sling it with the best of them! "Huh?"

"Change it!" she ordered.

I cringed, looking around the corridor to see which office doors were open and who may be hearing our skirmish; I shakily said, "The grades have been in the book for months; I can't change them on a whim."

"Not a whim. You made a mistake. Tell them that you made a mistake!" she clamored.

Not bad logic, but not an attractive option under these conditions, so I shook my head. "I can't say that now."

"You can go in there right now," she gestured toward the open office, the one that she knew housed academic records. "Nobody is looking; you can go in there right now and change his grade to an A."

She must have noticed that a couple of my chins dropped a few feet, for she added, "That is what he deserved you know. And it will help him get into Chi-cago. This also is what he deserves."

Honestly, the rest is a blur. The conclusion of our exchange had been choked off in my mind, after hearing her *suggestion* that I march into the office *while no one is looking* and change her son's grade.

I had the power to change grades. The procedure is simple: It merely required me to ask the records clerk for a change-of-grade card. Changing grades is the sole discretion of a teacher; no one else is allowed by law to do that. Lawsuits have revolved around school administrators or district personnel who have unilater-ally attempted to make grade changes; the teachers, however, have always won their cases. Quon had not followed my class rules. And neither had some others.

They all received just consequences for their infringements—their tardies; yet, in Quon's case, I had almost abandoned my principles, letting my heart get the better of me. Although I can't remember how it eventually panned out, I know that I had become quietly indignant after rebuking her blatantly unethical instructions.

Until a year later, when Quon's father ordered Quon to quit the debate team, I had encountered Quon's mother on only a few other occasions. She was always high-strung, aggressive; but maybe that's just who she was. Maybe boys like Quon have to live with these kinds of mothers until they finally graduate high school and manage to flee their homes—and mothers—for saner ground.

Quon never went to the University of Chicago. Besides the D in speech that I gave him, he also received a C in his Advanced Placement English class during his 12th-grade year, sealing his fate.

His mother complained to that teacher and accused her of bias against her male students, particularly Asian boys.

Quon wound up with the C anyway, and continued on to the state college system, where he did just fine.

MR. G.'S HOME-GROWN ADVICE

My advice on this rather sensitive topic is based on my own experiences with overachieving teenagers; it comes from the heart. I'm absolutely certain that this powerful angst—the kind that ruins young lives and even drives some to suicide—can be assuaged by huge, groundbreaking changes in attitudes. Unfortunately, without major shifts in the way we adults see school, learning, and success, not a flicker of hope exists for those obsessive-compulsive students of the future.

Parents

Which hill will you die on *here?* You can't pester your kids about *everything;* soon they turn you off. During the brief moment I've been parenting, I've already found much to be disgusted with in myself, especially when it comes to my perennial nagging. I tell my students that when you become a teacher, you become a mega-nag. You nag your students all day, and then you go home and nag your own kids. You never stop nagging—at least, until you sleep. And even then, you dream all night about nagging.

What I haven't clued them about is my nagging strategy; it's hard to master a flawless one, but one of my own nagging tactics is the concept of *priority nagging.* Simply put, we can't badger them about *everything;* so from an early age, we have to decide over which issues we're going to pester our children. For instance, my wife and I wouldn't jump for joy if our kids received terrible grades in school. But we've decided to give a little on grades. Exceptional grades will not be the Holy Grail in our family. We intend to emphasize character and honor and dignity and honesty and kindness and loyalty and decency and altruism a lot more than we will stress grades. Teachers who tell us that our kids are wonderful people will make our day! We'll be on our way to reaching our goal as parents: *turning out quality human beings*. Each one of you must determine a direction for your children. Since they cannot get to the Holy Grail without your help, guidance, and support, your children look to you as role models; and they usually build a hierarchy of values based on what you have instilled in them. If an A is more important to you than knowing your children usually do the right thing, your grandchildren will be brought up the same way. You can count on it: "Cheating is no big deal, if you don't get caught. If you don't get into the college of our—er, your—choice, you have already failed in life." Young people entertain memories of their parents for the rest of their lives—long after their parents have lain in their permanent resting place. Sometimes kids don't understand why they do the things they do, why they feel the way they feel; they just have a vague sense that it has to do with the way they were brought up, but they aren't sure. So for parents I have five crucial pieces of advice about education, school, and success:

1. Back off. From the beginning take an active interest in your child's learning. Help her with her homework. Don't worry about academic perfection; but let your critical eye look for rude, obnoxious, or selfish behaviors that need work, instead of ragging on your kid because she colored imperfectly between the lines.

2. Don't compare. The experiences of siblings, friends, other kids, and your own childhood are all different. If you compare them to your teenager, he will think he has come up short in every comparison, even if you intended to flatter him.

3. Make sure that he has fun. And this goes for school days, too. If your child busily engages himself in homework for several hours each day, *when does he relax?* Remember when you knew that you had to have some down time and couldn't figure out a way to work it out? Now is the time for you to solve that dilemma with your own kids: Movies, video games, television, exercise, recreational sports, family games, acting silly—these all serve to fulfill the chill-out agenda.

4. Compliment. Not the phony compliments educators tell us to bestow on kids, even if they haven't done anything to deserve them, but well-deserved compliments are in order. If you have a hardworking, conscientious

darling, then she needs to *hear* about it. Make it short, and don't load it with saccharine.

5. Emphasize her *other* options. Some parents cringe when they hear this, but becoming a Rhodes Scholar is not the only path to success. Inform your children early and often of the choices they have: community colleges, tech schools, the military, apprenticeships, low-pressure jobs, and so on. When teens realize they have several roads they may take on their life's journey, they may find inner peace within themselves; for not only do they believe they *can* realize their dreams, they also know there are several ways of pleasing *you*. Make it clear to your teenagers that one of their primary goals should be to please *themselves*; after all—and I do hate to remind you of this—they're going to be here long after you have already left the building.

Teachers

Just yesterday an 11th-grade girl came to me during our lunch break and asked me to sign a standard recommendation form that would gain her acceptance into the senior Advanced Placement English class. I'm usually pleased to endorse students; however, in this situation the girl had received a D grade in my English class for the first semester. And now her grade rested at about 62 percent, also a D mark.

I said, "I'll sign that, Mary, but I'm obligated to put down next to my name that you received a D last semester and are on course to get another D this semester."

Her grin became a scowl, and I inquired, "Is that okay with you?"

"No," she replied gently.

"Or," I continued, "I can call your guidance counselor and explain the situation to her. Do you want me to do that?"

I took her silence for a no.

I realize this sounds callous to a lot of people who are thinking, "Why does he have to be such a jerk? Just sign the paper! She'll find out soon enough if she can handle AP work or not!" But that misses the point: I won't help this kid by testifying she can succeed in an advanced English class, when she had already demonstrated she could not succeed in a regular English class. The school also loses when it engineers yet another 12th-grade failure; in fact, our limited financial resources would go to support Mary's repetition of senior English. Also, my name means something to me; if I sign a lie, my name would mean less. I imagine there's unreasonable pressure from someone—probably a parent—being applied to Mary. She's a sweet girl who will probably do well in life, but dissecting 24 novels next year may not be for her the most direct path to success.

Here are five tips for teachers:

1. Remember that she has five other classes. Yeah, yeah, yeah. Heard that one before. Right. But keep thinking about it...because it's *oh so true!*

2. You were once a student. And how did you feel then? Imagine how they feel today. It's a lot harder to be a student today than it was then. Stop rhapsodizing about education during your youth; it's much tougher now.

3. Be flexible. Teachers who make exceptions and deal with each of their students as individuals manufacture a better product in their class-rooms. Not all kids fit a cookie-cutter mold. If you must make a deci-sion regarding a specific student, ask yourself, "What is the best thing for this particular kid?" And then go from there. Some will cry *foul*— but—hey—you did what was right for *that* kid.

4. Your students are human beings. Oh, yeah. Forgot about that little tidbit. And just how should we treat human beings? The dignity and respect we afford others are also the dignity and respect we should give to our stu-dents; they're people, too. Sure, sometimes they relinquish that dignity and respect, and we're forced to cope. But until then, remember their humanity.

5. Honesty reaps; phoniness reeks. You look like a big, fat liar when you make a big deal out of things that don't matter. When the standardized test *really* counts, say so; when it's just another bureaucratic order com-ing from the dopes downtown—make *that* clear. Your students need to know which hill to die on, too; and your blunt, honest appraisal will help them decide. You should steer your top students to where they should put their best efforts—blood, sweat, tears—and precious time. But be brutally honest with those who would be temporarily better off taking it easy, joking around, or making fun of weird-looking people at the mall. You should say this delicately, but *college isn't for everyone*. Remind them that other teachers might have different opinions; however, *you* think they would be happier in the military or preparing gourmet Italian din-ners at Antonio's Pasta Factory.

Teenagers

Flat out: Despite what others may have you believe, *it is your life*. I understand this; *you* understand this. Your parents understand this.

Or they may not.

You should always pay close attention to what your parents say. Most parents do not tell their kids to do things that are illegal, immoral, or fattening (unsafe or unhealthy), so parents do have the last say. They are responsible for you. They have the awesome burden of making sure you are safe. Parents *protect* their children; so even if they tell you to do something and they are wrong, *they have the right to be wrong.* In the long run, you will be glad they made nuisances of themselves.

However, long after they are dead, *you* will be here. Children outlive their parents by trillions of years; it's the natural order of things. So, whatever job you are doing, whatever career you have settled into for the rest of your lives—it will no longer matter to your parents. *You* are the one who will have to grin and bear it.

Basically, when it comes to education and the direction your lives will eventually go, the decision is *yours.* Sometimes parents hope their children will attend college, simply because *they* did not. Sometimes parents hope their kids will attend a specific college, because it's the college they had dreamed of going to themselves. Although rarely, parents may discourage college, because they have latent jealousies of their children—jealousies that have emerged during their own kids' high school years. A small minority of parents does *not* wish to see their children do better in life than they have done.

Beware! Parents should guide, aid, support, provide, and advise you about colleges or careers.

And then back off.

Yes, you could make a hideous error in choosing the rest of your life. You may think back to the seemingly misguided advice your father once gave you and regret that you had not taken it. You may curse the moment you read the advice in this book and hate me for offering it. But you are the planner of your own destiny and the master of your own soul. When it comes to mapping out the next 70 years of your existence, ultimately you will live—and die—with the decisions you make now.

Long ago, my cousin Brett telephoned me in great despair. Almost 15 years younger than I, Brett had looked to me for assistance on numerous occasions. I didn't get the chance to see him very often, because of the geographical distance between us, but I made it my business to know what was going on in his life. Brett had attended college and earned his bachelor's degree in business—or something else equally useless—and then proceeded to move back with his parents. At 22 years old, Brett withered in a state of confusion, oblivious to what he wanted to do with his life.

Brett confessed to me that his parents had decided to kick him out of the house. They gave him 60 days to find an apartment, offering to pay his first and last month's rent; the rest, they told their son, was up to him.

"What happened?" I inquired.

"They got fed up with me."

"Why?"

"I'm driving a taxi, Bruce. I have a college degree, and I'm driving a *taxi*."

"That's respectable," I tried to convince him.

"Not with a college degree," he replied.

"What do you want to do with that degree, Brett?"

A long pause ensued; then he said, "Nothing."

"No wonder they're impatient," I told him. "They think you're wasting your degree. You *are*."

"But *music* is what I want, Bruce! Music. I'm in a little band and we play coffee houses three or four nights a week. I'm never happier than when I play my music with the guys in the band; that's what I want to do."

"You want to play in coffee houses at night and drive a taxi during the day?" I asked.

"Exactly," he didn't hesitate to answer.

My cousin wasn't a teenager anymore. As an adult, no justification could be made for his parents managing his life; on the other hand, no one could defend Brett's leeching off his parents anymore either. But what I told Brett made a difference; at least, he acknowledged that to me later.

I encouraged him to follow his desired goals. Brett continued to play music, barely supporting himself with his sporadic job as a cab driver. A few years later, however, he met a beautiful young bank teller. Their attraction was mutual, but she hesitated to get serious about marriage when he had maintained that he could go on driving a cab while she worked as a teller.

"You'll have to do better than that," she maintained.

And he decided that she was right.

Brett spent the next three years in law school, passed the California bar exam on his first attempt, and became a prominent criminal defense attorney. She applauded his efforts, married him, and today they have two beautiful children.

Brett's parents had demanded that he become a lawyer, but to no avail; Brett's girlfriend also demanded that he become a lawyer, and three years later he's fighting it out in San Francisco courtrooms.

We shouldn't lead our lives by what other people want us to become; however, sometimes what we call *making a life for ourselves* entails pleasing others so they may respect us more—and maybe even marry us! Of course, we should never take a job or choose an occupation because someone is threatening to dump us if we don't conform to her notions of success, but earning the esteem of others is dependent upon our sense of self-worth and personal dignity. And we usually attain self-worth and personal dignity by staying in school, doing homework, overcoming obstacles, and tenaciously dealing with the everyday rigors of life. Sometimes we're forced to peel off the prying fingers of others—even those who love us—knowing that we *alone* will determine our future by the choices *we* make and the passions *we* hold. One of the genuine keys to happiness is having numerous options for our future—right at our fingertips.

Side note: In 1994 Brett had a near-fatal heart attack that put him in the hospital for triple bypass surgery. Skeptics have said that Brett would have avoided the heart attack if he had continued strumming on his guitar in those coffee houses. But I doubt it. Brett survived this health crisis because he finally had so much to live for: a wife and two daughters, who made certain that the most important man in their lives would be hanging in there for them a whole lot longer.

17

You Mean, When You Die, You're Dead?

LATE-NIGHT BANTER AT THE OL' DORM

The 5-foot-10-inch star varsity basketball player stood at the head of his English teacher's desk. As he cradled his textbook and notebook, his face beamed the familiar, charming smile many had found irresistible. Thursday afternoon promised to be a special time for both of them: in about one hour, the teacher would be headed to San Jose with the debate team; the basketball player would be attending his first cabinet meeting. He had just been elected student body president.

"I got a problem, Coach," Johnny said.

"Shoot," the teacher urged.

"Well, I got a really busy weekend. I mean, I could go into it, if you want me to, but—"

"No, Johnny. Just tell me what you need," the teacher said amiably.

Johnny grinned. "I need an extension on the homework until, like, Tuesday. I got a few of 'em done in class, but no way I'll have 'em all done by Monday. No way."

The teacher had just introduced his class to Act I of the play *Our Town*, by Thornton Wilder. He instructed his honors students to write down and explain 10 significant lines from this first act of the play.

"No problem, Johnny," the teacher assured him. "Tuesday is fine; in fact, make it Wednesday, if that helps to relieve some of your stress."

Johnny's usually wide grin grew even wider, and he lightly punched the teacher on the shoulder—a playful gesture—as he moved toward the classroom's exit. "Thanks, Coach," was the last thing the teacher heard him say.

The teacher would forever have a snapshot in his head of that seemingly innocuous encounter. Some things are that way; we don't appreciate them at the time, but later we remember them as golden moments we can never have back.

In exactly one hour and 10 minutes, Johnny would be dead.

Shakespeare wrote in *Macbeth*: "Out—out, brief candle. Life is but a walking shadow that struts itself upon the stage and then is heard no more."[1] Such is the fleeting nature of life: a candle's glowing flame, giving the room joy and purpose. And then—*poof*—no more flame! Could something as weak as a small gust of air challenge this brilliance? The concept of that fire being extinguished by something so sudden and innocent juts from the scope of rational thought.

But it's not rational thought that guides a teenager's view of life and death; it's *irrational emotion*. Emotions lie to us. Emotions insidiously implode our sense of reality, of right and wrong, of the true nature of our existence. The impulsive decisions that come from our hearts—and our loins—do not guide us from positions of strength. They take us to the brink of death more times than we wish to admit—and far more often than our emotions confess, to our inevitable demise.

Teenagers do not possess a natural sense of their own mortality. Certainly, kids know they will die; they also have a good sense of what can kill them. Weirdly, what they do not seem to grasp is the permanence of death—that dead means *forever*.

Late at night many years ago, I sat with a good friend in his college dormitory room; he'd just returned home from a party. His candor had been heightened—not lessened—by his drunken stupor, as I listened to him rattle on cogently—albeit embarrassingly—about a cornucopia of topics. At one point in the "conversation" (he had done almost all the "conversing"), he paused, looked at me directly, and stared. I watched his eyes well with tears; he appeared ready to deliver the crescendo, the grand finale of all his wisdom, philosophies, and advice. Young and witless, I could have benefited from whatever my enlightened—through booze and whatever else—friend had to offer.

I inhaled, saying nothing.

In a voice riddled with deep emotion, he uttered the profound words I would relay to thousands of teenagers: "Ya know...it's like this, Bruce....*First, you die...and then...you're...dead.*"

I waited; assuredly more would come. But when more did not come, I burst into uncontrollable laughter. But the last laugh would be on *me*.

First you die—and then you're dead.

The importance of teenagers understanding this wisdom would become the framework—the bulwark—for countless lessons, lectures, sermons, and tirades in the decades that followed.

Scientists have taught us about the underdeveloped part of the teenage brain, the portion that lends ability for *thinking things through*, for digesting the pros and cons of a particular decision by weighing *logically* the various issues involved. For example, if teenagers should lock into the notion that fatalities happen only to *others*, they are far more likely to be careless, callous, and carefree—to the point of deadly fault.

"I know that I'll die someday," Chavonne recently admitted to me. "It's just that, well, I mean, I don't think about dying as being, like, death, and final and all that. I know people who have died, but I don't think it's going to happen to me. I mean, I know that it *can* happen to me, but, well—I mean—I'm all confused now."

Seventeen-year-old Chavonne's views of death and dying reflect the majority of America's teenagers' views on this subject. Young people have only an abstract sense of their own mortality. They know they're going to *die* some day, but they don't necessarily link that concept—dying—to an eternal *death;* moreover, death is something that happens to *others*—and the notion that getting into a drunk guy's car, playing macho with a kilo of cocaine, or standing too close to the railroad tracks can actually kill *them* escapes most teenagers.

Chavonne told me that she had lost her grandmother after a long bout with cervical cancer two years ago. "I've also known other kids who've died," she said. "I mean, I didn't actually *know* them that well, but I knew *of* them, and it was sort of eerie. But my grandmother is the only one close to me who has died. Does it make me think about dying? Not really. My grandmother was 70 years old. By the time I'm 70, I hope I'm ready to accept my fate."

Just a few weeks ago (in 2008), three local teenagers were killed in a car wreck right after leaving their prom; one teen drove recklessly, and their van overturned. Two passengers died on the street, and the driver succumbed later in the hospital. The police found several open containers of alcohol at the scene of the carnage. What did Chavonne think of that?

"You hear about that sort of thing all the time," she answered thoughtfully. "Especially this time of year it's a problem. But again, you never think it's going to affect *you* that much—and you really put off in your mind the idea that it can happen to *you*."

"But, Chavonne, can it happen to you?"

"Sure. But I don't dwell on it. Maybe I should, but I don't."

DEATH TAKES NO PRISONERS

In the distance we heard the faint sounds of sirens.

Our school is located in a suburban neighborhood; on one side is a large public park, and on the other side, a lavish country club with a golf course. Although the sounds of the city occasionally make themselves known, police cars, ambulances, and fire trucks are not a regular occurrence. Even though my classes and I acknowledged the sounds of the emergency vehicles, we all adhered to the principle of self-survival: *It ain't about me.*

Later that afternoon the principal summoned me to his office. Mr. Harris looked grim. "Hi, Bruce," he greeted me, shutting the office door behind him.

"Need to tell you something, but don't let it out, yet. Two of our students were killed this morning—just down the street—on the way to school. Another kid is in intensive care, and they don't know if she's going to make it."

"Who?" I faltered.

"Marcy Mancineras and Kiko Torres. Marcy's mother was also killed."

I thought to myself: "My God! Three people dead!"

He continued sullenly, "I'm warning these kids' teachers to prepare for the worst tomorrow. Your students are going to need you. But like I said, please keep it quiet for the rest of the day, so all hell doesn't break loose on campus. It's going to be bad enough tomorrow."

And then Mr. Harris did the darndest thing: He came around the desk and hugged me. His crushing embrace may have relieved some of the tension he felt and helped to transfer his powerful aching to another human being.

"So sorry, Bruce," he wept. "The last thing I ever wanted to do is break horrible news like this to you or anyone else."

Of the two teenagers killed in that accident, one had been a student in my honors English course. Kiko, an unusually quiet (for an honors class), sweet, little girl, sported an affable disposition. She had been struggling with her understanding of the more complex philosophies presented by our writers, but she worked hard and had conscientious homework habits. Viewing her empty seat tomorrow would be an agonizing experience for all of us.

The group of four, driven by Mrs. Mancineras, had been late for school. Mrs. Mancineras raced down a hill and lost control of her car, crashing into a brick wall on the side of the road. The fiery crash left Mrs. Mancinceras and two of her passengers dead at the scene, including her daughter Marcy. The fourth teenager, Karen Gomez, did survive, but her scars would probably linger forever. Emotional and physical healing may take an eternity, especially after a catastrophe like this one.

I remind my students that we constantly make monumental decisions—even on a daily basis—and sometimes we don't realize their significance until much later. We are so focused on the task at hand, person in the spotlight, or concept of current relevance that we often overlook the *ultimate* outcomes of our actions. That old line about not being able to see the forest for the trees rings relevant. I tell kids, "Don't be paranoid, but consider every decision you make and every action you take; know their impacts could be far, far beyond the scope of what you foresaw or intended."

Don personified this paradigm for tragedy.

Don stood about five feet tall by the end of his ninth-grade year. He would have grown taller; all kids do. But Don was a late bloomer in that regard, even though good looks were already his trademark. His bright blond hair and deep blue eyes threw sinkers into the hearts of ninth-grade girls and even a few older damsels on our speech team. That May afternoon in 1979, Don held the coveted position of lighting director for our spring play. I usually put the younger kids on the tech assignments, but I rarely beamed as much confidence with ninth graders as I had with Don: reliable, punctual, and serious, Don made sure the lighting effects burden would be lifted from my shoulders.

It was the Friday before Memorial Day, and while we worked backstage, Don reluctantly slithered over to me.

"Mr. G., uh, I don't know how to tell you this, but I can't be at rehearsal tomorrow. My dad is making me go with everybody to the mountains on a family getaway."

Exhaustion had already overtaken me, so rather than confronting his father, I resigned myself to a dress rehearsal without our ace lighting guy.

What I had *not* resigned myself to, however, was Don's sudden, tragic death the next day. At the precise moment our cast rehearsed the show with a temporary lighting director, Don had slipped and fallen while hiking in the mountains. He'd tumbled only about 12 feet off the side of a hill, but his head thudded into a rock, and he died in the mountain brush, his entire family looking on in horror.

Don's death did not prevent the show from opening on schedule. It did not shut down the school or bring the community to paralysis; it did, though, remind other students, especially the ones who were working on the play with Don, about the fleeting nature of life itself: Each of our lives hangs on a slender thread—that may be severed, cut, detached in an instant. A precious 14-year-old boy: alive and vibrant one moment . . .

And then is here no more.

I have counted 25 former students who are now dead (that I'm aware of). Most died in automobile accidents; some met their demises through a natural progression of insidious illnesses. Of course, the usual drug-related fatalities come to mind, along with one kid who died of AIDS years after he graduated high school. These were living, breathing human beings—teenagers at the time—who had sat wide-eyed in my classrooms, listening to poems by Robert Frost and Edna St. Vincent Millay. They asked questions about essays that dealt with mortality and the uncertainty of life; they pondered the tragic fates of students who came before them, and the deaths of kids they didn't even know.

And now they are gone, too.

Just today I clipped an article from the newspaper, an appalling story describing a 14-year-old girl who had developed an Internet relationship with a 30-year-old man. The girl's parents found the man's picture on her computer (on MySpace), and they immediately removed their daughter's computer from her bedroom. She then pursued the cyber-relationship through her friends' computers. (Don't you love some kids' definition of *friend?*) The 30-something adult arranged to meet

the 14-year-old child for sex; her parents intervened, and the predator was arrested for child molestation.

But then the heartbroken teenager hanged herself from a loft in their lavish
California home.

After reading that news piece, the depth of my anger knew no bounds. A little
girl had felt her life was over; she was despondent about the loss of her first love,
who came in the form of a grown man twice her age—a man who had molested
her. What went through her immature adolescent mind, no one will ever know:
"I'll fix my parents! They can't take everything away from me! I'm a person, too!
You wanna have something taken away from you—fine! How 'bout if I'm taken
away from you, Mom and Dad? How would you like that!"

And so she made certain that her small body, dangling from the rafters of her
Orange County house, would be discovered first by the people who loved her
more than anyone else in the world: her parents.

Impulsive decisions such as these do not communicate an understanding of the
absoluteness of death. Silly forms of gossip, pranks, and miniature teen dramas
play themselves out in minutes or days or weeks, while the state of being dead is
an *eternity*—the clarity of its permanence often brushed aside by the trivial and
the mundane. It's the *eternity* thing most teens fail to grasp. *Death is forever.* But
kids seem indifferent to this concept. The sixties encouraged, *Live for today!* And
too many of our young people have done just that. Living for today may sound
good, but without planning for tomorrow, *today* has a hollow ring to it.

Ask a few teens, "What is in your future?" And they'll probably answer as
these kids did:

Nothing. My parents have told me I won't amount to anything. And that's a
   big joke, because what have they ever amounted to? Nothing. So maybe
   they expect the same from me. Sometimes I feel like they hope I won't
   amount to anything because I would just show them up.

College. But when I get to college, I don't know if I'll make it. So, right now,
   I'm pretty worried and depressed.

Anger. I am still mad at my father for cheating with another woman when I
   was seven. I'll hate him for the rest of my life. I haven't heard from him in
   years, but when he dies, I want to know, because I will find his funeral—
   wherever it is—and go there just to spit on his grave.

Taking care of my parents. They expect me to take care of them when they get
   older. I've already been told by them and the rest of the family that I'll have
   to be their caretaker. It's getting kind of scary. Dad has smoked a pack a day
   since he was 14, and his lungs are already getting bad—and he's only 50.

Mom has been unhealthy almost every day since I was born. But here I am—and here I will be—the one to take care of everybody but myself.

The military. If I could have joined right after September 11, I would have. I hate the people who want to kill me and my family, and I think we should kill them before they kill any more of us.

The only thing absolutely certain about our kids' futures is that one day they will die. Years ago I offered to take some of my more depressed, disheveled, and distracted students for a little visit. "The visit will be short, and you won't have to write anything about it—or even talk about it with anyone—if you don't want to."

"Where's *that?*" the goofy boy in the back asked, half-mocking me in order to get a cheap chuckle.

"We'll go to a hospice. At a hospice, you will have the chance to see people—young and old—who are dying. Even children, who long for only *one thing* through all their pain and gross disillusionment. And do any of you have the slightest idea what that *one thing* is?"

A sprinkling of hands went up, and one of the kids yelled, "Pot!" But I ignored that dimwit, knowing some of the other students had the right answer. "These people in the hospice—the dying people—would swap any of your problems for theirs. They would swap *all* of your problems for theirs. We'll go there and watch them clinging to life—perhaps, praying—for any sign of improvement, all the while understanding that their dying is inevitable. That must be terrible, huh? Knowing that this room, these four walls surrounding you, are the only sights you will ever see, because in a few weeks, days, or hours, you will be dead."

The finality of death becomes much clearer when we have a concept of what death entails—what it means to *be* dead. Beyond religious views about death, the majority of us view death as mysterious at best, and horrific at worst. The everlasting condition of being dead suggests the absence of family, friends, movies, pets, baseball, and pizza. When we fully grasp this concept, one that teaches us we will never see our loved ones or friends again, never watch a movie again (no more Paul Giamatti, Denzel Washington, Keira Knightley), never stroke our pets again, and never eat pizza again—we can preview a more frightening realm of where death takes us. Perceptions, conceptions, or inventions of an afterlife bring debate and controversy; *the only assurance we have about death is the eternal loss of what life had offered us.*

Yes, former college buddy: when you die . . . you are *dead*.

Surveying teenagers about their attitudes on dying and death proved to be a futile experience. Since America's adolescents are far from stupid, asking them something like whether they know they will be dead someday undermines their intelligence. When teenagers actually think through these concepts, they know the obvious answers. The problem, as reiterated so many times in this book: the teenager's deficiency in the development—or the willingness to use—the part of his brain that *thinks things through*. Infamous for their impulsivity, teenagers drag race down residential streets *now* and think about it later.

Columnist Dr. George A. Sheehan had diagnosed his prostate cancer almost a decade before it killed him. For years, I have shared one of his most memorable, poignant essays with my students with the hope that they, too, would understand what Sheehan discovered about life. Sheehan teaches us to "Make the most of every second that you have. Enjoy the sun as though there will be no sun tomorrow.... Look at your precious loved ones and snap a picture of them in your mind. Carry that picture with you for your remaining days."[2]

Sheer *luck* (winning the lottery of life) has dictated that each one of us may live in the most powerful, compassionate, technologically advanced, and wealthiest nation in the history of civilization. Just think about it: we could have been be one of those kids on late-night television with the flies crawling all over him and his bones sticking out. But that isn't the case. Somehow—maybe by the grace of God—we are *here*, and *now*, not 200 years ago, with wagon trains thudding through mountains and valleys, and the pioneers battling deadly smallpox and angry Indians. Ignoring this miracle, making it an entitlement, devalues our existence, and pushes up our noses on the dearness of life.

In a San Jose hotel room, on April 30, 1992, my speech students and I sat in shock; the devastating information we had just received had begun its emotional toll. The phone call from a parent: Johnny Wilcox, newly elected student body president, star varsity basketball player, student in my third period honors English class, had been killed during lunch. He had hopped into the back of a pickup truck, driven by a good friend of his—another star athlete—Wesley. Speeding down a local street, the boys headed for a Taco Bell; and with only 30 minutes to get there, eat, and drive back before their next classes, time had become of the essence.

Witnesses claimed that another car, emerging from a driveway, had suddenly poked its nose into the street, scaring Wesley into turning the steering wheel too fast and too far. He overcorrected his maneuver, and the truck flipped on its side, throwing Johnny and another boy from the open flat back. Luckily the truck hurled the other boy free of its two-ton carcass; Johnny, however, was not as fortunate. The tumbling cab trapped his head flush against the pavement of the street, crushing his skull.

Moving his way through a carefree life, well on his way to a promising future, Johnny died on the street he had traveled so many times before. Full of charm, intelligence, and perseverance, Johnny had been moving toward the kind of stardom seemingly reserved for the most talented of teenagers and, ironically, the most fortunate.

In Johnny's funeral program, someone had inscribed this short paragraph: "When Johnny's locker was cleaned out on the day of his death, it was discovered that he had written this line from the play *Our Town* on a piece of paper he had placed in his textbook just minutes before he died: "The morning star always gets wonderful bright the minute before it has to go, doesn't it?""

The first of the 10 significant lines Johnny had chosen for his weekend homework assignment came from a character named the Stage Manager, who laments throughout the play about the uncertainty of life, the jaws of death, and the paradoxes of improper timing that surround our living and our dying. Johnny, a young scholar and athlete, arose that fateful day as the "Morning Star," only to be snuffed out by a series of immature, irrational, and impulsive decisions teenagers sometimes make—but can never explain; and, of course, none of us could have foreseen the tragic events lurking on the horizon, or the monumental irony that would haunt us for years.

Two thousand other teenagers had learned a lot about living and dying, and maturity and mortality. As for Johnny's classmates, the juniors who knew him so well: their irrational guilt paralyzed some of them for months. The boy, Wesley, who had driven the pickup truck that day, lapsed into a long, dark depression. The repercussions from this calamity created a shock wave that affected future generations at our school, making legends out of the teenagers who were involved.

Our students are no longer permitted to leave school to buy their lunches. Today when my students gripe about their closed campus, I tell them about Johnny; I talk about how a quest for tacos, the back of a pickup, and a moment of erratic driving stole a young life that had not come even close to reaching its potential.

MR. G.'S HOME-GROWN ADVICE

Unless a human being values his life, thoughts of death turn up as mere annoyances. Death doesn't matter as much: "Enjoy the moment! I'm gonna live forever, man! Life sucks!" Death looms only as an abstraction:

I will *die* . . .

But *other people* will be dead.

So, there are two keys:

1. Teenagers must value their lives.

2. Teenagers must realize the truth of their own mortality.

Parents

You start long before the initial blackhead of adolescence springs its first ugly pimple. When the kids are young—very young—get a goldfish. Very soon the fish will be floating belly up near the top of the water. Gather together your little tykes and point to the dead fish, explaining to them that, sooner or later, *all* living things wind up like that fish. You don't want them to summon a thought of Grandma lying silently on *her* back at the top of a swimming pool, but you get the idea: What happens to all of us at a given point is...*we die*.

And we don't come back.

I talk with my own small children about heaven and angels and God, and I think they're beginning to comprehend a little something about death. It's a very fine line: I don't want to terrify them; I also don't want them to see death as an inviting, attractive concept: "Daddy, when you're dead and in heaven, can I go to heaven too, so I can be with you?" Before the age of puberty, having some idea that death ends life and happens to everybody is enough information to fill their plates. But by the time they're teenagers, comprehending the tenuous status of their existence can make living more enriching. It's the old, tired question with the familiar, brilliant answer:

Would you like to live forever?

"Of course not; if I knew I would live on no matter what I said or did with my life—that everything had permanence—of what value would any of my individual actions be? Why would I appreciate—have gratitude—for anything, if I knew it would always be there: that I could try again tomorrow; that I could rewind the tape and watch it again?"

At their most effective, parents convey to their children that life is a most precious gift—and death takes that gift away: *Death ends life.*

But death also gives life its intrinsic worth.

Teachers

Maybe it's not our job to teach teenagers about death and dying. Optimistically, parents will do this, along with their religious institutions; however, with many teenagers void of meaningful understanding of their own mortality, what can teachers do to help their students grapple with death and dying?

Rather ghoulish to some people, but the sudden, untimely death of a 16-year-old may render itself purposeful, helping *others* to grow, mature, and prosper. If a boy is killed on a Friday night because he got in the car with a drunken friend, by Monday morning a couple thousand frightened teenagers are momentarily pondering how they *will*—at all costs—avoid similar fates themselves.

English teachers have a unique chance to bring a timely awareness to their students through various pieces of literature whose themes present these issues with amazing power. Thornton Wilder's *Our Town* is a must-read (or must-view) for all teens in America. There is a reason that this play, penned over a century ago, tops the list as the most performed play in the United States. The poignant, surreal scene in which the now-deceased character Emily dramatically focuses on everything she had previously taken for granted has become a classic. As for films that touch these themes, nothing beats Jimmy Stewart's George Bailey recounting how the world would have been worse off if he had not existed, in the holiday favorite, *It's a Wonderful Life*. And there's Adam Sandler's character in *Click*, Michael Newman, who so desperately wanted to slow his life down in order to relish the precious times he had callously ignored—or relive the rare and special moments he had heartlessly fouled up.

No matter what their subject matter, teachers are endowed with the ability to discuss topics like gratitude and appreciation for the little things in life. They can point to the United States of America and how blessed all of us are for living here. They might suggest the foolishness of some young people who wasted their lives by doing idiotic stunts that led to their premature demise. The closer to home teachers bring these examples—these anecdotes—the more impact they will have on kids who look to them for advice, guidance, and role modeling.

Teenagers

Here's a little tidbit: *When you die, you're dead*.

Dead.

Over.

Finite.

Nothing.

Gone.

Through.

Had it.

The *end*.

Is that direct enough for you?

Are you still planning your next life because this one is so boring? There aren't enough hot spots in your hometown? The beach gets too cloudy? There is *no* beach? Your boyfriend is a slug? You have *no* boyfriend? Life sucks?

You're, like, all . . .

Remember Sheehan—the writer whose pending death prompted him to appreciate every precious minute of life, to absorb the presence of every living thing around him, to enhance every sensory perception in his body? No longer was his goal to be careful so he would *not* die; death was a given. Sheehan found that when death is a given, life is a heaven. All of those little irritations—the people who cut him off on the street, the cigarette butts that sat on the ground, the store clerks who ignored his presence—they took on new meaning for him. They became a part of his celebration of life, rather than a constant reminder that life was a daily challenge, something he just had to put up with before he died.

And so: When you realize the certainty of dying, you live better. When you live better, life screams its immeasurable worth into every fiber of your being. When life screams its worth, you are oh-so-careful about what you do with it. When you are oh-so-careful about what you do with your life, you will live longer, probably avoiding the sharks, pitfalls, and booby traps waiting menacingly for their opportunity to do you in. You understand that when you die, you *are* dead. And—we aren't sure, of course—but death probably isn't much fun; undoubtedly it's more boring than even a Barry Manilow concert.

The previous paragraph is amazing, so I beg you to read it again.

Please.

I'll wait...

I won't remind you to be careful and refrain from taking unnecessary chances. I won't warn you to take care of yourself when you're sick and wear warm clothes in the winter. I'm not going to nag you about driving carefully, playing with fire, and doing drugs. These admonishments would be obvious, and, frankly, you're going to do...*what you're going to do*. However, once you have truly bought into the philosophy expressed in the previous paragraph—the one you've now read *twice*—you will see your life as a remarkable gift you will cherish for a very, very long time.

18

It's a Matter of Philosophy: Remedies Times 10

One way to use this book is to read only this chapter.

But to fully understand teenagers and develop some empathy for their world, you'll find that reading the previous 17 chapters lends more credibility—even urgency—to the ideas in this chapter. And examining the last two chapters seals the deal.

I have—maybe with just the right amount of arrogance—set myself up as an authority on teenagers. Almost 40 years among them—and from so many different venues and perspectives—has given me license to do this. Presumably, you are reading this book because you wanted some insight from *me;* you figured *this* reading material would provide you more cluck for your buck.

And you'd be right.

These comments preface this chapter because many of the ideas I present here are rather controversial. Not everyone will agree with me; counter sides can be argued fairly. Some people will turn up their noses at the whole book, simply because of what I have to say *here*. They're going to observe, "Yeah, sure, some of those stories about his former students and other teens were entertaining and moving, but when it comes right down to it, what does he *really* know about teenagers? His own kids aren't even teenagers yet!"

Even some of my closest friends don't see eye to eye with me on these topics. But I remind you of this: I have lived among teenagers for the last 37 years; I have been exposed to their private lives, their shenanigans, their secrets, their families—and thousands and thousands of pages of their writings. I have counseled them, cried with them, and thrown things at them. Frankly, I have never stopped talking to them, thinking about them, or praying for them.

From these interactions, I have developed 10 axioms for helping teenagers.

1. Letting the horse out of the stable is bad, but having no stable is a heck of a lot worse.

Teenagers need stability in their lives. They need to know that bad things—and, yes, good things—will happen to them on a regular basis. They need to know what to expect and how to plan for it. This is the primary reason divorce shatters the lives of kids: their stability has been devastated. When teens are batted back and forth through visitations and shared custodies—as pawns in the battles that ensue between their mothers and fathers—their world comes down and *crushes* them. Every time I hear a parent say, "Kids are durable. They can deal with it," or "They'll bounce back. They'll get over it," I look for some walls to pound. The parents' inability to choose decent spouses or to keep their marriage together cannot be rationalized by placing more hope in the artificial strength of their children than they have put into their own relationship. So many teens have shared with me their grief over their parents' divorces that my heart grieves every time I even think about it: moving *here,* visiting *there,* leaving *here,* going *there*—and I wonder how these kids can survive the messes their parents have created for them. Sure, most kids endure, and they live to tell stories of their heartaches to their own children. But they have been immeasurably affected by their lack of stability: never knowing the duration of their home in a certain city, the length of their stay at a particular school, the viability of their parents' marriage, and the certainty of their already dubious futures.

Tara said pointedly: "I hate my mother. She never knows if she's coming or going, and she never bothers to check to see where I'm coming from or where I'm going to."

2. Know what kind of a void I got in me? I'll tell you: It's an *empty* void.

Fill up teenagers with love and attention, or they will fill up themselves with something that you won't like. Just for a moment, look at teens as though they were gigantic digestive systems. Sure, most of us already look at teenagers that way when we watch them eat; but in this case, think of them more as *only* digestive systems: stomachs and livers and gallbladders and intestines, and so on that are crying out, "Feed me! Feed me! Feed me!" (remember the plant monster in *The Little Shop of Horrors?*). Teens are going to fill up with—whatever—eventually; so by the time little kids grow up and become big kids, they may already be filled up with those—*whatevers.* And here's the scariest part of all: All of us, parents, friends, teachers, extended family, and even the old man who lives in the scary house down the street have the power to *feed* our teenagers—to fill them up—either with the grains of health and prosperity—or with the poisons of illness and failure.

The Beatles had it wrong when they sang, "Love is *all* you need," because we need a lot more. But at least they had some understanding of the power of love.

Lacking love can make somebody feel very power*less*. One of the characters, Abra, in the classic film adaptation of John Steinbeck's powerful novel, *East of Eden*, tells Caleb's father, as the old man lies on his death bed after a stroke, "It's really an awful, terrible, terrible thing not to be loved, Mr. Trask. . . . It makes you mean and violent and cruel."[1]

Rodney's (from chapter 6) mother left him when he was just a baby and figured she had no reason to stay with Rodney's father, since they had not been married at the time Rodney was conceived. Rodney lived with his father, who wound up raising him into young adulthood. All this sounds like one of those rare, beautiful stories about a once irresponsible man who bravely rose to the occasion in order to lead his son into a model of adulthood.

Unfortunately, this story does not pretend any such claim. Rodney's father worked as a cop, and he ran his home with his cop-like iron fist. He remarried, and his new wife took over their household. She moved in her young son—who attracted all of the positive attention—and awarded him the prize of the only other bedroom in the house. Rodney had permission to sleep in the living room or on his stepbrother's bedroom floor, if Rodney promised not to touch any of his stepbrother's precious belongings. Mostly, Rodney saw his father when his father enforced one of his wife's inflexible house rules, although those meetings could not have been that pleasant (except for the occasional open hand to his face, Rodney vehemently denied that his father physically punished him).

The emotional abuse, however, mounted; Rodney had no one to talk to, no one to pay attention to him, and no one to show *him* even the slightest bit of affection. While everyone else in that house busily loved each other, Rodney felt like the odd man out. He possessed a big heart and a beautiful soul but had no place to go with them; furthermore, Rodney was not being filled up with love and attention. Far from it. His heart and soul were ripe for *other* kinds of filling up.

Luckily, Rodney joined the speech team and became successful in the tournaments. He was handsome, too, and sometimes the speech girls gave him the loving attention and kindness that he craved. Thank goodness the girls who took an interest in Rodney were nice girls; they only wanted to make Rodney better by feeding him lots of needed attention—mostly providing an ear for his sad stories—and nothing else.

Because he joined the speech team, Rodney filled up with the good stuff, instead of the bad stuff.

It could have worked out a lot worse for Rodney.

Occasionally, strokes of good luck happen. But usually they don't. We need to provide environments where teenagers receive love, affection, support, guidance, accolades, discipline, boundaries, and input. Without these, the pump is primed for loading the basin with poison.

3. **Telling kids *everything*, because, well, you're always honest with them is, like, incredibly unnecessary and counterproductive. And let me be honest: If you do that, you're, like, really dumb.**

Unless there is a need for them to know, don't tell teenagers everything. This axiom applies to everyone: teachers, friends, acquaintances, mentors, coaches—and especially parents. I wish I had a buck for each time I've asked a parent why she *told* her child about (her affair, her drug use as a teenager, her criminal past, her sex life, her problems on the job, her abortion, her five previous marriages, her—whatever). The usual responses: "Well, I wanted to be honest with him," or "I tell my children everything." Well, let me be honest with *you*: Giving kids information that is of no use to them is self-serving at best, and destructive at worst. Most information is better left in the hands of those who will protect its confidentiality.

One of my students, Jerry, faced devastation when his parents divorced. And his mother, whose sole purpose was to get back at his father, inflicted additional injury. She told him that his father was not his biological father. (She used the ridiculous, inaccurate term *real father*.) Jerry's mother admitted to a one-night stand that brought about his conception, and then she remarried as quickly as possible—evidently, too quickly—in order to conceal her "mistake." After calling this woman selfish, I told Jerry that his *real father* is the man who had raised him; and he would remain his *real* father for the rest of his life.

The biological father never contacted his birth son; the birth mother ran off with a new stud. Most important, Jerry's father remained in his life for two decades, until he died about five years ago. Jerry's mother had created chaos and confusion; *honesty*, if it were truly her goal, should have come 16 years earlier.

4. **Some traditions really suck—such as feeding cloves of garlic to pledges at initiation ceremonies; however, the traditional *family* cements a foundation that teenagers need to walk on when they sneak home in the middle of the night way past their curfews.**

The traditional family, a mother and a father who are married to each other, provides teenagers a better chance for success in life. You want to know all about the joys of commitment and love and giving and sacrifice and compromise and loyalty? Visit some of the families I have known over the years: The moms and dads are married to each other. The children all come from the same sperm and egg donors. The family fights through the requisite tough times together, finally persevering. Moms usually provide care for their kids, rather than sending them off to institutionalized child rearing (although sometimes it is the dad who stays home and takes care of the children).

Whether we like to talk about it or not, facts are facts: Children who come from intact, traditional American homes have less chance of becoming involved with drugs; they are also less likely to become alcoholics. Boys who grow up in homes with their fathers will commit fewer crimes than boys who go through their childhoods fatherless. Girls who have dedicated fathers are much less likely to become promiscuous, make babies out of wedlock, or get divorced.[2] Statistics abound to support this, but logic alone should prevail here. Sometimes, even though we are in self-denial, the obvious truth about a situation should suffice. Syndicated columnist Donna Britt observed, "It takes a *man* to teach a boy how to become a man."[3] Specific qualities have to be passed on to their children by adult men; other traits have to be taught to children by adult women. Men and women can be equally loving and attentive toward children, but *together* they act as a cohesive unit, each providing unique offerings, teaching and nurturing kids to grow into responsible, productive adults.

5. What's the purpose of caring about purpose, if the whole purpose of adults who mock purpose is to make purpose irrelevant?

Teenagers require clarity of purpose. A major premise of this volume is that teens are not stupid; on the contrary, many of them are a heck of a lot smarter than we were—than some of us are *now!* Today their brains can actually be a dangerous thing, for kids might start asking some serious questions we'd better be ready to answer: "Why am I here? Where am I going? Can you help me? Will you help me?" And my favorite: "Why did you do that?" If teenagers were robotic beings, life for them—and us—would be much easier. But the truth is, kids come into this world curious about everything, and later they point their curiosities in directions that prove to be embarrassing for some of the rest of us.

More than 40 years ago, when I sat in a high school classroom with other boys, we generally knew what we would be doing with our lives: we would go to college; we would find a good factory job that would support us; we would join the military; we would get married and have children; we would work to support our children; we would protect our families; we would do anything to please our women. Teenagers knew what it took to be a *man* in America. Our parents, teachers, and other adults told us stories of men who worked 10 hours a day in the coal mines, braving black lung disease, poisonous gases, and disastrous cave-ins, just so they could feed their children and pay their rents. That seemed normal. We, too, were ready to do what was necessary to live up to others' expectations. We had clarity.

But what is clear to boys who grow up in America today? Evidently, women don't need men to raise children anymore—just listen to those who sing the melodies of single motherhood. Women don't need men to make babies anymore. Madonna showed us that. So did Jodie Foster. And if a woman lacks the wherewithal to purchase sperm, she can always allure a "donor" for free. Women don't need men to protect them anymore either: Martial arts classes, paid bodyguards, and assertiveness training have all rendered men antiquated as protectors and hunters. And don't forget that the factory jobs have been outsourced, while illegal foreigners have driven wages way down, making it virtually impossible for a man to support his family on a single income. However, since the majority of college graduates today are women—and we hear that by 2018 more than two-thirds of them will be women—the chances of *his* earning a degree that is economically viable are disintegrating by the minute.[4] So if boys realize their future roles of protector, provider, and producer are irrelevant and immaterial, what are they to think about their purpose—*purpose?*—in this life?

Girls get confused, too. But no matter what, women will always have motherhood; they will always be the more nurturing of the two sexes. Having said that: what young American women face today is a very confused state of being a woman—and what that actually entails. Teenage girls today have been torn between *Girls Going Mild* and *Girls Gone Wild*. The mixed messages they receive—among all of the religious groups, the media groups, and the feminist groups—make their heads spin faster than did that chick's head in *The Exorcist*. Fifteen-year-olds have been bombarded by images of Paris Hilton and Lindsay Lohan, and their own reputations are cheapened when they attempt to emulate them.

We have pounded into girls' heads that dating only one boy is irresponsible, confining—even dangerous; yet, we mock girls who date several boys. Girls who are deemed unattractive have it worse: But why a double standard? Girls know when *men* get older, they get more handsome, distinguished looking, and desirable, but *women* are perceived as over-the-hill—distinguished looking is irrelevant—and less desirable.

The bottom line: Boys and girls must find a niche, a purpose, a passion—a meaning for their existence—so their lives will be conducted with poise, dignity, and humility.

6. Teens do not like compromise, but the alternative is flat-out sacrifice, and they despise sacrifice even more.

The parents set and enforce limits; input from their children matters, but parents should make the final decisions. That is not only the *ideal;* that is the *requirement.* A couple of years ago during lunch, Hailey came to me in tears. She said, "Mr. G., I got a problem."

"Everybody does," I answered, paying only half-attention until I could remove my sandwich, celery, and wafer cookies from my lunch sack.

"One of my girlfriends is having a sleepover tonight; it's Friday, and my parents usually let me go to sleepovers on Friday nights."

"So?" I shrugged, biting into a peanut butter and jelly sandwich.

"So the problem is that my parents found out we're going to be watching a certain movie tonight, and when they found out what the movie is, they said that I couldn't go."

I have a stock answer to situations like this, and I should have used it without probing further into the specific situation. But my curiosity took over. "What movie?" I asked, wishing that I hadn't.

"*Seven*," she said quietly, as though she were ashamed. "The one with Brad Pitt."

My shoulders relaxed: an involuntary reaction, which conveyed my lack of concern. To her, though, this was extremely serious. "Then don't go," I shrugged again.

She thought this response to be flippant and obnoxious, if not totally callous. But it was my way of falling into alignment with the following philosophy: "Your parents get to make those kinds of decisions," I said. "I can't make them; only your parents can."

"But do you think that movie is so bad?" she inquired with a hint of panic in her voice, perhaps realizing that she had mistakenly figured I would side with her. "I mean, what can be so bad about a movie? I'm 16."

Directly answering that question would have been another mistake. Again, I wanted for us to focus on the main point: "It doesn't matter what *I* think. It only matters what your parents think."

"But what if they're wrong!" she snapped.

I surprised myself by replying immediately, even as I stuffed the last piece of crust from my sandwich into my mouth. "If your parents are wrong—then—they're wrong."

"Huh?"

I swear, at this point, I thought she was ready to bawl. "They have a right to be wrong."

"What?" I expected her to hurl a book at me.

Deciding that the rest of my lunch would have to wait until after I emphasized the most important concept of our conversation, I sat up and rested my hands on my desk. "It's like this, Hailey: Your parents have the ultimate responsibility to make sure you're safe and healthy; it's their job to protect you. When you're over 18 and on your own and have all the responsibility for yourself, then you can do anything you want. But until then, your parents have that job—to protect you. So, if they think something isn't good for you, if they feel like you're in jeopardy, they have to put their foot down. In my opinion, if they thought something was bad for you, and they said or did nothing, they would be bad parents. So I guess what I'm saying is, yeah, sure, they can make mistakes about things like this—and they probably have made mistakes before—but by virtue of their authority as parents they have the right to be wrong."

After an initial period of shock, Hailey sneered at me. "Right, Mr. G., but what if they tell me to—I don't know—what if they say it's in my best interest to run some drug money over to the neighbor's house? What am I supposed to say to myself: 'Well, I think they're wrong about this, but they're my parents, and they have the right to make mistakes!'"

"No, Hailey," I calmly replied, thinking she had an excellent question. "As I've always maintained with everything—and you know this, because you've been in my class for almost a year—you should always draw the line at the illegal, immoral, or unsafe. Not letting you see a Brad Pitt movie is not unsafe; in fact, it may be that your parents are trying to protect you from what they deem is unsafe for *you*."

"Yeah," she sagged. "What *they* deem is unsafe..."

"That's the way it is," I sighed, noting her dismay at having come to me for advice. "They have the responsibility; they have the power." And then I forced a wry grin. "Any more questions for me?"

Parents and their teens can talk things over; they can give and take. They can discuss conflicts and differences of opinion until they're blue in the face; however, the parents are the authority. When the kids are parents, they will be the authority. When teenagers get older, they will look back and thank their parents for all they had done for them: setting boundaries, making up rules—and *enforcing* those rules. Teenagers think they know everything, but later they realize this hadn't been the case. A good parent reflects on when *she* was 16 years old, and the dumb choices she made before she finally learned her own lessons.

As a teacher, I know that the instructors the students respect the most are those who have high expectations, set clear boundaries, and consistently enforce their classroom rules.

And the same is true about parents.

Kids ultimately respect parents who *teach* them right from wrong, *model* for them what is admirable, *and expect the same of their children*. When a parent says in a genuine, matter-of-fact manner, "I love you. You are the most important thing to me in my world. My job is to help you grow into a good human being and be respected by others. Here is what I expect from you, and these are the lines you may not cross"—her children will grow to see her for the terrific parent she always has been.

Lottie, a student who eventually mired herself in the drug scene and dropped out of high school, learned nothing from me about leading a better life. However, she made a comment that has stuck with me for more than 30 years: "My dad—I never met him; he left when I was two months old. My mom—she wants to be my best friend and not my mom; so I guess I'm an orphan."

7. Playing a role is good, but *having* a role is better.

Teens should retain age-appropriate roles and identities. In *The Catcher in the Rye,* the protagonist, 16-year-old Holden Caulfield, is obsessed with protecting the innocence of children. He confesses to his 10-year-old sister Phoebe that he wants to stand at the bottom of a hill in a rye field, and as kids fell off the side of a cliff, he would catch them.[5]

Later in the novel, Holden is angered over his discoveries of the word *fuck* in several places frequented by little children: in particular, the staircase of the elementary school that his 10-year-old sister attends. He rages to himself that he wants to *kill* the guy who wrote on the staircase, because little children would see that ugly word.[6]

One of the beauties of this book is its poignant reminder of the dearness of childhood innocence; that during different stages of our lives—particularly when we're very young—we're so naive about the world, so oblivious about the evil that surrounds us and the adults who mess us up. Too many adults mistakenly believe that kids are better off if they grow up faster—that somehow an accelerated maturity is beneficial to everybody, including the children themselves. The push for children to grow up more quickly comes from an eagerness on the part of parents to rid themselves of the confining responsibilities of parenthood; it's also to satisfy the following philosophy: The faster my kids mature and are able to take on the challenges of the adult world, the better job I will have done in preparing my kids for the eventual challenges of adulthood.

Wrong!

What kids really require are age-appropriate hurdles into the inevitable glut of harrowing experiences they will encounter later on. A *gradual* immersion into adulthood allows kids to experience maturity without too much wear and tear—emotionally, mentally, spiritually, and physically—along the way.

I thought you would never ask me what that means!

Teens should not have jobs until they are out of high school. Their job is *school,* developing their academic skills and character qualities.

Teens should be held accountable for household duties and chores. Whether or not to pay an allowance is moot; however, having a solid family requires that everyone in the family pulls his own weight.

Teens should not be given unrestricted access to media or the Internet; this means, at school, at home, or anywhere else. Society must enforce its laws that protect minors, and parents must exercise good common sense about what media entertainment they allow their teenage children to indulge in.

Teens should be taught manners and common courtesy. Ideally, these kinds of teachings begin when the teen is a little tyke; however, they must be continued during the teenage years, as well. Rules of conduct revolve around the use of polite language, appropriate public behavior, and modest choices in attire and lifestyle.

Teens should be shielded from adult problems that plague the household and/or the family. They do not need to dwell on Uncle Ned's divorce, cousin Marta's abortion, or Dad's propensity to lose money gambling. Of course, these general issues should be discussed (age appropriately) at home and lessons may be learned from others' mistakes. But focusing on these adult plagues and making them a major part of a child's personal life is deleterious to her.

Fathers and mothers should talk to sons and daughters about issues related to sex, intimacy, and drugs and alcohol. Around the fifth grade is a fair time to begin, with more of the complexities weighed in later. Heavy issues demand parental guidance and strong adults' points of view, or else kids will get their morals from MTV and Snoopy Doogy Doo-doo—or whatever.

Teens should be encouraged by parents and teachers to speak up: when they have a problem; when their friends need help; when they have serious questions; when they are sick; when they are bullied; when they are frightened; when they feel helpless; when they are confused; when they are hurting. Every teenager should have someone to turn to in times of need—and teenagers, in particular, require responsible sounding boards.

Teens should not have to perform parental responsibilities. *Parents* are supposed to support their families and make contacts with teachers and other institutions of authority. While older children can—and should—have a role in the development of their siblings, they should not have the burden of child rearing and babysitting. I have heard too many stories of teenagers skipping school because they had been forced to watch a younger brother or sister. Parents have the obligation to provide for those needs, not their kids.

Teens should not have to help with a family business, the family finances, or family social dynamics. Children may be *introduced* to responsibilities like these—not *shouldering* these responsibilities.

Teens should not be adult confidants. Adults need *adult* confidants to share their woes. I wish I had a buck for each time a student wrote something like, "My mother is my best friend, and I am her best friend." I can see how a 15-year-old girl would think her mother is her friend, but a mother thinking *her* best friend is a 15-year-old is alarming. Shouldn't 40-year-old women have friends—best friends—in their adult age range? And since best friends share all sorts of secrets and problems, what business does a 40-year-old have sharing her secrets and problems with a 15-year-old? Adults are supposed to protect kids from ugly adult problems—*not the other way around.*

The adult world will arrive soon enough. Let's let children live as children and become gradually maturing adolescents for as long as we possibly can. Healthier, wiser, and happier adults will be the product of this endeavor.

8. R-E-S-P-E-C-T: I can't get no. I don't have none. We should give some—and other grammatical guffaws.

Teenagers require trust and respect. In the past 37 years, almost every problem I've watched teenagers encounter has been perpetrated upon them by *adults* who have used, abused, or ignored them. Yes, teens require adult *guidance* and positive role modeling, but kids also need to feel as though they have intrinsic *worth.* With older people constantly looking upon teenagers askance, with ridicule, and giving them a sense of ineptitude, our kids' self-worth sinks even further into the depths of narcissism and hedonism.

Danielle said, "My mother thinks I'm totally incapable of following directions, so she never lets me cook meals at home. Yeah, I've messed up a few times, but I think I learned from my mistakes and am ready to take it [cooking] on again, but she won't give me any more chances."

David lamented, "Everybody I know puts us [teens] down. My teachers are always making fun of teenagers and comparing us to the good old days, which I guess means when they were kids. But for once it would be nice to hear about the potential my generation has for making the world better. When you look at how things are today, I don't see how we can screw them up any worse than they [past generations] have."

And in a class discussion Elise added, "All you hear is how terrible my generation is. I don't think that we started out that way, but adults somehow made sure we wound up that way!"

When Chad shot a rubber band at the girl next to him, I asked him with obvious exasperation, "Chad, why did you just shoot a rubber band at Marlene?"

To which he responded: "Because I had the rubber band, and when you looked at me, I could see in your eyes that you expected me to shoot her. So I did it; I shot her with a rubber band."

Negative talk, parody, and tight reins on teenage conduct inevitably lead to a mindset that sinks—or rallies—to the level of others' expectations. Sometimes it seems as though there is no light at the end of the alien tunnel, and the darkness of disrespect and ridicule encourages teenagers to conduct themselves in ways that they will most certainly regret later. And much to their dismay, they invite the most dreaded of clichés: "See! I told you so!"

When kids are put in positions of responsibility and trust—heads of committees, public liaisons, appointed officers, money handlers, discussion group reporters, Scout leaders, caregivers, dog bathers—they usually come through. Sure, there are some kids who don't rise to the occasion, but the successes far outnumber the failures.

R-E-S-P-E-C-T breeds, well, even more respect.

9. Liking yourself and, like, respecting yourself are not the same; like, one is just liking and the other is, like, something else.

Teens require instruction in self-respect, not self-esteem. The self-esteem movement, rooted in the nineties, accomplished nothing. One recent international study reported that students in the United States were ranked 14th in the industrial world in math and 11th in science. However—*ta-da*—American high school students did sit on the very top when it came to their levels of self-esteem. Translated: "American teenagers are among the dumbest in the world, but they feel really good about themselves!"

A student who had attended a high school leadership conference told me that one of the speakers there had asked the hundreds of kids in attendance to hug the person sitting next to her and tell him *what a wonderful person he is.* She asked me, "How could I do that? I didn't even *know* the person next to me. For all I knew, he could have cussed out his mother that morning—or even killed his neighbor's dog; I might've been sitting next to another Jeffrey Dahmer—with body odor!"

Savvy kid. The *adult* speaker expected these impressionable teenagers to believe they were wonderful just for *existing!* Now their self-esteem should soar! We have been led to believe that high self-esteem is the key to everything: better jobs, better spouses, and better gas mileage on our cars. I read where Saddam Hussein once bought a political foe a new Mercedes—just before he sent out the order to have the guy beheaded. Gang leaders walk around looking as proud as peacocks, heads held high, their self-esteem flowing off the charts. The idea that feeling good about oneself is the key to better behavior, more success, and less acne has gone the way of the eight-track tape and the landline telephone.

Here's what teenagers *do* need: self-*respect*. And self-respect comes from being able to examine yourself and ask, "What have I *done* to *earn* respect? Certainly, if others respect me—then perhaps I am *worthy* of receiving respect from myself."

And what do *others* respect us for?

Accomplishments: awards, advancements, degrees, distinctions, victories. But *also*...decency, kindness, goodness, compassion, loyalty, integrity, honesty, sincerity, punctuality, bravery, and altruism. When teenagers encompass virtues such as these, perform noble acts, and develop their characters, others will respect them—and pay them further tribute proportionate to what they have won or achieved. It follows, therefore, that teens will have much greater respect for themselves.

Modern teenagers are much too wise, too sophisticated, to believe that a hug from a complete stranger at a student convention would lift them atop the personhood pyramid. Modern teenagers know that in this world you get what you pay for, and you reap what you sow. You give nothing; you get nothing. You don't begin the journey; you never arrive at the destination.

10. Yuck! Not *that* way! But, yes, they long to be touched.

Teenagers actively seek—and desperately need—affection. In *A Rebel Without a Cause*, the Natalie Wood character, Judy, craving the attention and love of her father, goes to him and begins to put her arms around him. Her father pushes her away, saying something like, "Go away! You're too big a girl for that sort of thing!"

Of course, Judy is at the age for needing "that sort of thing" more than ever. Children usually receive *that sort* of love and attention when they're very small, and then they watch it disappear. Most parents love their children up when they're little. They coo to them, pamper them, and hold them close every chance they get. They kiss them, rub their bellies, and stroke their hair. If other people are watching, these kids slink away in embarrassment—but all the while devouring the demonstrative acts of their parents. Ironically—the teen years are packed with irony—just at a time when teenagers need their warmth the most, parents believe it's acceptable to withhold their affection.

I came from a kissing family. My mother and father kissed me, and I kissed them. And we hardly ever thought about it, until we noticed that many other families were *not* kissing families. Before I left the house to go out with my friends, my father would call to me, "Hey, Bruce!" And then he would point at his face—an obvious invitation for me to run over to him and peck his cheek with a kiss. This ritual embarrassed me, until one of my high school buddies, George, said, "Hey, man, I think it is really swell how your dad and you always kiss each other. I mean, my dad never touches me, unless he's smackin' me across the face or somethin.'"

George had reminded me that my dad had never smacked me across the face or somethin', for *any* reason. But he was always eager to plant a kiss on my cheek, to embrace me in a hug, or to tell me repeatedly how much he loved me.

Lots of my friends were not receiving nearly the same amount of affection.

Lots of today's teenagers don't get much affection either—not from anyone.

These kids are *still* kids on the inside; they may have developed the bodies of adults, but they are still little children who have rudimentary little children's requirements: kisses, hugs, and words of affection. If a kid is never told that she is loved, cherished, valued, prized, and appreciated, her social development will be stymied, her views tainted, and her conscience dulled.

Children must fill up, or the absence of physical affection will take its toll. Elementary school teachers have been hit a direct blow by the politics that forbids hugs and kisses in schools. They work with little boys and girls who yearn for even a modicum of physical affection. Unfortunately, teachers are no longer allowed to hug a child in distress, or rub the hair of a small kid in need of a confidence boost, for fear of repercussions from sue-happy parents; as a consequence, these little children don't receive physical affection from their teachers. And they may not get any affection at home. They grow into mean, testy, callous young adults who eventually lash out at the society that has failed to show them any love.

I have observed too many parents like this: their hollow eyes coldly staring at their offspring. But I also have seen the nurturing gestures of loving parents who are not squeamish about hugging and kissing their children in front of me. Even a flick of a hair that says, *good job*, often generates a spark from a child who had been listless and sad.

Touch. Affection.

Kids crave it; they hunger for hands that show them they are loved (although they usually know the difference between a touch that communicates confidence and admiration and awe, and a touch that is inappropriate and lecherous). For whatever reasons—and there are too many—society has withheld its affection from its members who require it the most: teenagers.

In 2005 I asked my students to complete a free write on the following topic: "Of all the people in the world, whom do you love the most, and why?"

This paper is easily one of my all-time favorites. From a girl, age 16:

> I love my mother and father.
>
> I love them for loving each other so much—and for showing that.
>
> I love them for staying married all of these years, when so many other parents did not. I love them for nagging my sister and me, even though most of the time all of that nagging got on my nerves. I love them for always wanting to know where I am going when I go out, and for making me call home whenever I get there. I love them for calling my friends' parents to find out what kind of people those parents are, and then for judging my friends accordingly.
>
> I love them for their hugs and kisses and just holding me when I'm afraid. I guess what I am saying is…I love my parents for *showing* me how much they love me.

Some of life's greatest profundities—right there—in the words of a teenager.

19

Can't! Won't! Not!

JUST SAY NO! UH, REALLY?

Nancy Reagan's *Just Say No* ads begged to be ridiculed. I, too, scoffed at the notion that, if you tell a teenager *not* to do something enough times, he won't do it. I, too, pooh-poohed the idea that the best way to keep kids off drugs is to tell them they *shouldn't* do drugs. I thought it absurd that a teenager's best answer to another's inquiry about drug use was simply to say something like . . .

No—I can't do that.

I'm not doing that.

I won't do that.

After all, for sexual promiscuity—venereal diseases and pregnancies—didn't we have to sanction sex education classes? For underage drinking, didn't we have to engage a bunch of former drunks to speak at high school assemblies? For dangerous driving, didn't we have to establish government-funded drivers' training courses? For drug abuse, wasn't it always all about the same things: programs, rehabs, speakers, plays, deprogramming, threats, and compromises?

Enter the bandwagon effect. How powerful it can be! A bunch of us start to believe there is a better way of doing things; we begin doing it that way with some degree of success, and—voilà—it becomes the standard for the next four quadrillion generations. We get lost in our paradigms, settled into our ruts, until someone blasts us out with a symbolic stick of dynamite.

We need to give teenagers more credit. The *Just Say No* philosophy is still around, still being preached across the United States for one reason: when done right, *it works*. Oh, sure, the cynics can cajole and laugh all they want about old people shaking a wrinkled, stubby finger in the air right in kids' faces while telling them, *no, no, no*; and about those teens racing off, unable to contain their derisive laughter. But the boring truth is, *once teenagers have been conditioned to think for themselves, to do the right thing, to protect their own physical and emotional well-being,* they have the most authentic, effective tool available to them: the power to tell others, "Sorry, not right for me."

The main reason that we don't trust today's teenagers: We were once teenagers ourselves, and we know how messed up *we* were. My own generation was chucked down the tubes by the generation before mine—that of my own parents. I mean, when I was 11, would I have lit a match and set the neighbor's garage on fire (I *did*) if I *really* thought it might burn me up and leave my ashes around their banana plants? Once a strong deterrent to reckless, self-destructive choices is clarified for teenagers, a motivation for safer behavior becomes apparent even to the dumbest kids. *Motivation,* therefore, is the catalyst for precluding social and personal disaster; *self-control struts itself as a lifelong habit.*

Yeah, I know. Much of this book has been dedicated to the belief that teenagers are horrible at self-control; in fact, they are genetically predisposed to *not* being able to exercise self-control. But this seeming contradiction works out through these six paths to self-containment.

One

Some teenagers never get into serious trouble. Yeah, they're the minority, but what happens in their lives that rescues them from the throes of social and personal dysfunction? The answer is…*these teenagers have learned how to control their actions.*

But how? How have they learned to control their actions? The answer lies in…

Two

They have good genetics; for instance, some men are morbidly obese because they don't exercise and eat properly, claiming they *inherited* this problem: bad metabolism. Wrong! The truth is, it's not because of their metabolism—that, too, is aptly controlled by exercise and diet—they are destined to suffer; it's their *unwillingness* to control their metabolism that allows them their excuse of "genetic predisposition." But that can be worked on, too.

How? How can we work on our genetic predispositions to be *lazy?*

Three

Motivation, will you please come forward! I once got a traffic citation I didn't deserve. (That's true. Only *once,* I swear!) While the cop smugly wrote my ticket for my having gone the wrong way on a one-way street, I felt an intense desire to punch him in the nose. Then, when he began badgering me about my inept, dangerous driving—he had rejected my "A big truck was blocking the sign" excuse—my inner rage swelled to a level I had never known before. Boy! This arrogant bastard deserved a broken nose at my hands! He needed to be taught a lesson! Now, you can call me a coward (okay, maybe my face began to twitch a bit while waiting for a citation); however, I instinctively knew this was neither the time nor the place to slug a cop. Again—don't get me wrong—he definitely deserved it, but his badge, his demeanor, and his *size* persuaded me to exert some big-time self-control.

The point: I had powerful motives *not to do* what I really wanted to do.

So I didn't.

We often have powerful motives to do that which we *don't* wish to do (go to church, attend a funeral, offer an apology, make amends, attend a family get-together, do homework, get to school, plow through this book, ask for help—you name it)!

Therefore...

Four

Teenagers are capable of self-control. They have to *want* to control themselves. Knowing the difference between right and wrong isn't enough. Impulsive decisions become less frequent when we train ourselves on what to do and how to act. Finding motives for correct choices: that's the thing!

Once we have accrued enough powerful *reasons* to act in the best interests of others and ourselves, we are brought to the following conclusion:

Five

We should give teens *reasons* to find their own potential for self-control. We must supply teenagers with motives upon motives upon motives upon motives (Did I mention *motives* enough?) for their self-restraint, for the power to tap into their reserves for combating impulsiveness, for doing what they *know* is best, and for changing their mindsets when it comes to coolness, peer pressure, and legacy. The *we* here refers to teachers, friends, parents, other family members, neighbors, and society. Teenagers don't want to die; they don't wish to go to prison; they don't desire to be seen as the losers and rejects of society. *Motives sink deep.*

So what are some of those motives?

Six

Having just alluded to a few, I can crystallize it this way: In my first three plays for teenagers, the problems the kids face are largely a result of their lack of self-control. True, we should forever be aware of why teens have this tendency (hormones, brain development, crummy homes, etc.), but the definitive issue always becomes one of making good choices—and those good choices require patience, moderation, limitation, and restraint. And guess what: patience, moderation, limitation, and restraint are best achieved when pursued by the teenager herself. Parents can discipline. Teachers can nag. Friends can challenge. But what it eventually comes down to is the teenager making the right choices at the right times. *No Way to Treat a Lady* discusses the horrible societal and personal life-altering effects of teenagers having sex. *Out—Out, Brief Candle* clarifies the ultimate effect of drug and alcohol abuse on teenagers—death. *The Center of the Universe* teaches the meaning of compassion and empathy by describing the harms that have arisen through indifference, callousness, and bigotry. All three of these plays motivate our teens to make better choices, avoid compromising situations, and alter their lifestyles. And the way to do it: *self-control.*

INSPIRATION AND PERSPIRATION

The following is a letter that Phantom Projects (the youth-oriented theater group for which I write morality plays) received after the performance of one of these plays. Keep in mind, Phantom (and its creator, director, and producer Steven Cisneros) has received gazillions of letters in the past 10 years; this is but a sampling (from 2007):

Dear Phantom Projects:
   I saw your performance...and I thought it was great....I learned some interesting and important facts about sex and the effects it could have that I didn't know about on my life. I have been pressured to have sex with someone more times than I can remember, and I'm only fourteen. Sometimes it's so hard to resist. Your production helped me a lot.

Here are two more letters from kids in response to my self-control plays. Two other plays handled the theme of drug abuse, but one was written and performed in 1986, and the other in 1989. I have kept both of these letters for obvious reasons, not the least of which had become the motivation years later for penning more morality plays for teenagers—and maybe even some impetus to write this book:

From 1986:
   Dear Mr. Gevirtzman,
   Even though I am not in any of your classes and you don't know me, I just needed to tell you how you changed my life. My teacher gave us an extra credit to write a play review, but I wanted to write you a thank you

note too. Thank you! When I saw how ugly and stupid those kids on stage looked, I thought how I never wanted to be like that myself. None of my friends agreed with me about this, because they all thought it was only a play and not real, but I kept reminding them how it was not just a play and how it was real. We all have friends who drink and do drugs, and when they throw up in the toilet at a party or get into a car and drive away, we all wonder about what's going on in their heads. Well, your play showed me what was going on in their heads, basically nothing, and made me strive to avoid drugs and even the people who use the drugs. Thank you so much!

And from 1989:

Well, Mr. G., your play really freaked me out. The lectures you give us in class came to life in the play that I saw tonight, so I figured I would take the time to write this to you before I go to bed. When the girl sees her reflection in the pond, and through all of the ripples of the pond she sees her dead face, I got spooked. When I got home, I thought about how my father is an alcoholic and my mother left us all when we were young so she could do drugs with her new boyfriend, and then I saw the dead kid in your play...and I decided I was not going to be that kid. You do have a certain way of making everything so real, even in our class, so I wanted to let you know that the actors scared me a lot.

My plays are but a single cog in a wheel meant to steer adolescents on a path to self-control—toward a life free of bad choices and impulse-driven disasters. The last two letters—before the advent of e-mail—have had a profound impact on me, motivating me to write more on these topics. Steve Cisneros's Phantom Projects continues to produce my plays and embrace all that is good for teenagers. (They have also performed, among other well-known plays, *To Kill a Mockingbird,* *The Diary of Anne Frank,* and *Of Mice and Men.*) The kids even have a part in helping to streamline and revise my scripts, taming my hyperbole and flavoring my authenticity. The young people involved with Phantom Projects *live* the lessons of self-control; and as they tour the landscape, teenagers everywhere benefit tremendously from their interactions.

With so many negative influences infesting every aspect of American culture, I have found myself curious as to why some kids survive unscathed, and other kids dwell in the pits of hell. I learned some answers from five of my current students:

Jill: I don't like alcohol, so that's easy. Drugs—how do you get them? And having sex? Well, that would be the hard one for me, but since I don't even have a boyfriend, I don't have to worry. I won't have a boyfriend either, until I can sneak out of the house or my father dies. Maybe both.

Jason: Alcohol runs in my family and I've seen what it can do, so—no! Drugs, too. I won't touch them. I know how they can destroy you. I have also broken off all my relationships with friends who have done any kind of drugs. I know that sex is wrong, especially for a girl, and if I like a girl, I'm not going to hurt her; so, forget that, too. Whew!

Larry: I tried booze at a party and I felt really stupid—not cool. I've never seen anything drug-wise except for marijuana, and I can't stand the smell; it makes me gag. I'm not ready to have sex, yet. I wouldn't even know what to do, if you want to know the truth. Just don't use my real name, if you print what I just said here; I'll never live it down.

Liana: I'm a Christian, and so if I love God and want to have a relationship with Him, I can't do things that will harm my body. All the things you mention can harm my body; they would not please God.

Katrina: I know that booze is bad for you, and I don't need it to have a good time. It's really sad that so many kids my age think they have to get drunk in order to have a good time. Not me. Drugs? They're illegal. I don't want any part of it—and it wouldn't do anything for me anyway. Sex is something that can get me pregnant—duh—and I'm no way going to get pregnant! And no way am I going to have an abortion, and I don't want to carry a baby for ten months, so I am really, really afraid of getting pregnant—and if I don't do what can get me pregnant, well, I won't get pregnant! What did I just say? Was that clear?

Yes, Katrina, that was *very* clear. At least, it rang clear to me. If you make choices that have a good chance of hurting you, you will have a greater chance of getting hurt; if you make choices that have a better chance of not hurting you, you will have less chance of getting hurt. Just think of it this way: Teenagers *can* control the good and bad decisions they make. It's tough, *but once they have been convinced there are* strong enough reasons *to do the right thing, they will do the right thing.*

The actual *knowing* of right from wrong has never been the problem. When I sit down with a triple scoop hot fudge sundae, *I know I shouldn't eat it;* springing a few more chins would not be good for me. *But can I keep myself from digging the spoon down through the extra burnt almonds and creamy hot fudge?* Now, *that* is the operative question.

Somebody—quick! While I shove this spoonful of ice cream into my mouth—take a picture! No—better—let me take off my shirt, as I dump some of this fat-inducing, lard-manufacturing, physique-destroying gunk down my gullet! Maybe I never stood a chance of controlling myself when it came to ice cream sundaes. But if that photograph of me with my shirt off and the ice cream spoon in my mouth doesn't induce me to improve my self-discipline—*nothing* will!

20

When All Is Said and Done

BITTERSWEET

A paper from Ragan, age 17:

When I was really little, my father would pick me up and smother my face and tummy with kisses. He made all kinds of funny noises, and he would just lose all his problems in those few seconds he held me. And then he would gently put me back in my crib and say to my mother, "I'm a blessed man, Bianca. I don't know what I have done to be so blessed by God, but of all the men in the world, God has blessed me the most." Sometimes he would cry. My mother said that he would sob in her arms and not say anything, because he couldn't believe how happy he was. . . . And then, on June 15, 1983, when my father was on the roof of our house fixing some leaks, he had a fatal heart attack. The doctor said my father probably knew he was having an attack and just sat down so he wouldn't fall. He died up there in the sun all by himself. . . .

I don't really remember my father at all. I don't even have any memories of him. But I do have lots of pictures everyone took since I was born, and you can see me with my father until the very week he died.

My mother never really recovered from my father's death. He was only forty-two. She was thirty-eight then, but she never remarried—never even dated anyone else again. And she barely held up. She drank a lot after that, and she watched so much television!

My father left us a huge insurance policy, so she didn't have to work right away, but she still wasn't there for us much. She certainly wasn't there with her emotions. I guess the thing I miss the most about my father is the feel of him. Sometimes I just want him to be here so he can hug me and kiss me some more. I was way too young to appreciate it then—even remember it—but I'm so lonesome for my father's touch. My mother probably wasn't the most affectionate person in the world to begin with, but after my father died, she withheld all her affection for me. . . . I know it doesn't make sense, but I think it's the major reason I'm so messed up today.

During the nineties, I asked my honors English students to write a candid autobiographical sketch. The main requirement: the students would focus on an event(s) in their lives that most influenced them into being the people they are today.

By then I had already been teaching high school for 20 years; I knew the sorts of problems teenagers possessed. But my experiences with teenagers until this time had been mostly anecdotal; I had lacked general research, made excessive generalizations, and meekly coaxed students to provide details about profound events in their lives. Their autobiographical pieces, however, opened my eyes. I learned so much about teenagers—more than I had ever known before: Paper after paper related crushing events that happened to them; they came at me with the force of a word-driven tornado. The students I had been privy to in classes, the kids on my speech squads, baseball teams, and in my plays had been human, in-the-flesh *samples* of teenagers. Now the whole picture was beginning to focus like a blurry television set that suddenly received much clearer reception.

Ragan's autobiographical sketch displays some excellent writing skills; however, you may have overlooked them, because of the affecting—albeit distressing—rendering of her story. Her experiences could have been those of countless children in America. The brutal lives of kids who live without love and human touch pose constant reminders about the throngs of teenagers I come into contact with every day—and the horrendous hardships some of these kids must be enduring.

THE SCOOP

While at home recently, I had been in the midst of a whiny pontification about a few of my more slothful students, mostly dwelling on their lack of academic achievement, but sometimes commending them for their amiability. My wife, also a high school teacher, said gently, "They're good kids; they're nice. Give them a break."

"But they're not—" I began to protest, but as usual, my wife's more level head prevailed.

She interrupted, "These kids—so many of them are hurting. The fact that some of them can be polite and decent in light of what's challenging them ought to count for something, Bruce; cut them some slack."

I thought about the voids in their lives: a lack of touch; an absence of love; a confusion of direction; a deficiency of purpose; an abstraction of identity.... I also considered the hurdles in their lives: poverty, gangs, social strife, media, runaway technology, peer pressure, divorce, mix-n-match families, poor role modeling, hurdles to college, drugs, alcohol, sex, abusive parents, shrinking job markets, an erratic economy, racism, war, terrorism, crime.... And I wondered why *any* teacher expected them to give a rat's behind about something so esoteric and far removed from their own realities as the words of Hemingway or Steinbeck. And did it really matter to them how to combine two simple sentences with a coordinating conjunction? How much of their hearts and minds resided *outside* my classroom—even on days I thought I had done a decent job teaching them something! I mean, how presumptuous of me to believe that I could be the center of their universe for even five minutes!

What *was* on their minds and in their hearts?

I conducted surveys and did interviews of various teenagers in my high school, in the religious school that I taught on Sunday mornings, and with the students who sat in my classroom every day of the school year. Here are some of the questions I asked and the results I received:

1. Do you like being a teenager?

An overwhelming 76 percent said that they did *not* like being teenagers—or they *hated* being teenagers. The biggest reason: Adults don't respect them. Adults love the little ones and sit in deference to other adults, but teenagers remain on the back burner when it comes to getting respect.

2. Whom do you admire?

Most kids admire one or both of their parents; some mentioned grandparents or other members of their families, including siblings. Surprisingly, only a few mentioned rock stars or other media celebrities.

3. Who is the source of your biggest problems?

Very interesting answers poured in on this one: The number one answer: parents (32%), but a second choice came in unexpectedly high—the government received 27 percent. (Could this have had anything to do with government-mandated compulsory education?) The environment—though the response is a non sequitur—won the third slot. I'm wondering, however, how many teenagers can't finish their homework or get a decent job because of global warming or litter on the beaches.

4. What is your favorite thing to do?

If this were the Miss America Pageant, undoubtedly, they all would have mentioned working for world peace. But the frontrunners in this category came as rather ambiguous entries: A whopping 76 percent said they liked "hanging out with friends." Of course, what this *hanging* entailed is not exactly clear; it could have been anything from seeing a movie to getting plastered at a party. But friends rule!

5. If you could go anywhere in the world, where would it be?

Why 22 percent selected Amsterdam as a place to visit is a mystery. Ah! Now they tell me that Amsterdam has legalized marijuana, and the minimum drinking age is 18. Can *that* have anything to do with it? Nah! Anyway, Hawaii is second, and New York City third. By the way: 15 years ago—before Mayor Giuliani—not one teenager would have mentioned New York City as a preferred travel site.

And now for the juicy stuff.

6. Should teenagers have sex?

Define *sex*. I didn't. President Clinton wasn't asked, so I assume the teenagers thought this meant intercourse. Now that I think about it, I should have used the word *intercourse*. At any rate 40 percent responded in the affirmative; 47 percent were aghast. The rest, I suppose, have their own ideas about what *is* is.

7. Have you ever used illegal drugs (other than alcohol)?

Only 11 percent admitted to using illegal drugs. I would have predicted a much higher number. Maybe the teens worried that their answers would be traced back to them, and so they lied on the survey. Maybe some of them didn't consider marijuana an illegal drug, even though it's clearly illegal in California. The National Institute on Drug Abuse placed the number of teen drug users (in 2006) at closer to 30 percent, a more dismaying statistic.[1]

8. Which types of technology do you use the most?

Interestingly, the Internet (38%) nosed out cell phones (36%). Music and video devices (27%) slithered into third place. I'm surprised by the low cell phone statistics; more teens prefer phones for text messaging (56%) than voice communicating (42%). From my own observations in the classroom, kids seem to like conversing with each other much more than poking at a keypad. Some kids mentioned various handheld devices I couldn't identify even if one slammed me in the face.

9. After you are dead, how will this world have been left a little bit better because you lived here?

Of all the questions, this one solicited the widest variety of answers. Most revealing—or perhaps not—is that 24 percent of the teens responded that the world would *not* be a better place because they lived here. (Maybe that response simply revealed a lack of creativity.) The top comment was *don't know*— 26 percent. The most common answer as to how society would be affected in a positive way: "will help people" (in some way)—8 percent, although the kids rarely indicated specifics as to how they would accomplish this. Four percent of the students mentioned the possibility of becoming a teacher. Which is weird. Are there teenagers who actually believe that *teachers* do something beneficial? During the adolescent years, aren't teachers rather, well, yucky? Finally, an interesting comment made by some kids was "raise decent children"—which would be good for the world, indeed!

10. What is the one thing that you like most about school—and the one thing that you like least about school?

Homework nets the *stinky* label. More than half the students thought that homework was the worst thing about school, followed by the second-place bummer, having to get up so early in the morning. Their favorites: getting to see friends; meeting members of the opposite sex; participation in various clubs, sports, and activities. Barely 6 percent of the students mentioned anything about preparing them for life, the real world, or college; in fact, hardly anything related to academics per se received attention.

11. Do you have any concerns about homosexuality—either for yourself, others, or in general?

Among the population, teenagers are the most homophobic of all. Eighty-nine percent of the responses showed some concern about homosexuality. Not surprisingly, a miniscule less than one percent voiced any self-doubts about their own sexuality. At our school gays are overall treated fairly. There is a Gay-Straight Alliance club, and most of the kids seem ambivalent about it. I have, however, heard the usual hurtful, bigoted rhetoric directed toward homosexuals in general. One respondent wrote on the survey, "I hate fags!" Another voiced, "They [homosexual students] should be in their own special school—not our school." So, yeah, emotions run strong; hatred permeates the air. But most gay teens— especially the boys—suppress or deny their homosexual feelings altogether. Being a teenager is already off-the-charts difficult enough; thinking you are gay or that others believe you are gay may take that difficulty to catastrophic levels of self-loathing or self-destruction.

In speaking with today's teenagers, I gathered information through surveys, interviews, and class discussions. The kids had no reason *not* to be frank, every reason to be honest, and they participated in this project only if they wished to do so; in other words, student input was completely voluntary. The bulk of this book, however, is based on my personal observations and interactions with teenagers during the past few decades. Along with the 11 questions and answers I produced for this chapter, I also asked about a hundred other questions to kids; their answers provided background information about teen behavior and attitudes that are used throughout this book.

It was not random choice that I began this final chapter with an excerpt from Ragan's autobiographical sketch. Ragan typifies—on a grander, more intense level—the condition of most American teenagers: that their lives have been filled with ups and downs, peaks and valleys, structure and chaos. Ragan began her life with the ideal situation: two vibrant, adoring parents who loved each other, a secure home, and a promising future; after tragedy struck, she was left with a cold, listless mother. Distracted and paralyzed by circumstance, Ragan's mother became frightened by even her own shadow. Ragan's depression and loneliness then hurled her into a life of parties, boys, drugs, and fast cars; her mother rejected her, and her teachers neglected her. Ragan's body may have grown into that of a woman, but her emotional well-being, sense of security, and perennial optimism were left behind.

Ragan's craving—her intense longing—for physical affection had thrown her into the arms of every boy and girl who promised to fill an enormous void. Younger children get all the coddling and cuddling they can handle—and then, for myriad reasons, it stops; still, the yearning for a physical connection continues, and teenagers like Ragan wind up seeking and accepting affection wherever they can find it: For girls, this means sex, because sex and love for most teenage girls are interchangeable; for boys, it means getting girls to like them, to be jealous around them, and to fight for them. Boys, of course, know that sex is just *sex*, but they often exploit a girl's willingness to do sexual favors for them in order to receive attention, gain status, and validate their machismo. But girls, who substitute sex for love, are too often oblivious to this biological reality. That "filling up" process—this time with sex—can never be fully satiated by having intercourse or experimenting with fellatio. Not really. Not forever.

Sometimes not at all.

But even aliens require physical affection. Even aliens love to be noticed. Even aliens need to know that they *matter*.

Even aliens...are *human beings*.

In *The Center of the Universe*, my play about tolerance and the value of life, one of the characters makes the following observation:

> If we could only look at the person next to us and remember he is just like we are; he likes hot dogs and ballgames; he hurts when he is hit and cries when he is sad; he dreams, hopes, wishes, and prays; he wants, craves, needs, and lusts; he has fears, longings, frustrations, and confusions. *He is a human being, too....* If we remember this, we cannot possibly be cruel to him. And the world would be a more beautiful place—a more content, secure, loving place—for all of us to live.

After all is said and done, even aliens are people, too.

Notes

CHAPTER 3

1. American Accreditation Health Care Commission, "Complications of Anorexia," *New York Times*, December 31, 2007, Health Guide, p. 1.

2. Not his real name, Dr. Moxie did not wish to go on record with his rather candid description of the problem. The doctor's comments were provided in May 2007.

3. F. Scott Fitzgerald, "Winter Dreams," in *The American Experience* (Englewood Cliffs, N.J.: Prentice-Hall, 1989), p. 741.

4. Kristi Dyer, M.D., "Teen Suicide: Too Young to Die," *Palliative Care Newsletter*, p. 1, 5th paragraph, November 18, 2006, http://dying.about.com.

CHAPTER 6

1. National Highway Traffic Safety Administration, *Street Legal Drags*, "Illegal Racing Stats," 1st paragraph, 2003, http://nhra.com/streetlegal/stats.html.

CHAPTER 8

1. This interview was conducted on April 30, 2007. These kids responded to a general school announcement that the author sought to interview students about the drug problem. Unable to obtain permission to audiotape these teenagers, the author reconstructed the interview from his notes and the best of his memory.

2. Joseph Serwach, "Smoking among American Teens in Eight-Year Decline," *The University Record*, University of Michigan Regents, January 10, 2005, p. 1.

CHAPTER 9

1. Jay Boyarsky, *Case Disposition: "Parents Held Accountable for Underage Drinking Party,"* p. 1, December 18, 2006, http://www.Boyarskyforjudge.com.

2. Ibid.

CHAPTER 10

1. NBC News, "Profile," *The Nightly News,* March 4, 1999.

2. Gwendolyn Driscoll, "Leads Sought on Fullerton Girl," *The Orange County Register,* part 3, p. 1, November 25, 2005.

3. Benjamin Franklin, *Poor Richard's Almanack* (Englewood Cliffs, N.J.: Prentice-Hall, 1989), p. 118.

CHAPTER 11

1. William Pierce, *Where Have All the Babies Gone?* December 1, 1988, 2nd paragraph, http://www.cnnmoney.com.

2. Child Welfare Gateway Community, *Third National Conference of Child Abuse and Neglect,* April 16–21, 2007, http://nccanch.acf.hhs.gov.

3. Cynthia Harper and Sara McLanahan, "Boys without Fathers Grow up into Dangerous Men," *Wall Street Journal,* December 1, 1998, p. 1, paragraph 3, http://fathermag.com/news/2770-WSJ81201.shtml.

4. William Hillbury, "President's Budget Will Strain California," *L.A. Daily News,* April 21, 2002, p. 6.

CHAPTER 12

1. Meg Meeker, M.D., *Strong Fathers, Strong Daughters: Ten Secrets Every Father Should Know* (Washington, D.C.: Regnery, 2006), chapter 5.

2. Ibid., p. 13, 17.

3. Ibid., p. 255.

4. Ibid., chapter 5.

5. Dr. Laura Schlessinger, "Introduction," in *The Proper Care and Feeding of Husbands* (New York: HarperCollins, 2003).

6. Michael D. Resnick, "Protecting Adolescents from Harm: Findings from the National Longitudinal Survey of Adolescent Health," *Journal of the American Medical Association* 278 (1997): 823–32.

CHAPTER 13

1. Marshall Mathers, "Kim," *Marshall Mathers LP*, Interscope Records, May 23, 2000.

2. James B. Twitchell, *For Shame: The Loss of Common Decency in American Culture* (New York: St. Martin's Press, 1997), pp. 196–99.

CHAPTER 14

1. This is a parody by the author.

2. Insurance Institute for Highway Safety, 2004, *Partners for Safe Teen Driving,* 6th paragraph, http://safeteendriving.org.

3. Senator Joe Simitian, "Solutions for State and Local Governments in an Information Age," *Economic Development E-Gov*, August 28, 2007, 2nd paragraph, http://paloaltoonline.com.

CHAPTER 15

1. Edwin A. Robinson, "Richard Cory," in *The American Experience* (Englewood Cliffs, N.J.: Prentice-Hall, 1989), p. 682.

CHAPTER 16

1. Dennis Prager, *Ultimate Issues*. Prager wrote a quarterly journal in which he discussed ethics issues relative to education (and other social issues). The author obtained these data from Prager in 1997 from his KABC radio talk show.

2. Associated Press, *Girl Sues to Be Lone Class Valedictorian*, May 2, 2003, 4th paragraph, http://www.cnn.com.

3. All of these events had been referred to in the past tense; the author would have been required to take professional/legal action as a teacher if he believed them to be occurring in the present tense.

CHAPTER 17

1. William Shakespeare, *Macbeth*, Act V, Scene 5.

2. George A. Sheehan, M.D., "And Miles to Go before I Sleep," *Runner's World*, March 1995, p. 18 (summary of article).

CHAPTER 18

1. John Steinbeck and Robert Shapiro, *East of Eden*, screenplay, Warner Bros., 1955, from the last scene of the film.

2. Meg Meeker, M.D., *Strong Fathers, Strong Daughters: Ten Secrets Every Father Should Know* (Washington, D.C.: Regnery, 2006), chapter 5.

3. Donna Britt, "Feeling a Bit Scared in a Brave New Father-Free World," *The Washington Post*, September 4, 1998, p. B1.

4. Jonathan Rauch, "The Coming American Matriarchy," January 15, 2008, paragraph 3, http://www.reason.com/news/show/124402.html.

5. J. D. Salinger, *The Catcher in the Rye* (Boston: Little Brown, 1951), p. 201.

6. Ibid., p. 173.

CHAPTER 20

1. Terry Frieden, "Study: Teens Getting High on Legal Drugs," December 21, 2006, http://www.cnn.com/2006/HEALTH/12/21/drug.survey/index.html.

Bibliography

American Accreditation Health Care Commission. "Complications of Anorexia." *New York Times,* December 31, 2007, Health Guide, p. 1.

Associated Press. *Girl Sues to Be Lone Class Valedictorian.* May 2, 2003. http://www.cnn.com/2003/EDUCATION/05/02/valedictorian.lawsuit.ap/

Boyarsky, Jay. *Case Disposition: "Parents Held Accountable for Underage Drinking Party."* December 18, 2006. http://www.Boyarskyforjudge.com.

Britt, Donna. "Feeling a Bit Scared in a Brave New Father-Free World." *The Washington Post,* September 4, 1998, p. B1.

Child Welfare Gateway Community. *Third National Conference of Child Abuse and Neglect.* April 16–21, 2007. http://www.childwelfare.com.

Driscoll, Gwendolyn. "Leads Sought on Fullerton Girl." *The Orange County Register,* November 25, 2005, part 3, p. 1.

Dyer, Kristi, M.D., "Teen Suicide: Too Young to Die." *Palliative Care Newsletter,* November 18, 2006, p. 1. http://dying.about.com.

Fitzgerald, F. Scott. "Winter Dreams." *The American Experience.* Englewood Cliffs, N.J.: Prentice-Hall, 1989.

Franklin, Benjamin. *Poor Richard's Almanack.* Englewood Cliffs, N.J.: Prentice-Hall, 1989.

Harper, Cynthia, and Sara McLanahan. "Boys without Fathers Grow up into Dangerous Men." *Wall Street Journal,* December 1, 1998, p. 1. http://fathermag.com/news/2770-WSJ81201.shtml.

Hillbury, William. "President's Budget Will Strain California." *L.A. Daily News,* April 21, 2002, p. 6.

Insurance Institute for Highway Safety. *Partners for Safe Teen Driving.* 2004. http://safeteendriving.org.

Mathers, Marshall. "Kim." *Marshall Mathers LP.* Interscope Records. May 23, 2000.

Meeker, Meg, M.D. *Strong Fathers, Strong Daughters: Ten Secrets Every Father Should Know.* Washington D.C.: Regnery, 2006.

National Highway Traffic Safety Administration. *Street Legal Drags.* "Illegal Racing Stats." 2003. http://nhra.com/streetlegal/stats.html.

NBC News. "Profile." *The Nightly News.* March 4, 1999.

Pierce, William. *Where Have All the Babies Gone?* December 1, 1988. http://money.cnn. com/magazines/moneymag_archive/1988/12/01/84832/index.htm.

Prager, Dennis. "Should We Pay Kids for Grades?" *Ultimate Issues: A Quarterly Journal by Dennis Prager.* October–December 1989, p. 2.

Resnick, Michael D. "Protecting Adolescents from Harm: Findings from the National Longitudinal Survey of Adolescent Health." *Journal of the American Medical Association* 278 (1997): 823–32.

Robinson, Edwin A. "Richard Cory." *The American Experience.* Englewood Cliffs, N.J.: Prentice-Hall, 1989.

Salinger, J. D. *The Catcher in the Rye.* Boston: Little Brown, 1951.

Schlessinger, Laura. *The Proper Care and Feeding of Husbands.* New York: HarperCollins, 2003.

Serwach, Joseph. "Smoking among Teens in Eight-Year Decline." *The University Record,* University of Michigan Regents. January 10, 2005.

Shakespeare, William. *Macbeth,* Act V, Scene 5.

Sheehan, George A., M.D. "And Miles to Go before I Sleep." *Runner's World,* March 1995, p. 18.

Simitian, Joe. "Solutions for State and Local Governments in an Information Age." *Economic Development E-Gov.* August 28, 2007. http://paloaltoonline.com/news/show_ story.php?id=5682.

Steinbeck, John, and Robert Shapiro. *East of Eden* (screenplay). Warner Bros., 1955.

Twitchell, James B. *For Shame: The Loss of Common Decency in American Culture.* New York: St. Martin's Press, 1997.

Index

ABCs for Resisting Dumb Stuff, 76–78
Abortion: Eldridge, Mr., 141–42;
    emotional trauma, 144; Maxine,
    139–42, 152
Academic pressures, 197–215; Brett,
    213–14, 215; Emma, 202; Holy
    Grail, 210; honesty about college, 212;
    Mary, 211, 213; Oscar, 202–4; parent
    involvement, 210–11; Quon, and
    father, 199–201; Quon, and mother,
    198; 201; Quon's mother, conversation
    with, 207–9; teacher involvement, 212
Addam's Family, The, 47, 48
Affection: connection to others, 254;
    essay about, 241; from parents, 250;
    George, 240; lack of and effects, 241
Aliens, 1, 61–62, 254, 255
Allen, Woody, 31
"All Out of Love" (Air Supply), 105
American Civil Liberties Union
    (ACLU), 135
American Graffiti, 67–68
Annie Hall, 15
Anorexia nervosa (and other eating
    disorders), 33–34, 39, 41
Anti-Midas teens: breeds of, 58; Carl,
    63–64; Gergamister, Sam, 59–60;
    Harold, 56–58; Jake, 53–54; losers and
    winners, 58–59; Sura, 53, 62

Autobiographical sketch, from Ragan,
    249–50
Automobile crashes, statistics for, 171

Beatles, 65, 158, 171, 230
Ben Hur, 31
Best and brightest. *See* High achievers
Bitch, pejorative use of word, 4, 156
Boyarsky, Jay, 112
Boys, and communication (Scott), 9
Britt, Donna, 232

Catcher in the Rye, The, 177, 236
Cell phones: benefits of, 175; Bill
    (classroom disruptions), 176–77;
    cellular subterfuge, 177–78; as cheating
    devices, 175–76; distractions, 177;
    Mrs. Smith (parent encounter),
    177–80; while driving, 175
Center of the Universe, The, 245, 255
Charleston, 109
Cheating, 181–83, 199
Choking game, 70
Cigarette smoking, 94–95
Cisneros, Steve, 46, 245, 246
Click, 226
Clinton, Bill, 49; and Lewinsky, 151
Clueless, 2
Columbine High School, 56

Communication barriers: boys, 9; girls, 8–9; Miguel, 10
Cool Hand Luke, 17
Crystal meth, 93, 106

Dahmer, Jeffrey, 239
Dan the Van, 15–18
Dean, James, 19, 67. *See also under* Rebels
Death and dying, 216–27; Chavonne, 218, Don, death of, 219–20; dorm buddy, 222, 217; Harris, Mr., 218–19; hospice visit, 22; Kiko, Mary, and Mrs. Mancineras, 219; parents handling of, 223–24; permanence of, 217, 221, 222, 226–27; suddenness of, 217; 25 former students, 220; Wesley, 223, 224
Dignity, 20, 59, 76, 115, 214; sex and, 146–51; teachers and, 212
Dirty Dancing, 105
Drugs: Bryce, 92; coach's sermon, 91–92; confession, 103; death penalty for, 100; 15 reasons they suck, 102; Greg's essay about, 101; invasion of privacy, 100; selling to grade school kids, 92
Dumb Stuff, 65–78; Mario, 70; Melissa, 69; Milt, 70–74; Monique, 66; Paulina, 65–67; Roger, 70; Terence, 70

East of Eden (motion picture), 230
Efron, Zac, 19, 155
Eight track tape player, 174
Einstein, Albert, 65
Eminem, 153–54, 159, 167, 171
Emos, 49–50
Enchanted, 160

Fast Times at Ridgemont High, 92
Fathers: and daughters, 137–38, 145, 232; importance of, 157, 193; and sons, 232
Federal Communications Commission (FCC), 162
Feminism, 49
Fiddler on the Roof, The, 197
Fitzgerald, Scott, F., 34

Forbidden Fruit Theory, 149–50
Foster, Jodi, 233
Friends with benefits, 147, 151
Future, looking at the (poll), 221–22

Gangs, 129–36; defining characteristics, 130; Hector, 129, 136; observing a shooting, essay about, 131–32; teenagers' comments about, 131
Garden of Eden, 114, 149
Gay teens, 38, 253
Ghoul Squad, 51
Girls Gone Wild, 161, 233
Giuliani, Rudy, 135, 252
God, 149, 177, 195, 247, 250
Good kids, 186–96; everybody else, 191; Gerald and Jack, 186; God, 195; goodie two shoes, 190–91; Jack, 196; Jimmy, 193–94; Joyce, 192–93, 194, 196; misfits, 190; Paul, 191–92; Saul, 186–87
Gossip, 8
Goths, 47, 48, 51; Meg, comments from, 50
"Greased Lightning," 153
"Groovy Kind of Love, A" (The Mindbenders), 6

Head bashing game, 70
High achievers: comments from, 205; parent involvement, 206; pressures on
Hill, Faith, 105
Hilton, Paris, 233
Hiroshima, bombing of, 172, 183, 185
Hitler, Adolph, 20, 122, 125, 126, 187, 196
Hodads, 1–2, 47
"Hook-up," 161
Horror films: *Hostel*, 159, 165; Jerry's speech, 165; *Saw*, 160; sex and horror, 165–67

Impulsivity, 62, 76, 217, 221, 223, 224
Internet, 180–83; MySpace, 180–81, 185; Sasha, 181–83

iPod: rap music, 156, 168, 170, 171; restaurant use, 188–90; restrictions on, 184–85; school use, 172–74, 184
It's a Wonderful Life, 226

Japanese culture, 201–2
Jeanie (speech team star), 56–57
Jessicas, 32, 33, 38, 43
Johnny: conversation with teacher, 216; death of, 223–24

Kaczynski, Ted. *See* Unibomber
"Kim" (Eminem), 153–54
King Midas, 53, 55
Kutcher, Ashton, 155

Language of teenagers. *See* Teenagese
Las Vegas, visiting, 187–90
Led Zeppelin, 105
"Like," as language filler, 14
Little Caesar and the Romans, grammar error, 4
Lohan, Lindsay, 44, 233
Loyalty: blind, 126–27; friendship, 126–28; unconditional, 126

Macbeth (Shakespeare), 217
Madonna, 233
Manson, Charles, 196
Marijuana (pot), 23, 71, 73, 93–99, 178, 252
Married with Children, 63
Media, 153–69; advice to parents, 166; advice to teens, 167–168; Bryan, 162–64; movies, 159–61; MTV, 161; soul pollution vs. body pollution, 164–65; suggestive media, definition of, 154; television, 161–62, 164; video games, harms of, 162–64
Mega-nag, 209
Misogyny, 4, 151, 158, 164, 168
Miss Bikini Babe, 187–90
Mod Squad, The, 51

"Money is the root of all evil" (aphorism), 183
Motion Picture Association of America (MPAA), 160
Moxie, Dr. Robert, 34, 257n2
MTV (Music Television), 155, 161, 237
Munsters, The, 47
MySpace, 180–81, 185, 220

Nietzsche, Frederick, 12
No Way to Treat a Lady, 245

Opinions of teenagers (poll): admired people, 251; being a teenager, 251; biggest problems facing teens, 251; drug use, 252; favorite thing to do, 252; having sex, 252; homosexuality, 253; leaving a better world, 253; places to visit, 252; school, 253; technology, 252
Oral sex, 49, 141, 147
Orange County Register, 118
O'Reilly Factor for Kids, 102
Our Town, 225–27; Jimmy, 216; "Morning Star," 224
"Out—Out, brief candle…" *See Macbeth*
Out—Out, Brief Candle (play), 102, 245
Own Drummers, 47–48
Oxford American Dictionary, definition of *junk*, 163

Parties, 104–14; ala 1963, 104; ala 1988, 105; ala 2008, 105–6; cost vs. gains, 114; drug use during, 106; geeks, 109; Marcie, 108; parent involvement, 111–13; Randy, interview with, 106–7; Vera, 114; violence at, 110–11
Pet Shop Boys, 105
Phantom Projects, 46, 102, 261; letter to, 245–46; Website, 102
Piercings, 45–47, 50, 51
Porky Pig, 33
Poser, 1
Pound, Ezra, 187

Pregnancy, 49, 113, 139, 143, 146, 150.
    See also Sex
Priority nagging, 209–10
Prom, 24, 31–32, 47, 51, 84, 218
Protection of children, 236–37

Ragan, composition about loneliness, 254
Rap music: effect on language, 4, 5;
    Kelly's note, 168; original lyrics, 156;
    students' comments about, 156–59
Real World, The, 37, 145
Rebel paradox, 15–27
Rebels: Alyssa, 20; Gus, 25–26; Jackson,
    19; Jarrod, 19; Jay, 19; Jenny, 20; Mark,
    20; Monica, 22–23; *Rebel Without a
    Cause*, 19, 37, 240; Ronnie, 23–24;
    Sarah, 24–25
Remedies, 228–41; effects of divorce
    on, 229; Haily, 233–35; Jerry, 231;
    Lottie, 235–36; parent authority,
    233–36; Rodney, 230; sense of purpose,
    232–33; withholding information, 231
Respect: challenges, 238–39; trust issues,
    239
Restricted, movie rating:
    circumvention, 159, 166; effect of,
    161; *Ordinary People* and *Sideways*, 159;
    Saw IV, 161. *See also* Motion Picture
    Association of America
"Richard Cory" (Robinson), 194
Rick, death of, 73–75
"Run around Sue" (Dion and the
    Belmonts), 104

Schlessinger, Laura, 149
Sea of Black, 48–49
Self-control: letters from students,
    245–46; motivation for, 243–45
Self-discipline. *See* Self-control
Self image, 28–44; Annette, 43;
    Cornelia, 34–35, 36–38, 44; Diane,
    34; Isabel, 42–43; Laura's free write,
    28; Rachael, 32–33; students, looking
    in the mirror, 28–31

Self-respect, 36, 43, 77, 78, 88, 151, 161;
    contrasted with self-esteem, 239; how
    to acquire, 239–40. *See also* Dignity
Seven, 234
Seventies Show, That, 155
Sex, 137–52; abstinence, 150–51;
    AIDS and other STDs, 144–45,
    146, 150; bad reputations, 144, 146;
    communication about, 148–49; cost of
    an orgasm, 152; data about teenagers
    and sex, 141; harms of, 143–47;
    investment, 145; laundry list, 146;
    Mitchell, Billy, 140; parenthood, 144,
    152; parent role-modeling, 148–50;
    religion and sex, 147, 149; Suzie's
    discarded note, 142–43; unnecessary
    burden, 147. *See also* Oral sex
Sheehan, George A., 223, 242
"Sixty Minute Man" (The Dominoes), 153
Slayer, 105
Sluts Ahoy (with Richard), 49
Snitching, 115–28; badly behaving
    friends, 125; Candace, 125; child
    abduction, 118–19; family loyalty,
    122–25; John, 121–22; physical abuse
    case, 117; polls about, 116, 119–21,
    122–23; prison felon's mentality,
    115–16, 128; suicide, 121–22, 128;
    Washcloth, Mr., 123–24
Speech tournaments (and speech
    classes), 12–13, 16, 53–54, 57, 82, 98,
    199–201, 204, 207
Sperm donor, 233
Splendor in the Grass, 79
Sports, 79–90; baseball (Angelo),
    83–84; David, 83; football, 79; grade
    eligibility, 90; parent involvement,
    84–85, 89–90; Redhead with
    freckles, spirited, 87–88; why boys play
    sports, 82; why girls play sports, 85–86
Stereotypes, 45–49, 50, 87, 198
Stereotyping: Asian parents, 197; Jewish
    parents, 197; other cultures, 198
Street racing, 67–68, 195

Substance abuse: booze, 93–95; excusing vs. understanding, 96; parent role-modeling, 99–100; Rick, last conversation with, 97–98; round table interview with teens, 93–95

Suicide: academics-related, 205, 209; statistics, 35–36; Sura, 53. *See also* Anti-Midas teens; Snitching

Super Bowl, 42–43

Surfers, 1, 47

Tattoos, 19, 24

Teacher, as a professional ratter-outter, 118

Technology, 170–85; advice to parents about, 184; advice to teachers about, 184; advice to teenagers about, 185; costs vs. gains, 184; left behind, 174. *See also* Hiroshima, bombing of

Teenagese, 1–7; bad, 7; bitchin', 4; boss, 5–6; da'bomb, 7, 12; dope, 7; dude, 2; fabulous, 3; fantabulous, 3; far out, 5; groovy, 6; pimp, 4; radical (rad), 6; sick, 7; super, 5; swell, 5; tight, 7

Toilet papering (Paulina and Monique), 66–67

"To Know Him Is to Love Him" (The Teddy Bears), 153

Transistor radios, 170

Unabomber, 123, 125

Victrola, 172

Vietnam War, 110, 171

Wall Street Journal, The, 133

"Where or When" (Dion and the Belmonts), 104

"Whip It" (Devo) 153

Who's the Boss?, 63

YouTube, 178

About the Author

BRUCE J. GEVIRTZMAN is a high school English teacher who has also, across 34 years, served simultaneously as a sports and debate coach. Also Chief Playwright for Phantom Projects, an acclaimed youth theater group that has performed across several western states, Gevirtzman has authored and directed more than 30 stage productions. He has been featured in programs aired on NBC and PBS, and in the *Los Angeles Times*. Gevirtzman runs workshops for educators focused on teen issues.